Moralized Song

Moralized Song

The Character of Augustan Lyricism

RICHARD FEINGOLD

Rutgers University Press
New Brunswick and London

For Ralph Rader

A section of Chapter Two has been previously published as part of my essay, "Swift in His Poems: The Range of His Positive Rhetoric," in *The Character of Swift's Satire: A Revised Focus*, edited by Claude J. Rawson (Newark: University of Delaware Press, 1983); the material is reprinted here by kind permission of Claude J. Rawson.

Copyright © 1989 by Rutgers, The State University
All Rights Reserved
Manufactured in the United States of America

Library of Congress Cataloging-in-Publication Data

Feingold, Richard.
　Moralized song.

　　Includes index.
　　1. English poetry—18th century—History and criticism.
2. Self in literature.   3. Reflection (Philosophy) in literature.   4. Didactic poetry, English—History and criticism.   I. Title.
PR565.S44F45   1989   821′.5′09353   88-23861
ISBN 0-8135-1390-1

British Cataloging-in-Publication information available

Contents

Preface ix

Introduction Eloquence and Inwardness in Augustan Writing 1

1 Pope and Augustan Lyricism:
*The Second Epistle of the Second Book of Horace,
Imitated* 23

2 Swift as Lyricist:
The Poems to Stella and His Career in Satire 52

3 Teaching and Pleasing: Johnson's Lyric of Reason 94

4 *The Deserted Village* and Lyric Discovery 139

Appendix I William Shakespeare, *Cymbeline,*
IV.ii.215–281 187

Appendix II William Collins, A *Song from Shakespear's
Cymbelyne* 190

Notes 193

Index 217

Preface

This book is my effort to come to an understanding of some features of eighteenth-century literature—primarily its poetry—which have been of interest to me at least since my first professional engagement with it. These are its quite explicit didacticism and its peculiarly submerged representations of inward experience. My argument is that in its most interesting forms the didacticism common to the period's writing is closely associated with the representation of inward experience and that, whatever their ostensible genre, writings structured by that association have a powerfully lyric cast. Throughout, I have freely used the word "lyric" in its most common current sense to identify those moments in which the writer's engagement with inward human experience—either his own, or that of a represented figure—takes on the form of "passion brooding over itself," as Mill was to say. I have, of course, begun with the assumption that that experience was not foreign to the writers and the readers of the eighteenth century. My intention is to demonstrate the way in which an Augustan rhetoric becomes adequate to the task of representing it.

This issue is my central interest, and I have explored it here in a manner appropriate to a work of practical criticism. Only a small part of my purpose has been to consider the theoretical questions implied in my readings and findings. Certainly, though, the representation of inwardness in Augustan literature, and its association with a lyrical expressiveness, require theoretical inquiry. Some beginning was made in Donald Davie's brief but striking comments in the introduction to his collection, *The Augustan Lyric* (1974). More recently, Anne Williams in her book *Prophetic Strain* (1984) has sought to break the habits of familiar generic classification in order to discover the hiding places of the lyric impulse in neoclassical poetry. But the large questions still need to be asked and re-asked: how did the Augustan preference for submerging the experience of inwardness, for representing that experience impersonally, or distantly, or reticently, as if to do so were to rescue it from insignificance—how did that preference invent forms to suit its needs, what is the range of their variety, how adequate were they to their task, and why was that task important in the first place?

In its first form, this book antedated some critical studies that have been valuable to me as I have added to it and as I have, to some extent, recast it. The most important of these are Frank Stack's *Pope and Horace* (1985), Howard Erskine-Hill's *The Augustan Idea in English Literature* (1983), Roger Lonsdale's "A Garden and a Grave: The Poetry of Oliver Goldsmith" (1978), and Frederik Bogel's work on Pope and Johnson in his two books, *Acts of Knowledge* (1981) and *Literature and Insubstantiality in Later Eighteenth-Century England* (1982). Ongoing conversations with John Traugott, Andrew Griffin, Paul Alpers, and Steven Knapp have been as indispensable as they have been pleasurable. Ralph Rader's generous friendship and conversation over many years have been of special importance, far more than the several footnotes in my text might indicate. To Uli Knoepflmacher I owe many thanks, not only for his warm friendship, but also for the very valuable suggestions he made for presenting the argument. I am deeply grateful to Marilyn Shatz for her support as I was seeing this project through to its completion.

Berkeley, California
May 1988

Introduction

Eloquence and Inwardness in Augustan Writing

MY SUBJECT HERE IS the representation of inwardness in certain writings, usually poems, which, though they differ considerably from one another, still stand forth as easily recognizable documents of Augustan literary culture. My interest is in the writer's double effort to represent the experience of inwardness and at the same time speak to an audience imagined as present to him. This dual project is characteristic of Augustan literature and particularly of Augustan poetry: what it marks is the writer's insistent interest in the intersection of social and inward experience, an interest he reveals in his articulated and enacted wish to be seen as speaking with public authority even at the represented moment of self-absorption. To the effects produced by the rhetoric sufficient to that task I give the name Augustan lyricism.

The inwardness that the writer reveals may be his own, it may be another's—and that other may be either concretely imagined or universalized. As for the audience, it may be imagined as immediately, or as more distantly, present; it may be a figure in the text itself, explicitly addressed, or it may be constituted by the tacit yet clearly acknowledged presence of a reader. Whatever its form, an audience is always in some sense *there* as an object of address, and plainly or subtly the work enacts the writer's and the audience's contact with one another, a condition indispensable to the writer's assertion of his authority for speech. In the works discussed here, the representation of inwardness therefore, is always, in some sense a public occasion, a fact usually marked by the writer's didactic stance. Neoclassical poetry is unusually rich in writing whose explicit intention is didactic. Where this poetry is most accomplished, its didactic impulse is shaped to its representation of an inwardness that complicates the didactic material and, doing so, produces or enhances the effects I am calling Augustan lyricism.

An audience to speak to, a lesson to deliver, and a focus on inward experience—this complex blend of highly private subject matter and obviously public rhetoric is certainly a familiar feature of the most characteristic and significant poems of the eighteenth century. But the presence to the poet of his audience can seem to be a problematic—perhaps the most problematic—feature of Augustan representations of inwardness, especially to readers accustomed to romantic ways of representing the activity of the subjective consciousness. In recognizing the ubiquity of the imagined audience within Augustan poetry, we may easily recall John Stuart Mill's manifestly romantic insistence that in the specially charged species of writing he is willing to call "poetry," an audience can have neither place nor function. In Mill's scheme it is eloquence, but not poetry, which seeks an audience, for the purpose of eloquence is plainly to influence those to whom it is addressed, to convince them of notions, to induce in them feelings about notions.

These are social tasks above all, whereas for Mill it is solitude that marks the situation and the moment of poetry. In solitude, consciousness—determined and given shape by feeling—encounters itself only, and what it knows and says it knows and says for itself alone. Poetry is "passion brooding over itself,"[1] and its expression, though written to be read, is not written to enact the poet's *contact* with the reader; it is written, indeed, to feign the impossibility of such contact (p. 349). Hence Mill's familiar insistence that poetry is the species of utterance which is *overheard*. Almost inevitably, Mill would come to identify this overheard utterance with lyric, and thus to identify lyric almost with poetry itself.

> Lyric poetry, as it was the earliest kind, is also, if the view we are now taking of poetry be correct, more eminently and peculiarly poetry than any other; it is the poetry most natural to a really poetic temperament, and least capable of being successfully imitated by one not so endowed by nature.   [p. 359]

Mill's remarks about lyric, of course, hardly exhaust the subject; it is perfectly clear that he has no interest in what might be called the ceremonial or theatrical lyric popular in the seventeenth and eighteenth centuries, the greater and lesser odes of Dryden, of Gray, of Collins, of Smart, of Swift, and even, occasionally, of Pope. Nor is there in Mill's discussion of poetry any mention whatever of the writers of the two or three literary generations preceding William Wordsworth's, as if among them were none who found a rhetoric adequate to express "passion brooding over itself," and none who had recognized the possibility of such experience. And yet, whatever the limitations, and whatever the merits, of Mill's discussion, he seems to be implicitly responding to and providing a guide for inquiry into the poetic practice of those literary generations.[2]

What, after all, is signified by the scarcity in eighteenth-century poetry of the lyric writing that, pretending to be overheard, feigns the absence to each other of poet and reader or, more generally, of speaker and addressee? Nor is this a formal question only. For we are asking also about the experience that the formal situation is designed to represent: the experience of "passion brooding over itself."[3] What possibilities are there for representing this in a poetry whose commitment to public speech in public situations is marked by the insistent dominance of epistle, satire, and verse essay? In these forms, where so much that is said is meant to be *heard* (or read as if heard), how may the *overheard* component be recognized and listened for? And if in these public genres there is indeed a covertly present lyricism, what then of the *overtly* lyrical kinds—the elegies and the quiet odes, which even in their most intimate representations seem to seek a listener and perhaps a judge? These questions respond to the odd complexity of neoclassical poetry when the subject it engages is self-encounter, and when the experience it represents is primarily inward. They are questions that ask ultimately about the nature of lyric utterance within a rhetoric whose first task is to present the general experience of mankind as a knowable presence even in the moment of lyric solitude.[4]

———❖❖❖———

My emphasis in this book is on the covertly lyrical rhetoric of the more obviously public genres: epistle, satire, verse essay, conversation. But, to begin, some consideration of the more familiarly, more overtly lyrical Augustan writing will be useful, because, as the questions I have been raising suggest, the strictly formal distinctions between the apparently personal and the apparently public kinds of poetry tend to mask the presence in both of similar rhetorical tensions. Moreover, these rhetorical tensions themselves can become a poem's central subject.

I shall illustrate with an ode of Horace, simply assuming his paradigmatic stature for the English poets of the eighteenth century, who found in his work a variety of models for writing about the intersection of private and public experience; in Horace's work, indeed, public and personal are virtually forms of thought and feeling.[5] Nor was it only about the intersection of the private and the public that Horace wrote, but also about those boundaries between the two orders of experience which were not to be violated.[6] Here is *Ode I.24*, the elegy for Quintilius, which will illustrate the pressure contained within Augustan lyric utterance when it is given to the exploration of intensely powerful states of subjective consciousness:

> Quis desiderio sit pudor aut modus
> tam cari capitis? praecipe lugubres
> cantus, Melpomene, cui liquidam pater
>   vocem cum cithara dedit.
>
> ergo Quinctilium perpetuus sopor
> urget! cui Pudor et Iustitiae soror,
> incorrupta Fides, nudaque Veritas
>   quando ullum inveniet parem?
>
> multis ille bonis flebilis occidit,
> nulli flebilior quam tibi, Virgili.
> tu frustra pius heu non ita creditum
>   poscis Quinctilium deos.
>
> quod si Threicio blandius Orpheo
> auditam moderere arboribus fidem,
> non vanae redeat sanguis imagini,
>   quam virga semel horrida,
>
> non lenis precibus fata recludere,
> nigro compulerit Mercurius gregi.
> durum: sed levius fit patientia,
>   quidquid corrigere est nefas.[7]

[What restraint or measure should there be to grief for so dear a life? Teach me a song of mourning, O Melpomene, to whom the Father gave a liquid voice and with it the lyre. So now perpetual sleep presses itself upon Quintilius! When shall Honour, and unmoveable Loyalty, the sister of Justice, and plain Truth, ever find his peer? He dies mourned by many good men; by no one, Virgil, more than by you. In useless devotion you ask the gods for Quintilius, but, alas, he was not given to this life on such terms. Were you able more sweetly even than Thracian Orpheus to strike the strings the trees once heeded, still no blood would return to that empty shade, now that Mercury with his hideous rod has gathered it to the dark herd—Mercury, not easily persuaded to open the gates that Fate has shut. This is hard: but patience lightens the weight of those evils which it would be sinful to seek to set right.]

This poem, so obviously *about* an intense inward state, is nevertheless marked by language of an unmistakably public character. The poem's elegant and sometimes astonishing circumlocutions; the didactic charge of its concluding lines; the personified abstractions that suggest large attitudinal agreements, that is, Honor, Justice, Loyalty, Truth; and the poem's ceremonial manner—these register Horace's primary commitment to his hearers and thus to the decorums of a speech whose reticence must be the vehicle for its emotionally charged material. And that commitment is nowhere more plainly underlined than in the poem's opening. Here Horace's address to the muse acknowledges immediately that, between the powerful inwardness of grief and the act of speaking suitably about it, there must be some strain: "What restraint or limit should there be to grief for so dear a life? Teach me a song of mourning." In fact, the poem that follows is the very mourning song that gives answer to a question initially put as though no answer were possible or even desirable.

Such an answer must be complex enough not only to memorialize the dead Quintilius, but also to explore the problems inherent in such song as would meet that commitment. This task Horace accomplishes by his unexpected focus on the mourner, Virgil, whom Horace presents as both inconsolable and inarticulate. Once Horace has uttered his own memorial to the dead man, the accomplishment of his first two stanzas, he develops his poem as an address to Virgil. This address marks implicitly the contrast between what can be said and what *must not be said* ["nefas"], between Horace as artist and Virgil as mourner. It is Virgil, "frustra pius," who is represented as saying the "unspeakable"—beseeching the gods for the dead man's restoration. Perhaps most interesting and moving here is Horace's emphasis upon Virgil's fruitless speech, and upon the irony inherent in that supremely articulate man's incapacity for proper speech in this situation.

But Horace does not merely assert the fruitlessness of Virgil's speech; he emphasizes as well its *impiety*. In the beautiful moral lyricism of the two lines with which Horace ends his poem, the consolatory sympathy is obvious: "durum: sed levius fit patientia, / quidquid corrigere est nefas." But the final word surprises with its harshness. Heard in it is the deep connection between the idea of the unutterable and the idea of the impious, the unlawful, the unnatural. It is as if two kinds of speech are set in opposition to each other: the one, expressing Virgil's unutterable grief and *unspeakable* protest; the other, lawful, substantial, in accord with what is "right," what is "said," what "must be" (*fas—fari—fatum*)—in a word, with what is *authorized*. This is Horace's speech; it is the yield, finally, of his invocational request of the muse; indeed, his poem is bounded by that request, spoken in its opening lines, and by the final word of the final line—"nefas." And quite plainly, the muse gives, along with her lesson in the authorized sounds, a warning away from the sinful ones.

Now in aligning his own authorized song with what is pious, and Virgil's lament with what is unspeakable, Horace not only distinguishes between poem and outcry, but also between two kinds of poem. We see this in the question he sympathetically addresses to Virgil, the full force of which is not really clear until we have read to the end of the poem's last line.

>   quod, si Threicio blandius Orpheo
>   auditam moderere arboribus fidem,
>   non vanae redeat sanguis imagini,
>   quam virga semel horrida,
>
>   non lenis precibus fata recludere,
>   nigro compulerit Mercurius gregi.

The sympathy so obvious here is accompanied still by a subtle disclaimer: we hear it in the complexity of "vanae . . . imagini," in which, as against Virgil's desperate and fantastical insistence upon the continuing substantiality of the dead man, Horace asserts, plainly, his bloodlessness, his shadowiness. Once again, Horace's assertion implies a distinction between two kinds of utterance: the kind associated with miraculous and enchanting and unnatural speech, the speech of Thracian Orpheus (which can figure to itself as though still possessing substance the mere image of the precious dead), and the pious, the sane, the *eloquent and reticent* speech Horace is composing here. In the context of this reticent speech, "imagini" works to associate two ideas—first, the bloodlessness of the dead man, and second, the trope, the metaphor, the *imago* (one feels strongly the suggestion that this is the "mere metaphor") of the mad speech of the Orphic poet, the phantasm only, *vana imago*. Each—the dead man, and the poet's useless trope—is unreal, insubstantial, without blood. For all the sympathy Horace feels, his speech brutally insists upon this point.

But in aligning his style of speech with "what is said" (and in taking "what is said" to be synonymous with "what is ordained"), Horace is not merely dismissing the orphic impulse and its way. He is also acknowledging its rootedness in rich desire, and acknowledging too the tragic implications of his own choice of style. If indeed Virgil's speech—and the outcome it seeks—is impious, "nefas," what are we to make of Horace's description of Virgil as "frustra pius": "tu frustra pius heu non ita creditum / poscis Quintilium deos"? It seems an astonishing oxymoron: "deceived in your devotion [to Quintilius]" would be the primary reading here, but "pius" obviously registers also the sense of "righteous before the gods", so that Virgil is seen to be not only self-deluded in his insane wish for the return of his friend, but also "deceived in his righteousness" with respect to the gods. The ironic possibility here accords with the strong but not unlikely resonance of "swindled" in "frustra." These are meanings that certainly complicate Horace's role as spokesman for the authorized vision. Obviously, he has burdened this expression, "frustra pius," in order to suggest how complex and strained are the choices faced by a human speaker who would align his speech with that of the gods: what can it be but an implied indictment of their ways to say of the mourner that he has been deceived or swindled in his piety? Or wanton in his secular *devotions?* Certainly, Horace's exclamation in this stanza, "heu," tells us how aware he is of Virgil's victimization. Moreover, Horace's representation of Mercury is in obviously ironic relationship with his larger effort to align his speech with that of the gods and to define this effort as an act of authorized piety. Unmistakable here is the relentlessness of the figure of Mercury and his hideousness:

> non vanae redeat sanguis imagini,
>   quam virga semel horrida,
>
> non lenis precibus fata recludere,
> nigro compulerit Mercurius gregi.

Here the rhetoric makes it impossible to accept simply Horace's effort to distinguish his speech from Virgil's on the grounds of piety. The hideous figure of Mercury works decisively to limit our affective commitment to "what is decreed" (here "fata") and to the style of human speech that seeks an accord with it. Moreover, the image of Mercury compelling the beloved friend (*caput carus*, the dear life) into the "dark herd" is a terrifying expression of dehumanization; it stimulates our sympathy for Virgil's desire to see "the blood return to the empty [perhaps even here the 'drained'] shade," and it underscores how problematic indeed is Horace's effort to associate his vision and style with the way things are—a notion here complicated by its articulation in the word "fata," whose deep connection to the words *fari* and *fas* (and "nefas") is played upon richly. The irony of "corrigere" most powerfully acknowledges the insufficiencies Horace himself perceives in his effort to speak substantially for "what is ordained": "it is hard, but patience eases the weight of those evils which it would be sinful [unspeakable] to set right." That is, what is spoken is not right. To change it is to set it right ("corrigere"). But to set it right is "nefas"—unspeakable, an abomination. The richness of the irony here requires no comment.

   In its development, then, Horace's poem demonstrates that, to the question he initially addresses to the muse, there are two answers: Virgil's resists the limits that the decorums of substantial speech would impose upon speaking about grief (and perhaps upon imagining it), Horace's defines and enunciates them. The result is the reticent eloquence of the poem Horace gives us: a politeness that acknowledges and sympathizes with an experience that is, still, elusive and very threatening. Horace's reticence composes the poem, then, but it is Virgil's incapacity for restraint and for substantial speech which calls the poem into being and gives it shape.[8] In the play of Horace's way against Virgil's way, the poem's lyricism is made manifest, and what we *overhear* in this drama is Horace's coming to the recognition of the complexity of his stylistic and moral choices. Even in a poem so plainly marked by the gestures and conventions of social speech, much of what is meant is not finally *spoken out,* and though the poem's speaker is not situated in solitude, he is discovering the limits of the reach of his public voice.

———◆◆◆———

Perhaps the most obvious characteristic of Horace's poem is its intricacy. This intricacy is a function of the poem's attention to the ironies inherent in Virgil's, that supremely articulate man's, incapacity in this situation for substantial speech, speech that accords with decree and with fate, speech, therefore, that *speaks out.* Such substantial speech cannot be adequate to Virgil's inner situation, and intricacy of the kind manifested in the Quintilius ode is perhaps inevitable in Augustan poetry when it is about intensely inward states of mind. Perhaps this happens because in Augustan poetry eloquence is regularly understood to have primarily public functions or to be an essentially social display. The intricacy Horace's poem displays, generated by its search for a decorous eloquence at the same time that it articulates its sympathy for what must not be said, enacts the poet's experience of strain in representing or in honoring powerfully subjective experience. And this experience of strain is itself a tacit subject of Augustan poems when they are about such experience. The meaning of speech and the meaning of inarticulateness are perceived as rich and complex matters, problematized, as we might now say, whenever the rhetoric of social display seeks to reveal the contours of inward experience.

In Horace's poem, Virgil is not represented as being without words, but he is seen as essentially inarticulate. This crucial point is enforced by Horace's decision to keep him from speaking for himself within the rhetorical structure of the whole poem. That is, Horace attributes to Virgil a speech whose primary characteristic is its excess, but Horace does not *represent* that speech. Within *Horace's poem* Virgil himself has no voice of his own, and though the reader hears of Virgil's speech, he experiences it only as a silence. Now, especially interesting here is this enactment *within the poem* of the essential equivalence of verbal excess and silence, each a sign of a failure to reach substantial speech, each at the same time a sign of an inner experience of especial richness, in Virgil's case, his "unspeakable" desire for the "dear life."

In considering the association that Horace sees between Virgil's insubstantial speech, both excessive and unheard, and the intensity of his inner experience, we may call to mind those figures who belong to a later literary age but whose rhetorical situation is at least cognate with that of the Virgil we see in Horace's poem: figures such as Corporal Trim, Uncle Toby, Yorick, Harley. Excess and silence seem to mark their presence too, and the most eloquent moments of these heroes of sentimentalism are given out not by words, but by gestures; what we learn about them with most delight, we learn through feelings they enact rather than articulate, more accurately perhaps, through the fullness of feeling they point to. Indeed, the inarticulate eloquence of the hero of feeling, the sentimentalist, may well be a way of exploring concerns similar to those at the center of Horace's memorial ode. And more generally, in the overtly lyrical poetry of the eighteenth century, it is usual to discover the careful decorums of public speech shadowing forth and honoring certain rich states of mind of which speaking out is no necessary consequence. The complex ending of Thomas Gray's *Elegy*, for example, works to generate powerfully lyrical feeling without precisely defining it or describing its sources within the narrator. Indeed, the poem's concluding presentation of the speaker's own imagined monument, its reticent and unrevealing epitaph cut into it, clearly signals the way in which a public eloquence could be put to the task of honoring what it refuses to reveal, as if the refusal to reveal were itself an important constituent of valuable emotional experience. Here too, as in the Quintilius ode, intricate poetic activity will be generated by the poet's interest in the conditions of speech and speechlessness, but here the poet's refusal to commit himself entirely to his hearers even as he makes the sounds of public speech is more clearly brought forward than it is by Horace.[9] In the *Elegy* the poem's speaker is both Horace *and* Virgil: his is both the mastery of a reticent eloquence and the experience of a valued emotional excess.

Gray's gesturing at the presence of what he will not reveal I would define as a sentimental act; it marks the high value the writer places on inward experience, but also his somewhat contradictory suspicion that such experience can have no standing until it is translated into a heard language whose very good manners would give to the inward the grace and the status of the social. But then too, this uncertainty about the standing of the inward is accompanied also by the writer's hostility to the social, the speakable, the authorized. In Gray's poem, certainly, the public life is presented as knowable, as uninteresting, and as mean, and the poem's lyric effect is largely created by the speaker's incomplete effort at self-revelation played out against those assertions. What we are left with finally is the sense that having one's own story is all that counts, but publishing that story can only deface it. Gray's speaker wants, at one and the same time, the privileges of silence and of speech, to walk a stage where passion may brood over itself and still speak to a hearer. The special distinction of the *Elegy* is to have accorded moral dignity to this sentimental condition of mute articulateness.[10]

I want to turn now to a similarly revealing poem of William Collins in whose intricacies the rhetorical dynamics of Gray's *Elegy* can be seen to be played out in an even more complex fashion, all to demonstrate how an Augustan articulateness can be made to function in a situation in which, again, heard speech is situationally impossible. In A *Song from Shakespear's Cymbelyne* Collins has reimagined a dramatic action as a lyric poem, signaling in this his double effort to give standing to the experience of inwardness by linking it, if only allusively, to an originally public mode, the dramatic action, and *at the same time to resist the opportunities and obligations of public speech*. Collins's peculiar aim, like Gray's, is to honor silence and solitude, but also to authorize them—to be simultaneously inward and social, speechless and eloquent, sentimental and gentlemanly.

The intricacies of Collins's own *Song from Cymbelyne* result from its subtle use of the Shakespearean original, of course. But even the most cursory glance at the poem tells us that Collins had not only tuned his ear to "Fear no more the heat o' the sun"—the beautiful lyric that in the play ceremonializes the apparent death of Fidele, the real Imogen—but also drew together Shakespeare's "Song" *and* the dramatic movement immediately leading up to it. This he did, not merely to represent in his own terms the song of the two brothers at Fidele's burial, but to represent it by introducing into the situation a new line of sight altogether, one that would reveal the capacity of some distanced, indistinct, and generalized mourner for responding feelingly, *but without uttered words,* to that doubly fictional event. As in Horace's poem, it is the mourner and not the mourned who claims our central attention: but unlike Horace's dirge, and unlike Shakespeare's "Song," Collins's poem attenuates markedly its representation of the social dimension of the mourning situation.

Now in Horace's poem the social character of his response to Quintilius's death and Virgil's sorrow is perhaps most clearly marked in the plain didacticism of the concluding thought, however complex the implications of that didacticism may be: "durum: sed levius fit patientia, / quidquid corrigere est nefas." In Shakespeare's "Song" a similar didactic charge is expressed in the recurring rhyme of "dust" and "must"—that is, in the utterly realistic insistence upon the plain inevitability, finality, and democracy of death:

> Golden lads and girls all must,
> As chimney-sweepers, come to dust . . .
> The sceptre, learning, physic, must
> All follow this, and come to dust . . .
> All lovers young, all lovers must
> Consign to thee and come to dust . . .[11]

But this is only one of several sounds we hear in the "Song": this plain realism is blended with a note of genuine pathos itself articulated as elegiac circumlocution—"Thou thy worldly task hast done, / Home art gone and ta'en thy wages . . ."—and elsewhere in the most direct of sayings—"Care no more to clothe and eat; / To thee the reed is as the oak." In this, the utterance of a distanced but sympathetic consciousness, we can hear yet another music too, that of the small couplets chanting the ceremonial imperatives in which the song is concluded and which ordain, as if it were a ritual action, the reverential silence which is, oddly, to *mark* Fidele's grave.[12]

> No exorciser harm thee.
> Nor no witchcraft charm thee.
> Ghost unlaid forbear thee.
> Nothing ill come hear thee.
> Quiet consummation have,
> And renowned by thy grave.

This blend of realism, pathos, and ceremonial dignity gives the song its character and is the final style of the lyric utterance of the two brothers who had *in the dialogue immediately preceding the song* argued gently over what constituted speech proper to the occasion. The song itself is produced as the resolution of their argument, which was about the suitability of such excessive, such *sentimental* language as this to the fact of death:

> With fairest flowers
> Whilst summer lasts and I live here, Fidele,
> I'll sweeten thy sad grave. Thou shalt not lack
> The flower that's like thy face, pale primrose, nor
> The azur'd harebell, like thy veins; no, nor
> The leaf of eglantine, whom not to slander,
> Outsweet'ned not thy breath.

This, Arviragus's speech, is interrupted in the impatience of grief by his brother, Guiderius: "Prithee have done, / And do not play in wench-like words with that / Which is so serious." Guiderius objects to the apparent excessiveness of his brother's rhetoric, its inadequacy to the fact of death, while Guiderius reveals what he himself would take to be a more appropriate style in the brusque phrase in which he summarizes his impatience with his brother's speech. He says simply: "To the grave." And yet Guiderius had a moment earlier uttered his own "wench-like words," entirely in response to the shock of Fidele's apparent death:

> Why, he but sleeps!
> If he be gone, I'll make his grave a bed.
> With female fairies will his tomb be haunted,
> And worms will not come to thee.

This expression of a rich fantasy—"Why, he but sleeps"—with its merely subjunctive acknowledgment of the "truth" ("If he be gone"), its indicative assertion of an impossibility ("And worms will not come to thee"), and its transformation of a grave to a bed—all this is hardly the blunt realism that the speaker is himself to insist upon in a moment. It is, like Virgil's unheard speech, an excessive, a *sentimental* expression of desire for the "dear life." And only in the wonderful song to come thirty lines later are the realism Guiderius insists upon and the desire he feels brought together and harmonized. But in creating that harmony, Shakespeare has eliminated in the "Song" all trace of the sentimentalist's excess. That is to say, in the dramatic action, the sentimentalist's emotional excess is—unlike Virgil's unheard lament and Gray's unrevealed sorrow—plain and outspoken. But then this very outspokenness permissible in the dialogue—indeed, it is the subject of the dramatic dialogue—is entirely suppressed in the lyric movement that resolves the stylistic disagreement the dramatic dialogue articulates. And the new music of this "Song"—the ceremonial, the pathetic, the elegiacal chant—is entirely denuded of the language of flower and fairy in which the brothers had expressed their excessive, sentimental, and fantasized desire to preserve Fidele from death and corruption.

But, and this is especially interesting, Collins's *Song from Cymbelyne* is grounded entirely in that sentimental language of the two brothers. In Collins's reworking of Shakespeare's "Song" there is no reference whatever to the sententious realism of their new "Song"; nor is there any enactment of the small dispute over proper speech which precedes that song. Nevertheless, Collins clearly signals his attention to that dispute. For, in his *Song from Cymbelyne*, Collins reproduces the earlier sentimental language of both brothers—the language they will give up—but does so in the same ceremonial cadences *that had marked their abandonment of the sentimental style.* And, in this union of ceremonial and sentimental speech, Collins has discovered a public voice for the inwardness of the sentimentalist. We hear the ceremonial music in "No wither'd Witch shall here be seen, / No goblins lead their nightly Crew . . ." and in the following couplet, we hear the ceremonial and the sentimental: "The Female Fays shall haunt the Green, / And dress thy Grave with pearly Dew." The first two lines I have just cited plainly echo the ceremonial chant that concludes Shakespeare's song; equally clearly the second two lines pick up the excess of Guiderius's speech before it had been transformed into ceremonial song: "With female fairies will his tomb be haunted." Collins blends this, the language of Guiderius, to Arviragus's similarly expressed promise ("With fairest flowers . . . Fidele, I'll sweeten thy sad grave"), all in order to produce his new and now gentlemanly version of the speech of the young brothers: "The Female Fays shall haunt the Green, / And dress thy grave with pearly Dew."

What then has happened to the excessive, the sentimental utterance of the brothers' dramatic dialogue, which, as in Horace's memorial ode, represented a verbal fullness felt to be inappropriate both to the actuality of death and to the memorial song for the dead? Quite simply, Collins has pruned away that fullness. Arviragus's flowers—pale primrose, the azured harebell, the leaf of eglantine—each along with its analogue in some part of Fidele's anatomy, have been generalized to their simplest seasonal identity and ceremonial function:

> To fair Fidele's grassy Tomb
>   Soft Maids, and Village Hinds shall bring
> Each op'ning Sweet, of earliest Bloom,
>   And rifle all the breathing Spring.

Even more radical surgery is performed on Arviragus's robin, which Shakespeare gives us in this language:

> The raddock would,
> With charitable bill (O bill, sore shaming
> Those rich-left heirs that let their fathers lie
> Without a monument!), bring thee all this,
> Yea, and furr'd moss besides. When flow'rs are none,
> To winter-ground thy corse—

Here is Collins's version:

> The Redbreast oft at Ev'ning Hours
>   Shall kindly lend his little Aid:
> With hoary Moss, and gather'd Flow'rs,
>   To deck the Ground where thou art laid.

Obvious here is Collins's effort to do away with Arviragus's sententiousness and to tame his fervor; note the absence of exclamation, as well as the transformation of a desolate winter scene, spontaneously imagined, to an evening ceremony, regularly recurring. In this restraint Collins demonstrates that the reticence of ceremonial speech and the valued excess of the sentimentalist can, indeed, be harmonized, harmonized here in the generalizing decorums of Augustan eloquence, which has in Collins's version of the song become the sentimentalist's preferred style. Embodying these decorums, Collins's reworking of Shakespeare's scenario can give lyric articulation to the emotional and verbal excess which Shakespeare would dramatize in his dialogue but not allow in his "Song."

But the transformed sentimentalist who is the lyric speaker of Collins's poem and in whose Augustan decorums fullness of feeling has discovered its reticent eloquence—this lyric speaker has sought no occasion for speaking out. For, though he imagines the pastoral ceremony honoring Fidele, and even blesses it, he is by no means a participant in it. Indeed, he insists upon his separation from that ceremony and from its society, as his language makes clear: "soft Maids," "Village Hinds," "Shepherd Lads," and "melting Virgins"—it is for these that Fidele's tomb is a shrine. Not a member of this pastoral community (from which he excludes himself by the very act of naming it so conventionally and so elegantly), the speaker cannot appear in the poem as a presented figure at all. That is, he has taken from Shakespeare's play a dramatic action, and reimagined its cast of characters as a generalized and anonymous pastoral community; he then has excluded himself from participation in that community, but still asserted his own as the central consciousness of the scene he has thus re-created.

In this odd and intricate process, Collins creates a lyric poem out of a dramatic action and out of a set of actors, a single lyric speaker. Now this speaker, in his separation from a scene that is now not enacted but instead envisioned, can utter a speech that is not heard, but only *overheard*. But—and this is very important—the politeness and the ceremony of this overheard and entirely inward utterance are still the hallmarks of social speech. Were this a lyric constructed according to Mill's specifications, we would not expect to see written into it—at the moment, and at the site, of lyric speech—so clear, if tacit, a representation of the speaker's social self-awareness, here made plain in his insistence upon his separation from the very scene he broods over and claims emotional kinship with. But it is Collins's achievement to have represented the speaker's social self-awareness at the same time as he has made that representation the very condition of our entering into earshot of his *overheard address,* and thus into contact with his inwardness. Overheard address—this paradoxical, or at least odd, designation—best describes the character of Collins's lyric speech. It is the vehicle for the social display of inward experience.

Indeed, in transforming Shakespeare's dramatic action into a lyric poem, Collins seized the opportunity to create a new line of sight and with it a new register of feeling, the sight and feeling of the cultivated consciousness itself, socially and intellectually distinct from the pastoral milieu of both play and poem, but emotionally involved in it, as the last two stanzas show:

> When howling Winds, and beating Rain,
>   In Tempests shake the sylvan Cell:
> Or midst the Chace on ev'ry Plain,
>   The tender Thought on thee shall dwell.
>
> Each lonely Scene shall thee restore,
>   For thee the Tear be duly shed:
> Belov'd, till Life could charm no more;
>   And mourn'd, till Pity's self be dead.

Note the primacy here of the "tender Thought": thinking it is not represented as an experience the speaker sympathetically shares, if only from a distance, with the pastoral characters, as are the ceremonies of the earlier stanzas at Fidele's shrine. Now instead, it is his alone, available to him either when pastoral society is unable to assemble for its pleasures ("In Tempests"), or when it is inappropriately engaged in them ("midst the Chace on ev'ry Plain"). So the shrine built in the previous four stanzas has all along been intended for this new speaker, not as a place at which he and the pastoral characters might "assemble," as in a dramatic action embodying the experience of an acknowledged community of feeling. The shrine is instead a stimulus to the speaker's own capacity to think the "tender Thought," to weep, to love, to mourn, and to pity. The initial representation of the speaker as in sympathy with the pastoral characters is somewhat inconsistent, then, with the poem's concluding emphasis on his social and psychological isolation from them, an inconsistency that reveals the poem's straining point. Nevertheless, what Collins has done seems an exquisite feat of language; he has fully articulated a scene of solitude in which eloquence has been associated not with public utterance or even with the participation in public ceremony, but rather with inwardness itself—the thinking of the "tender Thought," "each lonely Scene," the tear "*duly* shed" (note the insistence upon decorum in that adverb even as the action it describes is entirely private). These scenes of solitude and acts of silence are the home and deeds of the inward consciousness itself, for which the restoring of loss is equivalent to thinking about the lost object—"Each lonely Scene shall thee restore"—just as loving and mourning are equivalent states. It is finally that quality of consciousness, the sovereign inwardness of which is demonstrated in its extraordinary command of social speech and *simultaneously in its freedom from social declarativeness*, that Collins's poem is all about. That is, its subject is "Pity's self," and "Pity's self" is actually the poem's speaker—Pathos, the very muse of inwardness. The poem's *action*, moreover, is to represent Pathos or Feeling coming to consciousness of itself, or as Mill stipulated, "brooding over itself." But what Mill would have deemed generically impossible is the poem's remarkable accomplishment: the demonstration that only a social eloquence (the poem contains no more obvious a public locution than that final personification, "Pity's self") can fully honor and make intelligible what must be experienced only in solitude and can be known only inwardly.

Now, it is an oddity of Collins's *Song from Cymbelyne* that it is presented entirely without irony, because the opportunities for irony here are considerable. The most obvious is that, though Shakespeare's Fidele will almost immediately in the play awake from what has been only the appearance of death, as Collins's poem is given, Fidele's death is not to be undone. His (or her) life is now newly bounded by the poem, for the poem is complete in itself as the contemplation of Fidele's memorial, and in that, of Feeling's coming to the awareness of itself. The poem does not question, parody, nor ironize that experience, it just presents it. At the same time, then, that the poem calls our attention to its rather subtly elaborated system of allusions, it also insists that we willfully refuse to look beyond the single moment in the play to which they immediately refer. Were we to look beyond that moment and then to read the poem in the light of our better knowledge, it would be difficult to take its lyric speaker seriously. He would be read as a figure mourning a death that has not happened, he would become therefore vulnerable to irony, and the poem would be open to a more complex reading than our experience of it can verify. If we were, in a triumph of judgment, to see the speaker ironically, we would be undoing our own rich act of sympathetic reading, and the poem would become pointless. For the very purpose of its rhetoric is to cause the reader to become aware of himself resisting that interpretive temptation. In this he gains a power to resist the full claim of the sophistication which the poem's brief allusion to *Cymbeline* has itself called into play.

Collins's willingness to resist that full claim seems to me central to his lyric success in *A Song from Shakespear's Cymbelyne*. In fact, his insistence on calling attention to the bounds he is willing to impose on his literary sophistication is a quite explicit indication of the importance he attached to the freedom thus gained, a freedom he did not always command as a writer of lyric poetry. For, in fact, Collins's extraordinary literary sophistication is more usually the subject of his poetry than are the feelings and the visions that give names to his poems and that he pretends to invoke. In the very midst of his *Ode to Fear*, for example, at what might have been a moment of great intensity, are two footnotes he himself places within his text to cool it down by calling attention to his sources in Sophocles. If this is not a simple act of pedantry, it is certainly a complex one, central to his intention in the ode, which is not, after all, to represent his being overcome by Fear, but politely to represent a sophisticated literary consciousness toying with that possibility and enjoying its distance from it. In his *Ode to Fear* Collins depends upon his reader's similarly sophisticated pleasure in catching the allusions, noting the discrepancies between source and poem, and deriving from this activity an affirmation, not of his power to feel Fear, but of the power his literacy gives him to make a game out of that possibility. The bond between poet and reader here is formed not by feeling, but by intelligence, by judgment, by sophistication.[13]

But the poise that characterizes Collins's *Song from Cymbelyne* seems to me a sign of sentimental expressiveness working its most interesting effects: such writing registers the author's awareness of the possibilities for ironizing his manner or parodying his material, but then his conscious resistance to doing so. To acknowledge those possibilities is to acknowledge the social claims of intelligence and judgment, to resist them is to embrace the pleasures of inwardness, and still to have one's intelligence and judgment endorsing that choice. Precisely this pointedly articulated, sentimental drama between intelligence and feeling produces the characteristic blend of lyricism and intellectual adroitness which is the special distinction of eighteenth-century poetry. Again, Gray's success in the *Elegy* in drawing the full evocative force from his rural material at the same time as he creates room and opportunity for the critical play of intelligence upon this rural material will stand as the primary example of the kind of pleasure a sentimental rhetoric can yield.

But when this kind of writing does not succeed—as, for example, in Gray's Eton College ode—the play of eloquence upon emotionally evocative material will seem intrusive. In such situations we can sense the poet reaching out too directly to his audience of readers, as if to assure them and himself that his lyrical material is not too much his own, not disruptive of the bond that social experience, intelligence, and literary sophistication have formed between them. The writer's fussiness rather than his intelligence is the most obvious message in the signals he sends out to assure the reader that despite the poem's personal charge it still is a record of shared public experience: it will pass judgment's muster. An example is Gray's use of the word "redolent" in the Eton College ode: it is not a bold straining beyond John Dryden's "honey redolent of Spring" to test the limits of our language (as Samuel Johnson disapprovingly thought),[14] but a fussy *reminder of* Dryden's usage. With that word Gray plays it safe, calling for support from Dryden's eloquent precedent to help establish his own authority for personal expression in his own poem. Gray's uncertainty in the personal and lyrical stance is evident also in the ode's shift into declamatory and pointed utterance, thoroughly inconsistent with the initially private and meditative situation the poem springs from: "Alas," "Yet see," "Ah, shew them," "Lo," and, of course, "No more: where ignorance is bliss, / 'Tis folly to be wise." The poem falls short in lyric power because it is not so much a record of what the poet felt and thought from his distant prospect of Eton College; it really registers instead his concern for his authority to speak about the experience.[15]

It is this concern for authority, this sense that poetic speech is warranted by a bond of intelligence, education, and sophistication between writer and reader, that often vitiates the portrayal of inwardness in the eighteenth-century lyric. The poet seems to think of his authority as a property of that bond, which he seeks to affirm, looking to it and not finally to his inner experience for the justification of his poem. When this happens, declamatory speech usually follows, since declamation more easily than the overheard speech of the lyric can stand as a demonstration of the intellectual and social bond the poet seeks with the reader. It is not surprising, therefore, to discover a mixture of lyricism and declamation pervading the period's lyric expression despite its formal variety, from Collins's visionary odes to William Cowper's unbroken conversation. Even so genuinely lyrical a talent as Robert Burns's, so late in the period, is disrupted and distorted by this mix, as in *The Cotter's Saturday Night*, where the charge of personal feeling so strongly binding the poet to his rural material dissipates itself in his search for a style to *distinguish* him from the peasantry. He tests no fewer than three languages in his effort to connect with his readers rather than with his subject: these languages are the dialect of the poor themselves, the "standard" English that sets the poet apart from the peasants, and then the borrowings from other poems that serve to link him in consciousness and sophistication with his readers and with high culture.

The most usual form of the poet's declamatory utterance in the lyric situation is didactic. In didactic address the eighteenth-century writer most regularly asserts his authority for speech; in didactic address he most often reveals himself in the role of writer, bonded to his audience by literary tradition, by intelligence, by judgment. Of course, the great variety of uses to which didactic address could be put, and of forms to which it could be shaped, itself speaks for the variousness of the conceptions of literary purpose and of literary *being* in the period. Jonathan Swift's pamphlets, for example, whether straight or satirical, all assume a writer in a position of some authority, with something *to say to* an audience, whatever the result of that saying may come to be. Alexander Pope's *Moral Essays* reveal by their very title their at least initially didactic intention, and his poetry throughout is rich in its presentation of serious and improving conversations in which the delivery of a lesson, as in Bethel's "sermon," is an important moment in a poem's thematic and emotional development. In the finest didactic literature, of course, an initially didactic stance will become richly complicated, and in this process the positive assumptions about the writer's bond with his audience which are implied in his didactic stance will be scrutinized; they may be rejected, or reaffirmed, or redefined.

In the obviously public poetry of the period—the poetry written for an audience, even if it be an audience of one, as in Swift's poems to Stella, even if it be a meditating reader, as in Johnson's *Vanity of Human Wishes*, or the recipient of an epistle, as in Pope's Horatian imitations—in this obviously public poetry, the representation of inwardness will usually be a function of the poet's scrutiny of his didactic stance. His rejection, or his reaffirmation, or his redefinition of it, will be seen as a humane complication of his lesson; and, in the process of complicating it, his poem will develop dramatically. The pleasure we derive from such writing comes from our sense that, shaping the lesson with which these poems directly address us, there is in them a curve of feeling to which we become alert, and that in this curve of feeling we overhear something of the poet's inner experience as the lesson's teacher. Our responsiveness to the poem as such a record of the poet's inwardness gives us our sense of its lyric force, and in the dramatic accord the poet establishes between his didactic manner and his inwardness is to be discovered the largest lesson of his work, its yield of instructive pleasure.

What I am describing here I have earlier called covert lyricism—covert, because the poet's inwardness is not his ostensible, his first subject. Nor can we see from his rhetorical situation, his "speaking out," that it can *become* his subject. Thus, Oliver Goldsmith's *Deserted Village* begins with an explanatory letter about, of all things, a matter of historical fact, and proceeds as a discourse on social policy. But this covertly lyrical poem soon enough comes to reveal the remarkable resources for the representation of inwardness which were inherent in the forms of its public address, of which the didactic was Goldsmith's favorite. In their discovery of the resources of a covert lyricism, the poets I discuss in the following chapters were able to satisfy two demands that were soon to seem incompatible: that they speak out with authoritative eloquence, and that they still reveal their own rich inwardness. It was a project that the overt lyric approached with uncertainty, never commanded, and usually failed at.

1

Pope and Augustan Lyricism: *The Second Epistle of the Second Book of Horace,* Imitated

FEW WRITERS HAVE MADE themselves their own subject so often as has Alexander Pope, and, in the process, few writers have displayed themselves as theatrically. This is an interesting contradiction, since in his mature representations of himself Pope's first insistence is upon the sufficiency of his private being, and his second, upon its integrity. Certainly the theatrical representation of one's integrity and self-sufficiency is an odd project, for its very goal is to display precisely that which declares itself free of the need for display. In Pope's case the oddity is enhanced by his making not simply himself but *his own inwardness* the central display of those poems in which he is most interestingly his own subject. In this peculiar blend of theatricality and inwardness we see the characteristic union of the social and the private which produces the effects of Augustan lyricism, and in Pope's management of those effects we have perhaps the richest, the most complex rhetorical performances in Augustan poetry.[1]

Pope's self-display is a carefully crafted presentation of a life made intelligible by the interaction of the public and the private experience of itself. As they were for Horace, the categories public and private are for Pope forms of thought and, indeed, of feeling; by them, the poet's being becomes aware of itself, and by them, others reveal themselves to him. In the smallest details of the poetry we can see the shaping presence of those categories.

> Is there a Parson, much bemus'ed in Beer,
> A maudlin Poetess, a ryming Peer . . .[2]

Here, for example, we derive our sense of *personal* disorder in these three figures by noting first the markers of their public identities: Parson, Poetess, Peer. Against these, the personal attributes—the drunkenness, the mawkishness, the inauthentic versifying—take on their meaning. With some surprise, and in the clarity now of a satirical judgment, we can see them as equivalent to each other and equally inappropriate: the rhyming of the peer, the mawkishness of the poetess, the drunkenness of the parson. Moreover, the ironic logic of the adjective-noun connections refines these definitions of skewed being: what, after all, is the nature of the connection between the poetess and her mawkishness, and again, between his rhyming and the peer? In the first case, the adjective and noun define an integral, if ridiculous personality: in some poor sense, being maudlin *is* being a poetess. But in the peer's case, he is all peer; his rhyming is, as its adjectival subordination to the noun that defines him implies, merely an adjunct to, an affectation of, his title. Again, later in the same poem, Pope's distillation of the tragedy of "Atticus"—"Who but must laugh if such a man there be? / Who would not weep, if *Atticus* were he!"—is presented as a small social drama of conflicting elements within the person judging Atticus: in conflict are the social impulse toward ridicule, seen as compelled, and the private experience of regret, presented as an effect of sympathy and choice.[3] Each of these instances—Atticus, the three would-be poets—presents a miniaturized parable whose implied subject is the nature of human identity, and whose vehicle is the public/private trope.

Pope's acts of self-display are also expressions of his almost constant interest in the constitution of personal identity, and they too are shaped by his imagination of the self as an entity produced and made intelligible in the dialogue of the private and the public. It is the distinction of his best poems that in them self-display in all its theatricality will function in the name of self-scrutiny, and that their essential poetic act—what builds and shapes them—will work as an agent of self-scrutiny.

Pope's poems are shaped not primarily by a network of small elements cohering as an organic union of metaphor, image, or allusion, but rather by an organization of tonal effects, each one built up within the unit of the verse paragraph, each one contrasting with, or intensifying, or complementing the sound that has come before and the one that will come after, all in order to give shape to a sweep of feeling that finds an appropriate rest, resolving itself in the full revelation of the poet's being that his poem's end brings. This is the *poesis* of Pope's mature poetry, the building of an emotional curve whose movement we *overhear* as we listen *to* the poet's overt address. What the reader overhears is the inner drama that accompanies, shapes, and is shaped by that overt address, and that gives to the poem its lyric force.[4] In the *Epistle to Arbuthnot*, for example, the long movement through several styles of address each according with the several roles within which Pope displays himself, his anger rising and falling as he marks the gaps between his adumbration of an ideal image of the poet's career and his own actual experience of it—this long movement toward the conclusion, with its grand assertion of the integrity of his identity against the play of forces working to pull it apart is itself a "meaning" of Pope's poem: "Thus far was right, the rest belongs to Heav'n." Our sense of lyric presence in this final line is produced by our awareness that during the poem's development it has not been clear that "Thus far was right." The grand assertion is itself a "coming to," an inward realization that sets the speaking poet apart even from the friend he blesses.[5]

The lyric beauty of the *Epistle to Arbuthnot* is generated by the poem's movement toward the resolved quiet in which Pope presents his final version of himself: that image simultaneously heroic and domestic in which the homeliest of details can support a grand assertion of self-sufficiency, and in which even the celebration of a friendship works to emphasize the rich solitude of the speaker's being. In this assertion of self—one wants to say this triumph of self—all the intricate investigation of the constitution of personal identity has its conclusion. A similar assertion of high self-awareness can be seen in the vastly different tonal environment of the *Epistle to Burlington*. Here, the conclusion in hortatory address represents the poet in his most obvious public role, a didactic and, indeed, a prophetic presence issuing the visionary commands of an inspired speaker. But if *Arbuthnot* emphasizes in its final movement the grand selfhood of the speaker, in *To Burlington* the transcendence of personality and the assertion of role is instead at the core of the poem's dramatic movement:

> You too proceed! make falling Arts your care,
> Erect new wonders, and the old repair,

> Jones and Palladio to themselves restore,
> And be whate'er Vitruvius was before:
> Till Kings call forth th' Ideas of your mind,
> Proud to accomplish what such hands design'd . . .
> (191–196)

This hortatory and vatic address could hardly have been anticipated in the poem's opening manner, whose chatty informality is just the right style to establish Pope's easy equality with his addressee, Lord Burlington: "'Tis strange the Miser should his Cares employ / To gain those Riches he can ne'er enjoy." (1–2). Immediately defining this informal ease as its central voice, the poem draws a circle around its speaker and his addressee, a circle that excludes, of course, the objects of their troubled amusement: the Miser, the Prodigal, the "wealthy fool," the "Coxcomb," the "brother Peer." And, having drawn the circle, Pope can define more precisely the complexities constituting the equality of the two men it contains:

> You show us, Rome was glorious not profuse,
> And pompous buildings once were things of Use.
> Yet shall (my Lord) your just, your noble rules
> Fill half the land with Imitating Fools;
>
> . . . .
>
> Oft have you hinted to your brother Peer,
> A certain truth, which many buy too dear:
> Something there is more needful than Expence,
> And something previous ev'n to Taste—'tis Sense.
> [23–26, 39–42]

This celebration of the shared taste of poet and peer is obviously complicated by questions of decorum and address. Perhaps most interesting here is the parenthetical "(my Lord)" of line 25 cited above. It marks the class distinction between Pope and Burlington in the very act of asserting their more essential equality as artist and architect—an essential equality even more strongly emphasized by the complex hauteur of "your brother Peer." The exclusion of the "brother" from the circle that bounds Pope and Burlington makes Pope's acknowledgment of the class distinction between him and the nobleman seem so easy, so free of invidious force.

In the context of this complex marking and then delimiting of the social distinction between the poet and peer, the poem's hortatory conclusion takes on its interest. For in that conclusion Pope, now emphasizing his role as poet, assumes the authority of the high didactic role that the peer, earlier in the poem, had been seen to fill—"You show us Rome was glorious, not profuse." But as the poet's, Pope's voice now moves to a register entirely different from the easy informality that has been celebrating and rehearsing these lessons of the peer. The intensity of Pope's new language accords, of course, with the monumental and also epic character of the work he as poet now envisions:

> Bid Harbors open, public Ways extend,
> Bid Temples, worthier of the God, ascend;
> Bid the broad Arch the dang'rous Flood contain,
> The Mole projected break the roaring Main;
> Back to his bounds their subject Sea command,
> And roll obedient Rivers thro' the Land . . .

The extraordinary contrast this prophetic and visionary mode makes with the chatty informality of the poem's body now marks the poet's movement into a role that will distance him from and place him above his noble addressee in authority. For not the projects but the *envisioning them* generates his rhetoric here. And as he assumes his own high role as civic visionary, the poet establishes and emphasizes his authority to direct the work of both the nobleman-architect and his executive—the king. That is, he establishes and emphasizes his absolutely central position in the life of the polity. It can be said, then, that the *Epistle to Burlington* in its celebration of a vision of what the kingdom might be is also a record of the poet's coming to awareness of himself as the source of that vision. As the easy but deferential informality of the poem's earlier manner yields to its closing vatic rhetoric, we have the lyric experience of *overhearing* the poet's own inward assumption of his highest public role. Consciousness comes to awareness of itself within an entirely public theater, and the assumption of the prophetic voice is represented as the outcome of the inner drama marked by the poet's movement from role to role, voice to voice—confidant, raconteur, celebrant, satirist. This movement has shaped his poem and gives it meaning.

———— ◆◆◆ ————

In producing his vision of the poet's function and authority in the ending of the *Epistle to Burlington,* Pope makes his highest claims for the didactic stance as he promotes it into a way of speech more usually associated with the "higher" genres. And reaching the language of those higher genres is the result of conversing, arguing, exhorting, mocking—all social acts whose outcome finally is the poet's new and heightened recognition of self, a recognition he marks by his highly theatrical representation of self.

I want to turn now to the most interesting—and most surprising—of Pope's theatrical self-representations, his imitation of Horace's *Epistle II. ii,* entitled *The Second Epistle of the Second Book of Horace.* Nowhere else has Pope made himself the subject of so intense an act of self-scrutiny as in this imitation of Horace, and nowhere else has he represented the outcome of that act as so triumphant a display of self-possession. Yet this is the most inward of his poems. In it, Pope displays an unsurpassed mastery of the rhythms and dramatic transitions by which a verbal structure may stand as a representation of a state of mind and soul. In his representation here of mind and soul, moreover, we may observe Pope's most intricate use of the materials that constitute his mature writing: the didacticism, the theatricality, the lyricism. For the lessons he now teaches are lessons to himself, and the theater he performs in is entirely the theater of his own mind. Yet the *sounds* he makes are the public ones of conversation, dialogue, exhortation:

> Learn to live well, or fairly make your Will;
> You've play'd, and lov'd, and eat, and drank your fill:
> Walk sober off; before a sprightlier Age
> Comes titt'ring on, and shoves you from the stage:
> Leave such to trifle with more grace and ease,
> Whom Folly pleases, and whose Follies please.
> [322–327]

This is the poem's resting place, a concluding moment remarkable for its resemblance to Horace's original, and also for its divergence from it.

Pope has certainly reproduced the quiet resolve of the original, and along with it, the moral lyricism of Horace's concluding lesson. But nothing in Horace's ending suggests the literally theatrical gesture with which Pope articulates his lesson to himself and by which he reveals himself publicly to others.

My interest is in the rhetorical and emotive movement that brings him to this point. This final divergence from the original is but one of many that mark the poem and call our attention to the intricate system working to make it Pope's own at the same time as it links him in a bond both social and imaginative with a valued other. Here, for example, is a passage much discussed for its striking differences from the easier, more offhand manner of the Horatian original:

> Years foll'wing Years, steal something ev'ry day,
> At last they steal us from our selves away;
> In one our Frolicks, one Amusements end,
> In one a Mistress drops, in one a Friend:
> This subtle Thief of Life, this paltry Time,
> What will it leave me, if it snatch my Rhime?
> If ev'ry Wheel of that unweary'd Mill
> That turn'd ten thousand Verses, now stands still.
>
> But after all, what wou'd you have me do?
> When out of twenty I can please not two;
> When this Heroicks only deigns to praise,
> Sharp Satire that, and that Pindaric lays?
> One likes the Pheasant's wing, and one the leg;
> The Vulgar boil, the Learned roast an Egg;
> Hard Task! to hit the Palate of such Guests,
> When Oldfield loves, what Dartineuf detests.
> [72–87]

The reader cannot fail to hear the abrupt shift in tone as Pope moves into the second paragraph, as if he were snapping out of himself, collecting himself suddenly and readdressing himself to the friend to whom he writes. The moving elegiacal quality of the first paragraph, created by the obvious personal focus and then by the repetitions of word, phrase and rhythm—years, steal, in one, this subtle thief, this paltry time—is abruptly broken by Pope's smart return to his imagined reader with chatty and sharp observations about the insufficiencies and inanities of the poet's audience, in contrast with the previous paragraph whose concern was with the poet's self and whose elegiac manner communicates that concern in a moment of inwardness, of self-absorption suddenly broken.[6] This movement into and out of himself, the shift from private to public address, creates a moment whose dynamics, as it were, correspond entirely to the larger subject of the poem, the costs of the life in literature with its strain between private and public commitment.

This subject can yield such intensities in Pope—it may be said to be his constant subject—precisely because he comes to poetry with the sense that its function *is* didactic, that its maker speaks with special authority, and that he addresses an audience who acknowledges, or should acknowledge, this authority. In this set of attitudes are certain inherent ironies that can be movingly exploited in any number of ways. In this epistle, for example, Pope feels the ironies inherent in the situation of one whose public duty to teach prevents him from experiencing in his own being the very lesson that is the burden of his public effort in poetry. But to put the matter as baldly as this is insufficient to the intensity and beauty of this poem; the adequate reader apprehends something more than a set of troubled ruminations on the hazards of a high occupation, rendered in ironic self-consciousness. He feels instead in the poem's development a rich process of inner exploration in which the highest values of the poet's career are inwardly rediscovered and seen to be compatible with the longings of the enriched self. Deftly and movingly that rediscovery is represented to occur in the very formulation of a didactic commitment and in its realization in words.

> Soon as I enter at my Country door,
> My Mind resumes the thread it dropt before;
> Thoughts, which at Hyde-Park-Corner I forgot,
> Meet and rejoin me, in the pensive Grott.
> There all alone, and Compliments apart,
> I ask these sober questions of my Heart.
> [206–210]

These well-known lines ostensibly represent the poet preparing for the *otium* in which he seeks release from a world of poetic business. The whole poem has been presented as a series of arguments *against* writing poetry, so that this prelude to its final movement appears at first to be the beginning of a vindication of those arguments. Indeed, Pope has just represented the making of poetry as entirely inconsistent with the act of asking, all alone, "sober questions of the Heart."

> To Rules of Poetry no more confin'd,
> I learn to smooth and harmonize my Mind.
> [202–204]

And throughout the poem, his device has been to identify the poet negatively (especially 115–125, 135–146, 198–205). With this in mind we come to the poem's final didactic movement, which is precisely an enactment and discovery of the *power* of poetry "to smooth and harmonize" the mind, its adequacy to the inner needs and being of the poet. And the vehicle of that discovery is the presentation of a lesson ranging over a variety of subjects, in a variety of tones—but a lesson to the self, a meditation, whose movement toward the resolved quiet of the poem's end itself demonstrates Pope's need for poetry as an agent of inner integration. Again, that this discovery of poetry coincides with the recital of a series of moralizing meditations signifies a tendency to identify poetry's didactic function *with* its capacity as a medium for inwardness, an agent of self-discovery. This tendency is especially striking in this poem, which has all along presented poetry as a business and care inconsistent with the inner needs of its maker.

Any discussion of Pope's Horatian poems, in which the blend of didactic utterance and personal revelation is especially marked, runs into the issue of Pope's relation to the original. Good scholarship has helped us to see that Pope's imitations are marked by his intensification of those elements in the originals which lend themselves to self-revelation. G. K. Hunter especially has shown that Pope's sense of his career emphasizes far more than Horace's the poet's subjectivity and individualism. For Hunter, and correctly so, this new quality of Pope's Horace comes out of his more openly satiric intention, his more obviously antagonistic relation to society.[7] This is what Hunter means by "the romanticism of Pope's Horace" in a reading that marks this crucial development of Pope's *away from* Horace. Indeed, the poignancy, the power, and the emotional curve of Pope's later poems are in large part created by the poet's awareness of his new direction, his awareness of both the value to him and the limited sufficiency of his model, his awareness that he cannot be what Horace was, and that therefore the act of imitating Horace is for him the necessary and entirely conscious act of establishing the distinctness of his own self and situation against those of a valued precursor.

Early in the poem, Pope offers as an account of his disinclination for poetry the example of the soldier who fights fiercely one day because he himself had been robbed the night before, but who on a subsequent occasion responds sluggishly to battle because his purse is now full. The working poet then is like the man who,

>   in such a desp'rate Mind,
> Between Revenge, and Grief, and Hunger join'd,
> Against the Foe, Himself, and all Mankind,
> . . . leap't the Trenches, scal'd a Castle-Wall,
> Tore down a Standard, Took the Fort and all.
>   [36–40]

The Horatian original is different: "In his ravening rage / The soldier grew fierce as a wolf, mad at himself / For losing the money and mad at the rascal who stole it." Pope's changes are intensifying additions that emphasize the play of motivation within the man and add a significant third element to the objects of his fury: "all Mankind." Horace's soldier is only "vehemens lupus," not driven and torn by Revenge, and Grief, and Hunger, and his fury is quite properly directed at himself and the thief, not at "all Mankind." These additions of Pope's are consistent with Hunter's point: they reflect more accurately and precisely than their model the motivation of the poet *as satirist*, whose work is a complexion of inner turmoil directed outward toward a fiercely generalized victim. This is an important point, and it seems to suggest the way in which the nature of Pope's whole poem must inevitably be affected by the fact that he is not, like Horace, forgiving himself merely for not writing, but for not writing *satire*. Pope's poem is a set of reflections on the cares and misgivings of the satiric poet, the cares and misgivings that explain his insistence that to write poetry is to engage in nasty business, to seek out trouble. And this helps to explain why, as his poem swings into its didactic conclusion, Pope, unlike Horace, will first particularize the scene for the meditative movement in his country house and "pensive Grott," the more to emphasize the contrast between meditative *otium* and poetic *negotium*.

The whole poem, however, is pervaded by Pope's awareness that for him poetry *is* satire and therefore his apology for not writing is an apology for not writing satire. The poem's most moving effects are responsive to that difference between himself and his model. The imitation of Horace in this epistle is a continuing metaphor of difference, therefore. Horace is, and is not, Pope's model, and in large part the poem probes the implications of Pope's admiration for a model whose career authentically embodied the *positive* functions of poetry, its celebrative rather than adversary relation to culture and society.

This inquiry involves Pope in a reflective survey of his own career, rather like that in the *Epistle to Arbuthnot*. Here, however, surveying his career is not the explicit process and subject it is in *Arbuthnot*. We hear it as an undercurrent: in a long passage, for example, where Pope illustrates the foolishness of the figure cut by the poet in London's feverish streets, he creates comedy by apparently accepting the judgments and perspectives of the London crowd, quite unlike the manner of his apologia in *Arbuthnot*:

> The Man, who stretch'd in Isis' calm Retreat
> To Books and Study gives sev'n years compleat,
> See! strow'd with learned dust, his Night-cap on,
> He walks, an Object new beneath the Sun!
> The Boys flock round him, and the People stare:
> So stiff, so mute! some Statue, you would swear,
> Stept from its Pedestal to take the Air.
> [116–122]

This mocking of the poet is in accord with the general comic movement that depends for its effects on our implied assent to a higher sense of poetry and the poet, the sense of their spiritual force and authority. But placed within this comedy there is this couplet: "How shall I rhime this eternal Roar? / How match the Bards whom none e'er match'd before?" (114–115). In the force of the last line, the comedy is momentarily displaced. All the deprecation and ridicule of poetry is quietly, momentarily diminished by the stern and austere sense of career Pope feels here, with its tremendous demand that the true poet's task is to "match the Bards whom none e'er match'd before." Again this intensifies the Horatian original, which merely has "Tu me inter strepitus nocturnos atque diurnos / Vis canere, et contacta sequi vestigia vatum?" Horace's line has the poet following the trail of his predecessors: Pope has him in a kind of struggle with them, an effort to become as they were.

In hearing the almost accidental intensity of this, along with the momentary dissonance of its music against that of the prevailing and deprecatory comedy, we overhear an inner event that quickly but decisively colors the burlesque and the comedy within which Pope had even played at likening himself to Sir Richard Blackmore. We see this for a game, serious as it may be, and we are unmistakably led back to the earlier years of Pope's career, when matching the old bards *was* the heady and beautiful ambition he could define as the object of his career in poetry, as in *An Essay on Criticism*:

> Hail *Bards Triumphant!* Born in *happier Days*;
> *Immortal* Heirs of *Universal* Praise!
> Whose Honours with Increase of Ages *grow*,
> As streams roll down, *enlarging* as they flow!
> Nations *unborn* your mighty Names shall sound,
> And Worlds applaud that must not yet be *found!*
> Oh may some Spark of *your* Coelestial Fire
> The last, the meanest of your Sons inspire,
> (That on weak Wings, from far, pursues your Flights;
> *Glows* while he *reads*, but *trembles* as he *writes*)
> To teach vain Wits a Science *little known*.
> T'*admire* Superior Sense, and *doubt* their own!
> [189–200]

It is not surprising that echoes of the *Essay on Criticism* with its positive vision of poetry and culture pervade Pope's later poem even to the point of direct quotation. Direct quotation occurs at the end of a long passage (153–179) contrasting the complacent ease of "bad rhimers" with the demanding severity of the true poets. It is a complex passage, reflecting now negatively on the value of that "ease" in the name of which Pope has been arguing throughout against poetry, then developing a genuinely celebrative, even heroic music in its account of the true poet, much like that in *An Essay on Criticism*.

> In vain, bad Rhimers all mankind reject,
> They treat themselves with most profound respect;
> 'Tis to small purpose that you hold your tongue,
> Each prais'd within, is happy all day long.
> But how severely with themselves proceed
> The Men, who write such Verse as we can read?
> Their own strict Judges, not a word they spare
> That wants or Force, or Light, or Weight, or Care,
> Howe'er unwillingly it quits its place,
> Nay tho' at Court (perhaps) it may find grace:
> Such they'll degrade; and sometimes, in its stead,
> In downright Charity revive the dead;
> Mark where a bold expressive Phrase appears,
> Bright thro' the rubbish of some hundred years;
> Command old words that long have slept, to wake,
> Words, that wise *Bacon*, or brave *Raleigh* spake;
> Or bid the new be *English*, Ages hence,
> (For Use will father what's begot by Sense)
> Pour the full Tide of Eloquence along,
> Serenely pure, and yet divinely strong,
> Rich with the Treasures of each foreign Tongue;
> Prune the luxuriant, the uncouth refine,
> But show no mercy to an empty line;
> Then polish all, with so much life and ease,
> You think 'tis Nature, and a knack to please:
> "But Ease in writing flows from Art, not Chance,
> "As those move easiest who have learn'd to dance.
>   If such the Plague and pains to write by rule,
> Better (say I) be pleas'd, and play the fool;
> Call, if you will, bad Rhiming a disease,
> It gives men happiness, or leaves them ease.
>   [153–183]

The passage begins with the suggestion that the inner ease and contentment Pope has all along set up as inconsistent with the career in poetry are, in fact, the pleasing possession of "bad rhimers": "Each prais'd within, is happy all day long." In contrast with these, the true poet is represented as a public figure: Pope sees his career as in accord with "all Mankind," in a kind of fruitless union against the powerfully complacent subjectivity of the bad writer. This conception pulls against the argument Pope has all along been advancing in pretending to accept the perspective of the crowd (especially in 108–125), and it works to suggest an ideal union of good audience and good writer who together compose the positive culture within which a positive art flourishes. As the passage develops, this conception grows more powerful, and the figure of the good poet begins to assume heroic proportions as he is represented to be a steward of civilization, possessing special authority and exercising didactic function: he *marks* and he *commands* (165, 167), and, in linking these two words to define his work, Pope unmistakably supports the union of imaginative mind and governing authority which defines the good poet's function at the center of his culture, forming it indeed in the dynamic process that continually creates civilization by building its language from the valued words of the past toward the eloquence of the future. And, whereas initially the passage had presented the good poet as a public figure of severe selflessness to contrast with the foolish inward ease of the dunce, now as the positive conception grows in intensity another kind of ease and another kind of inwardness are defined as the achievement of the true artist, who pours "the full Tide of Eloquence along," then polishes

> all, with so much life and ease,
> You think 'tis Nature and a knack to please:
> "But ease in writing flows from Art, not Chance,
> "As those move easiest who have learn'd to dance.
> [176–179]

The emphasis on ease here conflicts markedly with the earlier sense of the passage (and the sense of the passage immediately following) that the good artist is "severe," that his task is "plague" and "pain" (180), that his poetry is, in short, an expression of character, not self. Instead, Pope here defines the ease of the true artist as an ideal blend of personality and tradition; his ease signifies the realization of self achieved in the successful integration of self with culture, the achievement of substantial identity in a union with one's valued precursors—and heirs.

The direct quotation from the *Essay on Criticism* is of crucial importance here, and it distributes its force in several ways. Above all it functions at this moment in the poem as reminiscence as well as doctrine. At the very moment that Pope completes his ideal portrait of the poet as hero, he reaches back to an earlier moment in his life and his career in which this positive doctrine came more easily to him, came to him, indeed, as an "essayist." If we read this imitation of Horace with a full sense of the career of the actual man who is now writing and publishing in 1737, we will discern an inner movement. The force of this movement reveals Pope's awareness of the humane complication his positive doctrine has undergone as he reaches for it now from an earlier work across a career that has developed so differently from any expectation the young author of the *Essay on Criticism* might have had. As readers of his poem, we become aware of Pope's own recognition that the positive doctrine he expresses here is a more difficult and complex truth than it was at that earlier time when he wrote it down in almost the same words.

The achievement of this passage is its representation of the good artist in terms of his ideal public character, at the same time as it communicates Pope's troubled private experience of that ideal image; it is simultaneously a statement of doctrine and a revelation of self, a revelation of how that doctrine has complicated and been complicated by the life of this poem's author. We are helped to feel this play of experience against belief by the poem's emotional curve, by the way it builds toward the celebration of the ideal and falls away from it, as it does, for example, immediately in the next lines, with their abrupt turnabout: "If such be the Plague and pains to write by Rule, / Better (say I) be pleas'd, and play the fool" (180–181). Here, as earlier, the poem's movement suggests a sudden coming-to, as if Pope's reminiscence stretching back to the celebrative vision of art and culture in the *Essay on Criticism* functions in this poem as a kind of epic reverie, a vision valuable for itself but requiring redefinition now to acknowledge fully the poet's experience of the career in art subsequent to his first commitment to its most magnificent possibilities. That subsequent experience, of course, is of poetry as satire, of an adversary rather than a celebrative relation to culture. If, in the passage I have been examining, Pope so late in his career writes of the heroic poet as a maker of culture, he writes this knowing fully that his own heroism has been of another kind, that in his work the isolated anger of the satirist has blazed into its own heroic commitments, as he was to say explicitly in the two dialogues he entitled *Epilogue to the Satires* in the next year.

Pope's imitation of Horace, then, in this case is a vehicle for inner exploration, and its central concern is the changing sense of self, the mutable identity of the poet. His ostensible argument against poetry provides Pope the opportunity to review a career that has developed away from his own initial sense of it, and the poem's power to move us is certainly strengthened by our own awareness of the distance between the positive vision of the early career and the satiric commitment of the later. What moves us is our sense that across this distance there has been growth as well as disillusionment, that against all the forces that can have worked to undo the integrity of his identity, Pope has been able to maintain and to enhance that identity. It is not surprising, therefore, that we can feel the presence of the *Essay on Criticism* in this later poem, both as an explicit and implicit reference point. For in the earlier poem, the sustaining celebrative idea is that the young poet can create his identity by assimilating his being with his valued precursors. Just as Virgil became fully himself only after acknowledging in astonishment his need for Homer and Aristotle, the young Pope could seriously hope to discover his own self fully as it grew toward the character of those he chose for his models:

> But when t'examine ev'ry Part he came,
> *Nature* and *Homer* were, he found, the same:
> Convinc'd, amaz'd, he checks the bold Design,
> And rules as strict his labour'd Work confine,
> As if the *Stagyrite* o'erlook'd each Line.
> [133–137]

But writing and publishing now in 1737, Pope expresses an oblique and troubled awareness that this process can yield different results, moreover, that it can be aped in the name not of culture but of duncery:

> Thus we dispose of all poetic Merit,
> Yours *Milton*'s Genius, and mine *Homer*'s Spirit.
> Call *Tibbald Shakespear,* and he'll swear the Nine
> Dear *Cibber!* never match'd one Ode of thine.
> Lord! how we strut thro' *Merlin*'s Cave, to see
> No Poets there, but *Stephen*, you, and me.
> Walk with respect behind, while we at ease

>   Weave Laurel Crowns, and take what Names we please.
> "My dear *Tibullus!*" if that will not do,
> "Let me be *Horace,* and be *Ovid* you.
> "Or, I'm content, allow me *Dryden's* strains,
> "And you shall rise up *Otway* for your pains."
>   Much do I suffer, much, to keep in peace
>   This jealous, waspish, wrong-head, rhiming Race,
>   And much must flatter, if the Whim should bite
>   To court applause by printing what I write:
>   But let the Fit pass o'er, I'm wise enough,
>   To stop my ears to their confounded stuff.
>   [135–152]

In these complex lines, whose force is satirical rather than celebrative, Pope reflects obliquely on "the uses of the past," playfully associating himself with the duncery of the present only to pull himself abruptly away from the game (in "Much do I suffer, much, to keep in peace / This jealous, waspish, wrong-head, rhiming Race"). As the passage concludes, he communicates clearly to us his own positive sense of self now, but to do so he has had to speak from the periphery of his contemporary public culture, whose center is now occupied by men whose lives travesty the effort he could celebrate in his *Essay on Criticism.* *Their* effort to identify themselves with Milton, Shakespeare, Homer, Tibullus, Horace is in the name only of that insubstantial and complacent inner ease Pope will in a moment attack in the portrait of the heroic poet.

Certainly throughout all this satire of others and scrutiny of himself, Pope retains his earlier commitment, but he feels it in a different way, feels it as the cause of his movement over to the periphery of his own literary world. In this new place Pope remakes and reaffirms his earlier commitment to culture, but not in language whose "pull," as William Empson has said of the *Essay on Criticism*, is toward the drawing room, but rather toward the "pensive Grott." The movement in this poem toward the grotto and the country seat acknowledges fully the complexity with which Pope now experiences the positive values of the literary life, his sense of it now as a commitment that can pull the personality apart as it has his, from the young celebrant to the older satirist. Milton, Shakespeare, Horace, Tibullus, Ovid, Dryden—even the dunces can play at mimicking them and the triviality of their game is an oblique suggestion of the dangers and insufficiencies of his. Now required of the heroic poet is that he use the old models not as icons, but as guides to a new identity of his own—that he speak for his models in his own voice with an angry energy that sets him apart from them, and that he discover in his very distance from his models the authentic style of his likeness to them, the substance of his own self. And this effort now is implicated in another—the effort to see what kind of wholeness the poet can forge between his earlier and his present self. The resonance in this later poem of the *Essay on Criticism* is thus an indication of the deepening of Pope's sense of self across the space of his career, an acknowledgement that his own being has been made not in the imitation of his models but rather in the translation of their spirit into his own proper form. The echoes of the earlier poem work to make us feel how much has changed and still how much has remained the same. The dunces may now imitate the greats: Pope can be their transfiguration, not as the maker of epics or pastorals or georgics, but as the poet of satire.

This intense self-scrutiny requires the special blend of expression that distinguishes Pope's Horace from Horace himself: the intensification of Horace's satiric effects, the greater exploitation of Horace's resources for representing inwardness, the subtly but importantly changed relation between Pope's didactic conclusion and the body of his poem. The intensification of satiric effect acknowledges in itself that for Pope, poetry has become identified with satire; the intensification of lyric expression acknowledges Pope's use of his model as a vehicle for an introspective review of his own career. And in the deepening of the didactic lesson we feel the poem responding to the inner drama of self-discovery that leads to and culminates in that lesson. In this play of difference against sameness, of Pope against Horace in a poem that is still "Horatian," we have the very embodiment of a growing away from the letter and toward the spirit of his models which is the central fact of Pope's inner career, the central subject of this poem.

The long didactic meditation that concludes the poem and occupies one-third of its more than three hundred lines must, in its manner and substance, be considered a consequence of the inner drama preceding it. This long lesson is itself the resolution of that drama, and in its quiet conclusion the long shape of the poem's curve of feeling is closed. What may seem strange at first is the apparent thematic distance between the matter of the final lesson and the preceding argument with poetry which has been Pope's vehicle for the introspective survey of his career. For there is no explicit connection between the meditative lesson and Pope's argument with poetry. As he swings into the poem's final movement, our first sense is that Pope is demonstrating for the addressee of the epistle the pleasure of his escape from his career: "This is what I do, and this is the kind of thing I say, when once I'm free of London, and dunces, and poetry, in short, of all I've been complaining to you about."

> Soon as I enter at my Country door,
> My Mind resumes the thread it dropt before;
> Thoughts, which at Hyde-Park-Corner I forgot,
> Meet and rejoin me, in the pensive Grott.
> There all alone, and Compliments apart,
> I ask these sober questions of my Heart.
> If, when the more you drink, the more you crave,
> You tell the Doctor; when the more you have,
> The more you want, why not with equal ease
> Confess as well your Folly, as Disease? . . .
> [206–215]

Then follows a series of short lessons against ambition and avarice, each given its own brief verse paragraph. These, however, are all pointed toward the major thematic material of the meditation, whose central subject is the nature of possession and sufficiency. Pope comes to this first as a discussion of property—its ownership and use—and from this lesson, presented initially in legal terms, he develops his concluding argument in its largest, ethical implication: self-possession, self-sufficiency, the life well lived.

What at first seems detached from the poem's body is thus ultimately implicated with it and indeed resonates with it throughout. For the argument with poetry all along has had at its center the poet's apprehension that his inner being has been wrenched apart in his pursuit of his own business, his own career. Against the loss of self threatened by the career in poetry, Pope has shown already the manner in which the earlier career and the later have been forged into a new wholeness. What is so moving about the long didactic meditation in which this new integrity is ultimately enacted is the functioning of its lesson on property to generalize the case of the poet to the situation of all men. The legal fictions of the landholding lord—his inheritances, his perpetuities, his bequests—are all a form of the poet's ideal and early dream of culture as the sustaining element of his identity. And, therefore, Pope's lesson to the landholder is implied in his earlier discovery of himself: as the inner making of the self sustains culture, the moral will properly exercised in "use," in right living, gives meaning to possession:

> Heathcote himself, and such large-acred Men,
> Lords of fat *E'sham*, or of Lincoln Fen,
> Buy every stick of Wood that lends them heat,
> Buy every Pullet they afford to eat.
> Yet these are Wights, who fondly call their own
> Half that the Dev'l o'erlooks from Lincoln Town.
> The Laws of God, as well as of the Land,
> Abhor, a *Perpetuity* should stand:
> Estates have wings, and hang in Fortune's pow'r
> Loose on the point of ev'ry wav'ring Hour;
> Ready, by force, or of your own accord
> By sale, at least by death, to change their Lord.
> *Man?* and *for ever?* Wretch! what wou'dst thou have?
> Heir urges Heir, like Wave impelling Wave:
> All vast Possessions (just the same the case
> Whether you call them Villa, Park, or Chace)
> Alas, my BATHURST! what will they avail?
> Join *Cotswold* Hills to *Saperton's* fair Dale,
> Let rising Granaries and Temples here,
> There mingled Farms and Pyramids appear,
> Link Towns to Towns with Avenues of Oak,
> Enclose whole Downs in Walls, 'tis all a joke!
> Inexorable Death shall level all,
> And Trees, and Stones, and Farms, and Farmer fall.
> [240–263]

In this passage critics have pointed to a darkening of what they have in other places called Pope's Augustan vision. Aubrey Williams has finely commented on the way Pope here has deepened his original and expanded it "into a much wider and grander vision: he asks the same questions as Horace, but he also demonstrates that not man alone, but the whole universe, is caught up in an earthslide of Time and its inevitable changes . . . within a melancholy pattern that nature itself must endure."[8]

This is, indeed, a remarkable passage; in it we can hear echoes and ideas from Pope's most important works, from the urgent manner of his didactic address in *An Essay on Man* (252) to the melancholy reflection of the imperial vision of the *Epistle to Burlington* (258–264), as if the works of his own hand and the best thoughts of his mind are included also within the enlarged and deepened range of his imitation of Horace's lesson to the landholder. In Pope's version of Horace's lesson, we see the development of the poem's earlier inner drama into the concluding didactic celebration of a self-possession that is strength even against one's deepest awareness of the ultimate anonymity of his works and his name. We feel the generalizing tendency of Pope's version of Horace in, for example, the force of "all" in his lines, "Does neither Rage inflame, nor Fear appall? / Nor the black Fear of Death, which saddens all?" (308–309). This amplifies Horace's "caret tibi pectus inani / Ambitione? caret mortis formidine et ira?" So that in the intensified emphases of Pope's didactic rumination we feel the longing for privacy he expresses in the earlier part of the poem in one sense satisfied, and in another enhanced. It is satisfied in the very act by which the poem concludes, that is, in its representation of the poet alone, asking sober questions of his heart.[9] It is enhanced, however, by the universalizing tendency of those same questions. In fact, in the largeness of Pope's vision here, which resonates with but expands beyond the issues that had informed the poem's earlier movement, we can feel him working within the range of purpose and function he had imagined, in his early career, as that of the great public poet, the minister of culture, possessor of its moral heritage and of the authority to speak in its behalf.

Most remarkably however, Pope has represented this most heightened of his poem's movements as a *refuge* from poetry, a sample of his speaking with himself when he has fled its cares. His most public address he has imagined as a most private moment, and what the reader feels as a dialogue is in fact a meditation, a dialogue of one. The entire final movement of the poem may be said, therefore, to contain and resolve the stresses of its earlier argument. That earlier argument had expressed the poet's recognition of the inwardness that makes the poet and his poetry; its stresses were created in the clash of this awareness against Pope's ideal image of the public poet. Now, in the inner dialogue of the didactic meditation, we observe the poet in private possession of his public function, experiencing in his speech to himself the universal implications of his discovery of himself in the earlier part of the poem. This most Augustan of poems is also Pope's most lyrical, and the didactic matter that he represents as his escape from poetry in fact, contains what was for him poetry's highest, most characteristic value. Within the *Epistle*, the didactic matter is the final agent for the integration of Pope's youthful with his mature visions of his career and of his being.

The discovery of self *is* the discovery of poetry, and in the authority of the didactic address in which Pope comes to this realization, we feel his closest approach within the poem to the public manner he had envisioned as the voice of the good poet speaking to and for a good people. But we should also be alert to another music in it—the music of the satirist. For even here, as in the body of the poem, Pope has intensified his original's potential for angry expression, and many examples can be given which have a very different ring from Horace, whose anger is either muted or absent. But in Pope's Horace, the presence of an angry voice is essential, even in the movement toward the quiet of the close, precisely because it *is* a mark of the poet's present identity, precisely because he *was* writing satire even as he wrote this retrospective and introspective judgment of his life. The quiet of the poem's conclusion suits the dignity of its vision, but the plainly evident satiric impulse, so different from anything in Horace's lines, enforces our sense of the angry energy that must be assimilated to the whole poem's positive conclusion:

> Learn to live well, or fairly make your Will;
> You've play'd, and lov'd, and eat, and drank your fill:
> Walk sober off; before a sprightlier Age

Comes titt'ring on, and shoves you from the stage:
Leave such to trifle with more grace and ease,
Whom Folly pleases, and whose Follies please.
                    [322–327]

Pope has markedly increased the stature of the imagined addressee of these lines, who is also, of course, himself. Whereas Horace emphasizes this figure's vulnerability to the appropriate mockery of the young, Pope demonstrates his authority to *judge them:* they come "titt'ring on," they "trifle," and Pope's rendering of Horace's "lasciva" as "folly" removes from it entirely the positive possibility of sportiveness or play, just as "Walk sober off" colors Horace's "Tempus abire tibi est" more somberly and with a stronger suggestion of a motion of controlled and directed moral will. The dignity of Pope's conclusion is made in part from these small differences, which convey a positive sense of the satirist's acerbity, his moral resources.[10] But, of course, it is more than this. These last lines demonstrate and enact the assurance of a man who masters his perception of his own ultimate anonymity, who can do this because of the substantial identity he has made and possesses, and whose assertion of self has been earned in his inner struggle with those forces that can pull the personality apart. The loss of self the poet fears in his argument against his career has been entirely repaired in his resolution of that argument, and the "black fear of death," to which the earlier fear for the integrity of the poet's identity has been universalized, is now subjected to the force of Pope's lesson *in* poetry made from his argument *with* poetry.[11]

The imitation of Horace's *Epistle II. ii* by Pope is only one of his many poems in which a strong didactic movement is charged with personal purpose and meaning, but in this poem's procedure we have an unusual demonstration of the resources Pope discovered in didactic address. In Pope's *Epistle II. ii*, the didactic movement stands as an ostensible demonstration of the distance between the poet's public and private experience of himself. In the implicit and universalized resonances that harmonize the didactic meditation and the preceding personal material of the poem's body, however, we discover their essential compatibility. The long didactic meditation stands in this poem as a kind of symbolic utterance: the didactic mode is itself demonstrated to be a vehicle for the profoundest development of the personal material.

Within the long didactic close, represented in the poem as a sample of private dialogue rendered as though it were public address, we feel the presence of a public, satirical voice as well as the dignified and elegiacal rhythms of inner discourse. This tonal contrast is also a feature of the poem's earlier movement, but there the alternations are move violent; they are contrasts that in themselves portray the emotional uncertainty of Pope's movement into and out from himself, his uncertain effort to understand the integral connection between his earlier and present sense of self. By the end of the poem's first movement, however, the values Pope associates with his earlier career have been sustained in his later and very different identity. It remains for him to demonstrate in the long didactic close the look and feel of that new integrity; we perceive it in the assimilation of satirical impulses and manner within the beautiful concluding lesson on self-possession.[12] We feel it in the long movement to the resolved quiet of the poem's end in which a greater judgmental acerbity than is to be found in Pope's model sustains the image of dignified self-possession which is the poem's final lesson. Here there is none of the self-deprecatory comedy which, earlier in the poem, had served to link Pope with, as well as distinguish him from, the dunces. This rhythmic development, this movement from sharp tonal contrast to sustained and level feeling, closes the poem's emotional curve. The long shape of the poem becomes in this way a mimesis of the poet's inner experience as its writer, of his movement from emotional uncertainty toward emotional rest. And again, the work of criticism with such a poem requires a primary emphasis upon the tonal play and development within the poem; we need to feel the effects created by the play against each other of large units with their abrupt contrasts or their sustained rhythms.

The tonal play of Pope's poetry is a constant adjustment of public voice to private feeling. The public voice of didactic address sustains a positive sense of the poet's identity; in its private modulations, we overhear the reservations and judgments of the private man in whose life that ideal identity was sometimes realized, sometimes missed. It is perhaps true that as his career developed in satire, he discovered the height of his own powers in the freedom satire could provide from his ideal sense of himself and of his models. In the obscenity, violence, and negative intensity of the *Epilogue to the Satires* and *The Dunciad* we may sense the widest range of feeling and perception of which he was capable, and Pope may have become most himself not in his wish to imitate epic but in the work that travestied it. But even in *The Dunciad*, where Pope's imaginative power reveals a fascination for disorder and anarchy and suggests a peculiar sympathy as well as detestation for the objects of his attack, our sense of the man behind the poem is created by the play against each other of the poem's broken acceptance of epic and its violently farcical and tragic deviation from it. If Pope's greatest achievement in art is in the satiric violence that images the death of art, it is still in the antagonism of the positive public form of epic against the private fascinations of the satirist that we overhear the complex inner drama of the poem's maker. The larger pattern of revelation is still made from an elusive positive intention tested against a private energy seeking accord with it. I have described this pattern in Pope's *Epistle II. ii*, however different its effects are.

The Augustan poet regularly discovered the opportunity in didactic address to assume a positive, public identity; didactic address is the sign of his possession of his culture's moral and imaginative heritage, and the teaching of its lessons is also often their celebration. At the same time, the profoundest of this poetry explores a complex inner struggle in which the claims of individual experience are placed against those of a positive heritage; in this struggle the Augustan poet reveals his lyric capacities and the Augustan self encounters the complexity and richness of its public and private identity. If Pope's is the most significant achievement of Augustan art, it is because he explored his being and his career with greater freedom and within a wider range of forms than any other poet of the age. In his work a central task of his age is defined and clarified—the establishment of an authentic adjustment between a valued past and an uncertain, compelling, and fearful modernity. In this respect his explorations of himself, with their play of didactic intention and lyric effect, of public voice against private feeling, of culture against self, compose the first body of work entirely characteristic of what has come to be called modernity.

In the works I study in the following chapters, the resources of didactic address are everywhere evident and serve to illuminate the effort of the self to achieve authentic being within culture. For Johnson,

Goldsmith, and Swift, as for Pope, didactic address and intention reveal powerful lyric resources, are entirely adequate to the poet's efforts at self-discovery. As we might expect, however, the adjustment of private voice to public role is a very different matter for each man, and the blend of didacticism and lyricism in the work of each signifies a very different achievement. Johnson's empiricism, for example, along with his painful and private awareness of the aberrant power of the inner life, gives to his didactic demands of art an intensity that art can hardly sustain or satisfy. His effort to speak to men in art and in behalf of culture is managed with far less confident reference to an inherited set of normative attitudes or literary forms than is the case with Pope, and the authority of Johnson's didactic voice arises always from his awareness that it must be personally discovered and worked for. In his judicial criticism he resists invoking familiar formal considerations according to which he might vindicate an individual work that otherwise fails to meet his didactic demands of it, and in his own imaginative writing he asks from his reader a responsiveness undetermined by anything but the reader's humane and rational alertness to the events Johnson passes before him. If we miss in Johnson Pope's ease of movement through literature from form to form, from voice to voice, from Virgil to Horace to Milton, it is not merely because of Johnson's reduced range: it is rather because culture is for Johnson a continuously created accord between inwardness and experience. His didactic lyricism is the record, therefore, of his own tumultuous inner life at the same time that it is an acknowledgment that the resources of the past are less meaningful as public heritage than private opportunity. Johnson's is the authentic voice of enlightenment humanism, adjusting the claims of a radical skepticism to the social and rational needs of an often violent self.

In Johnson's work, his criticism and his art, the pressure of his rich and difficult inwardness is always near the surface. His remarkable achievement is to have forged from the public commitment of didactic address an instrument of expression and judgment entirely adequate to the depth of his private being. For all the breadth of his engagement with literature, therefore, we sense his possession of it as a series of discrete experiences, each judged for its own value by a mind not primarily engaged, as was Pope's, with the *idea* of literature, with the shape of its history or the pantheon of its forms. This perhaps explains the oddity of his remarkable criticism of Shakespeare: it is certainly a criticism that "places" Shakespeare and that recognizes the value to culture of such an effort. But then, precisely what the act of "placing" might preclude, the presentation of strictures "independent of place or time," comes to absorb Johnson's primary energy, and the Shakespeare he gives us is a genius to be placed with Homer and Sophocles, but also a man careless of the most significant of art's functions. In the idiosyncrasy of this judgment we have our best example of Johnson's characteristic engagement with culture: he is connected with it entirely on his terms and it yields to him the opportunities he most personally required. Yet the wonder of the *Preface to Shakespeare* is the unmistakable public authoritativeness with which it still resounds and which can be explained, after all, as an effect of its essential adequacy. Of all the reasons for Shakespeare's greatness, Johnson has emphasized the most important and was able to do so even as he insisted upon faults he felt more keenly, perhaps, than any other reader has.

The inward energy of Johnson's criticism and art entirely shape his appropriation of the didactic voice whose familiar presence in the eighteenth century is a sign of the writer's public commitment and of the authority his audience accords him. In Goldsmith's *Deserted Village*, however, the nature of that commitment and the sources of the poet's authority are reexamined as if by inadvertence: Goldsmith's poem is a strained mixture of compositional and rhetorical purpose, shifting between two very different justifications for poetic utterance, two very different conceptions of culture and of the poet's relation to it. Goldsmith's concluding assertion that the moral authority of poetry is fled with Auburn's vanished villagers has always been difficult to understand, especially with respect to the didactic authority with which he invests his own stance as poet. His concluding identification of poetry with the vanished villagers is a sign of uncertainty about his stance, about the public authority and identity of the poet, and indeed Goldsmith's whole poem becomes an effort to discover the inner sources of his own didactic purpose as the village's messenger to the larger world. *The Deserted Village* records an extended process of inner speech as the only authoritative vehicle for a didactic purpose. In its formal conception, the poem strains against Goldsmith's developing sense of poetry's character and the poet's identity; in its formal inconsistencies and compelling lyric impulses it demonstrates the difficulty a poet could face, late in the century, in his effort to establish an accord between his sense of himself as a spokesman for culture and his private impulse toward poetry. The ultimate adequacy of the poem both to its private and public purposes is certain, but so is the strain between them, and the poem's management of its didactic and lyric material reveals the direction to be taken by the next literary generation. *The Deserted Village* is a preromantic poem: it is also Augustan, and in exploring Goldsmith's work with respect to its responsiveness to the didactic and lyric impulses that shape so much of the poetry of his century, I have tried to invest these familiar and useful terms with some precision.

We have often been more fascinated (if not as pleased) by the developments at the end of the century than by those nearer its start. It is near the end of the century that we perceive the "shifts in sensibility" which register the birth of the modern self and along with it the imaginative forms adequate to the expression of its sovereign inwardness. We think of this as a momentous set of events in the history of culture, an adventure formed from the struggle of that new sovereign self against the restraints and conventions suitable to the language of a being with some considerable public component to his identity. Goldsmith's poem certainly contributes to this later process; but for Swift also, much earlier in the century, the experience of the sovereign self was no new discovery, and the distinctive force of his writing arises from his efforts to register the energies of an often anarchic personality against the recognizably social restraints he acknowledged in the character he assumed as the Dean. Swift's satire is unlike any other precisely because, as we have begun to understand, its ostensible targets are often versions of himself and because its horrific visions therefore have a force that works to undermine the positive ideas by which he probably meant them to be controlled. Swift's satiric art vexes us because, as F. R. Leavis showed long ago, it provides us with no assurance that our best beliefs are sufficient to withstand Swift's representation of all that deviates from them. His satire has the feel of energy released but not commanded, and if it ultimately delights and liberates us, it is into a freedom from intellectual restraint perhaps valuable in itself but with no clear object in sight.

This is Swift's memorable manner, and significantly it involves him in the pretenses of didactic address, pretenses that are typically turned to the purposes of bitter satire the radical force of which is to undermine entirely the claims of positive culture in whose behalf the satirist pretends initially to speak. And yet on rare occasions Swift explored the possibilities for a sustained positive address. The most moving of these occasions are in the poems to Stella, in which he created the opportunity to speak to Stella as an audience-of-one from whom he would not withdraw in irony and subversive play. With Stella as his surrogate for a community of virtue he knew had no public existence, he could speak directly in his character as Dean and, restraining the play of his personality, he could in these circumstances explore the positive possibilities of his character. The moving lyric force of these poems is in the discovery of self they portray, but here it is the discovery of the richness of a public self, of the authentic being possible to one who embraces his station and his best beliefs. Usually Swift addresses Stella in these poems with an explicit didactic lesson, as on honor or virtue, and the lesson will then modulate into a mimetic movement, sometimes an event, in which Swift expresses and explores his awareness of the value, the cost, and the reality of the ideas he loved and doubted, and which elsewhere in his work were more usually the occasion for the aggressive and corrosive irony in which they withered. The lyricism of the poems to Stella is the lyricism attendant upon Swift's discovery of his best self, in possession of his best beliefs. Of all the Augustans, Swift maintained the most ambiguous connection with culture, and his satire most intensely questions the hope of authentic accord between the self and culture; yet the resources of didactic expression for marking and achieving that accord are most clearly evident in those rare and anomalous poems of his in which he speaks to Stella in behalf of culture and of himself. Of the writers studied here, Swift's achievement in the didactic lyric is perhaps the narrowest, but the anarchic character of his imagination which would explain why this is so also provides the surest test of the value to the Augustan mind and self of their didactic art.

2

Swift as Lyricist: The Poems to Stella and His Career in Satire

No ARTIST IS MORE playful than Jonathan Swift, and no criticism more suited to his play than ours. He toys with and devastates meaning; we can at least understand the design of the assault. Our critical poise, moreover, is accompanied by a social one. Not like William Thackeray, fulminating in wonder at the human monstrosity of Swift, we can speak more easily of him even as we see as deeply into the horror managed by his play. As teachers, surely, more of us have encouraged our students to see the Swiftian worst than have advised them to spare themselves the experience.[1]

Certainly the Swiftian worst is a sublime cultural possession: Swift is a giant because he has defined a human possibility we might otherwise not have known. No other art springs so directly from the energies of hate as does his; no other art has, with hatred for its spring, revealed so much of reality. And no other artist has, with so small an estimate of the value of his enterprise and the worth of his audience, still urged himself toward the attention of the race. To accumulate these negative superlatives is to approach a judgment and a definition of Swift's achievement and of its anomalous character. Where could we find, until near our own time, a theory of art which could explain his imagination, which did not centrally affirm art as the work or the product of mankind's positive energies? And when was the pressure of this prejudice more heavily felt than by artists of Swift's own time, indeed, by Swift himself? The central judicial task of Swift's critics, therefore, will always be to explicate and insist upon the Swiftian worst even as they permit the pressure of positive ideas appropriate play in shaping their judgments. And the critical success we have been having with Swift is certainly explicable by the habitual poise we command as critics nowadays, poise being essential to so delicate a management of worst and best as Swift demands. In our poise we can communicate at least *something* and come through such cognitive devastation as the digression on madness or the fourth voyage, not unscarred, but certainly not incapable of speech. We can follow the devastation of argument which *is* Swift's argument and acknowledge, for instance, the hatred of the poor issuing in the details of the Irish feast. Swift did not love those he labored for and to see his hatred still produce such strenuous moral exertion is indeed an experience we are enriched by, a human possibility we might not, by ourselves, have guessed at.

But poise may protect too well against the occasionally valuable benefits of misunderstanding. Johnson, for example, was plainly unsettled by Swift, and his discomfort led him to some illuminating misjudgments. Johnson's estimate of Swift's achievement was, of all things, that he mastered a style whose strength was the "safe and easy conveyance of meaning."[2] It is no wonder to us that Johnson, thinking that, would have to retreat in confused irritation from those features of Swift's work which are neither safe nor easy. Only in the last paragraph of criticism proper in his life of Swift does Johnson raise an issue he does not mean to pursue: "The greatest difficulty that occurs in analyzing his character, is to discover by what depravity of intellect he took delight in revolving ideas, from which almost every other mind shrinks with disgust . . . what has disease, deformity, and filth, upon which the thoughts can be allured to dwell?"[3] It is to Johnson's credit that even in his irritation he could recognize—the words "delight," "revolving," and "allured" prove it—the obsessiveness that springs forth in the characteristic Swiftian play. Sensing the obsessiveness and the allurement and the delight that Swift released and experienced, Johnson could not integrate such a perception into his judgment of Swift's achievement. The safe and easy conveyor of meaning becomes a mystery as a man, and Johnson speaks of Swift's character rather than his work when he confesses his bewilderment at the most characteristic feature of the work. So Johnson gives us a master of didactic style and a monstrosity of a man—one who took delight in what "almost every other mind shrinks [from] with disgust." Our criticism, on the other hand, more successfully brings together the two. To us, Swift is a safe and easy conveyor of meaning least of all—he is an anarchic, aggressive assaulter of it. And for us, the value of his art is precisely that, the release it provides through play of what we all shrink from with disgust and fear.[4]

And yet Swift would have valued Johnson's judicious approval could he have won it. Swift, for whom poise was always suspect, for whom poise and complacency were difficult to distinguish, would have honored the moral intelligence that could not stand gracefully before games as dangerous as he played. Poise before such games, such disfigurations of meaning, risks being no more than the bland sophistication Swift hated in the human race above all else. What is the target of his *Modest Proposal* if not poise—the social poise that can accept the sight of the poor and the literary poise that can discover the *Proposal*'s joke. The two kinds can be the same, and John Traugott is right to say that the joke is on the reader who too quickly catches the joke of the *Proposal*—or who sees a joke in it at all.[5] If we consider that depopulation, either through celibacy, famine, or emigration, *has been* the historical politics of Irish poverty, we can sense the rightness of Traugott's judgment and the seriousness of Swift's proposal, his joke that is no joke at all. And if we consider that in writing down dreadful things there may be more strain than in doing them, we can recognize, beyond the positive intentions of the *Proposal*, the furious personal energy that seethed in ambiguous bondage to them. Swift must have hated the poor for the spectacle they presented; violent, filthy, promiscuous, abject—the poor of the *Proposal* are among his most horrific images of humanity, images that tell us how insulted he must have been by his daily sight of them, and may explain his detailed imagining of the uses to which their flesh could answer. In that imagination we should sense the desire. In this respect the *Proposal* is a great fiction as Plato understood fiction, the medium in which a mime becomes anything he wishes: thunder, wind, a wheel, a pulley, a dog, sheep, a cock, or, in this case, a murderer.[6]

Plato, who admired the safe and easy conveyance of meaning, despised the pantomimic gentleman. The trouble with him is that he does not speak in one voice—he has too much personality and not enough character for that; he needs to be too many people. Art is his way of giving each part of him, whatever its value, its play. For Plato the process is destructive of meaning, whatever other worth it may have. And Swift's *Proposal* can stand as an example of this, for how can we speak of the meaning of that assault upon meaning: the joke that is no joke, the murderer's hatred disguising itself in the moralist's zeal, and the other way around. The *Proposal* is Swift's way of being several of the people he was, and Johnson's praise for his style—"that he always understands himself, and his reader always understands him"—seems especially wrong, though consistent with his other judgment about Swift's safe and easy conveyance of meaning.

But again, Swift would have wished to deserve this praise. For, whatever direction he finally takes, whatever energies he finally releases, whatever meanings he ultimately destroys, his art derives its peculiar character from what must have been his haunting wish that meaning—direct, pure, true—might still be known and communicated among human creatures.[7] Swift's way of imagining virtue was to imagine a time or place or condition that was safe and easy for the conveyance of meaning. It was his favorite fantasy and can be seen in the pattern of his production. The meaning he assaults in *A Modest Proposal*, he asserts in *The Drapier's Letters*; the church he takes down in *An Argument against Abolishing Christianity*, he justifies in *The Sentiments of a Church of England Man*. Each of the "satires" is a kind of companion piece to a "straight" piece, indistinguishable in its superficial stylistic character (so well described by Johnson) from the other. *The Drapier's Letters* presume a community that can be directly addressed: "Brethren, Friends, Countrymen and Fellow Subjects." "I will therefore first tell you the plain Story of the Fact." "But a Word to the Wise is Enough." "When once the Kingdom is reduced to such a Condition, I will tell you what must be the End." "Therefore my Friends, stand to it One and All, refuse this Filthy Trash."[8] Here there is no play, and perhaps, little opportunity for explication. This style of the Drapier is the style of the Dean, nor was there any desire for that identity to be a subject for playful speculation. Assertiveness is the style, didactic authority (not down-home plainness) the stance, just as in the sermons, in which we can hear the same ring: preaching on the Trinity, Swift says of his style and of his subject, "I hope to handle it in such a Manner, that the most ignorant among you may return Home better informed of your Duty in this great Point, than probably you are at present."[9]

This is language without play, the language of character—wise, authoritative, socially and intellectually stable—not the release of personality. It conveys meaning safely, easily, and confidently. "I will tell you" is the characteristic configuration. It is, as Plato would have approved, the language of the speaker's single self. More, the integrity of that self is a function of the presumed integrity and coherence of its audience.

"Brethren, Friends, Countrymen, and Fellow Subjects," this salutation to the readers of *The Drapier's Letters* defines an audience for the style Johnson said was Swift's special achievement, an audience to whom meaning could be safely and easily conveyed. It is also an audience before whom, as Plato preferred, a writer could speak in his own voice, be his sole self. Such an audience is open to didactic address because between it and the writer language is a common ground. A word to the wise is enough when words are not tricks, when the writer understands himself and is therefore understood by the reader. To take the didactic stance before such an audience is to join with them, to direct their attention to common beliefs, shared positives: to instruct is only to remind and almost to celebrate. In the program and pattern of Swift's writing he regularly takes the didactic stance, pursues a didactic intention, presuming to teach or remind, all on the assumption that between him and his reader meaning can be clear and easy.

If we ask, then, what distinguishes the great satires from the didactic and straight, purposeful pamphlets, one way to answer would be to say that the satires only imitate didactic manner, only pretend to speak to a good audience, only pretend to arise from the cognitively fruitful opportunity that such an audience provides. The great satires become in effect fictions whose central subject is the absence of the good audience, the consequent devastation of cognitive opportunity and the anarchy of language. A notorious sentence from *A Modest Proposal* can stand as an example: "But I am not in the least Pain upon that Matter; because it is very well known that [the poor, aged, diseased and maimed] are every Day *dying*, and *rotting*, by *Cold* and *Famine*, and *Filth*, and *Vermin*, as fast as can be reasonably expected."[10] This sentence is the speaker's answer to a request that he instruct the populace on the welfare of the aged and the sick, but its true subject is the revised meaning of the words "Pain" and "reasonably," or, more accurately, their meaninglessness. And the pamphlet as a whole is about the revised meaning, or the meaninglessness, of the Irish nation and community. In the vicinity of the butcher's stall, who is an Irishman? What is an Irishman? Is the question real, and with what resources of language can an answer now be even contemplated? The pamphlet becomes an imitation of a world and a state of mind whose linguistic experience is only prattle because its ostensible debates must be conducted with words that have no moral meaning—nation, Irishman, man, reason. If what distinguishes Swift's satiric art from his didactic polemic is irony, then his irony might be described as the inevitable result of meaning's decay. Irony is what we perceive as meaning when once the communal conditions for direct cognitive interchange have been lost.

What kind of meaning survives in Swift's irony, then? It is the kind of meaning art has.[11] Swift's irony is not the eloquent medium of his didactic purpose, although it arises in works whose strategy is to imitate the appearance of such purpose. It is instead the vehicle that transforms this ostensible end into the less immediately utilitarian processes of art. A *Modest Proposal* becomes, through its irony, not the agent of the author's reforming zeal, but rather the expression of his insight into the moral shapelessness of a world beyond reform. In this sense too the *Proposal* is less a satire (in Swift's own reformist's sense of satire) than a fiction, a self-enclosed poetic whole in which language is freed for play, the self-referential play possible where ordinary words are freed from the ordinary constraints and references by which they ordinarily take on meaning. Freed in this way, language may become as in poetry the vehicle of the most devastating inquiry into ordinary meaning. Whereas the initial utilitarian or reformist purposes of the *Proposal* may be, like those of *The Drapier's Letters*, based upon the values of community, patriotism, and reason, the artistic *effect* of the *Proposal* is to raise the most radical questions about those very positives. Are they real or illusory? Are they effective standards of conduct, rooted in experience, or are they instead the self-serving illusions by which human creatures indulge a pleasing complacency, sweetening their fantasies of what they are? The chill in the proposer's view of the aged and the maimed is generated by his play with the word "reasonable" in a way that excludes from it any overtone of "humane." The effect is double. It clarifies the richness of a lost usage by defining the values that healthy custom and healthy intellect have concentrated into the key words of a culture. "Reasonable" can be understood in its rich complexity as a lost concept, once encompassing "humane" in contrast to the proposer's implied simpler definition: "statistical." But at the same time, in its capacity as a fiction whose mimetic subject is a ruined culture, the *Proposal* tests that lost usage, toys with it, measures it against the facts of actual behavior, so that it becomes not so much the standard against which aberrant behavior is measured but rather the subject of a test for which aberrant behavior has become the measure. As a reformist's polemic, the *Proposal* vexes its readers by inviting them first to identify with the proposer, an irretrievable misstep, then to dissociate themselves from him; they may dissociate themselves from him by exclaiming "No, what you say is detestable, unreasonable, it is inhumane." But this is to invoke precisely those concepts and that once rich usage which do not pass the test of actual behavior. The polemical purpose is superseded in this way as the *Proposal* proceeds to demonstrate the self-serving nature of our best words, the way they help us to dissociate ourselves from a project so exactly framed on our actual behavior. And in doing so it raises radical and subversive questions about the very positives we invoke when our actual behavior is challenged. Community, reason, humanity—they may survive Swift's scrutiny as speculative possibilities, but they do not survive intact as moral ideas that function feelingly in actual life. There they function as self-serving illusions of indistinct value, not guiding actual behavior but screening it. Because a satisfactory answer, based upon our actual behavior, to the question, "Why not eat the children?" is not possible for Swift's audience, the relevance to human life of man's moral ideas—his positives—is not clear. And A *Modest Proposal*, in so vexing its reader, ceases to function as a reformist document and becomes the fiction it is—the mimetic presentation of a world foundering without meaning, and of the quality of mind and feeling dominating such a world of cognitive disarray.

In *An Argument against Abolishing Christianity* the same dynamics are at work. This piece bears a relationship to *The Sentiments of a Church of England Man* similar to that between A *Modest Proposal* and *The Drapier's Letters*. The rational compromise supported in *Sentiments* becomes the nominal Christianity of *An Argument*, and once again "our actual behavior" becomes the subject of a fictional presentation, the actual behavior of a people subsisting upon the shards of indistinct custom and belief. But the edge of this piece is threateningly sharp. The nominal Christian or nominal Christianity is not so much the object of its polemical attack; instead, the phenomenon of "nominality" itself is the subject of its piercing inquiry. Issuing from Swift's involvement with the politics of the First Fruits and the Test Act, and probably initially intended to advance the same polemical ends as the later *Sentiments of a Church of England Man*, *An Argument* develops in oblique relation to the position of that moderate document. For, after all, despite the argumentative subtlety, despite the skill with which it preserves its appearance as a conciliatory document even as it acts to trap the dissenting party, *The Sentiments* advances a moderate's position, and demonstrates the polemical functioning of a moderate position against those who favor repeal. But in the *Argument* Swift seems to be examining the meaning and value of moderation itself, that is, the meaning and value of *any* religious settlement whose virtue is that it *can* stand as conformable with the needs of a political settlement. Moderation in *Sentiments* is "nominalism" in *An Argument*, and matters that are of casual concern in *The Sentiments* therefore become central in *An Argument*.[12] In *The Sentiments*, the writer can admit, as if to show his fairness, that "in the lists of the National Church," are many who by their behavior, writings, and conversation show that they need reminding that they "ought to believe a God and his Providence, together with revealed Religion and the Divinity of Christ."[13] But in *An Argument* this marginal belief of the Church-of-England man himself is the central source of the irony. In *The Sentiments*, Swift notes that it "makes an odd sound" to advance the apparently minimal stipulation that the Anglican should be a believer, but in the *Argument* that odd sound and all its overtones ring through the piece. *An Argument* is no longer a defense of a reasonable religious and political compromise; it is rather about the spiritual meanness of such compromise and the meanness of institutions that make it possible. For the minimal demands of Occasional Conformity, understood as a virtue of the religious and political settlement praised in *The Sentiments*, are the very substance of the nominal Christianity that is the subject of *An Argument*. In this piece Swift has represented a situation that works: this is the speaker's central point, and Swift's goad. In this state of affairs the Sacramental Test and the practice of Occasional Conformity are identified with the Christian religion itself. In this politico-spiritual warp where Occasional Conformity sounds in our ears like casual Christianity, it becomes indeed conceivable that the Church can survive the abolition of its own proper foundation. That the abolition of Christianity only *may* put the Church in some danger is the possibility Swift sees into, a possibility that opens the subversive, generalized inquiry into the connection between spiritual ends and political means that the *Argument* in fact is. It is the very usefulness of a church, its undisturbing support of ordinary life, that enrages the writer we sense behind the speaker.

In this way An *Argument* probes the implications of "the settlement" celebrated in *The Sentiments*, probes them to raise questions not only about "the settlement," but about settlement in general. Swift does this simply by introducing into *An Argument* the notion of nominal Christianity, distinguishing the nominal from the primitive—that is, the true—version, and demonstrating the compatibility among the present settlement, current life, and nominal observance. The very Test Act that he labors for in his straight polemic he recognizes here as a support for a church whose connection with the Christian religion can be, for all essential purposes, accidental rather than necessary. He assures his readership that he is not

> so weak [as] to stand up in the Defence of *real* Christianity such as used in primitive Times . . . to have an influence upon Men's belief and Actions: to offer at the Restoring of that would indeed be a wild Project; it would be to dig up Foundations; to destroy at one Blow *all* the wit, and *half* the Learning of the Kingdom; to break the entire Frame and Constitution of Things; to ruin Trade, extinguish Arts and Sciences with the Professors of them; in short, to turn our Courts, Exchanges, and Shops into Desarts. . . . Therefore I think this Caution was in itself altogether unnecessary . . . since every candid Reader will easily understand my Discourse to be intended only in Defence of *nominal* Christianity; the other having been for some Time wholly laid aside by general Consent, as utterly inconsistent with our present schemes of Wealth and Power.[14]

As in *A Modest Proposal*, the joke here may well be on the reader who too quickly perceives this declaration as a joke. Actually, what has happened is that the attitude of "low-norm" satire (to use Northrop Frye's terms) in which Swift puts forth his defense of the settlement, has been simultaneously scrutinized from the perspective of high norms, of primitive, or real, Christianity.[15] From this perspective, such practices as occasional conformity and such acts as the Sacramental Test must themselves appear as shrewd compromises, wholly in accord with "our present schemes of wealth and power," which now emerge as the effective norms according to which a society judges and values its first things. This conclusion seems fairly to be drawn from the demonstration that the abolition of nominal Christianity only *may* put the Church in some danger. We can imagine Swift in writing *An Argument* warming toward that demonstration, seeing keenly and suddenly into the absolute incompatibility of true religion and any politics, and losing himself as a "low-norm" polemicist as he discovers himself as a high-norm satirist, a satirist who sees that the Church, its Test Act, and its dependence upon occasional conformity are all instruments of politics only, useful to civil society only insofar as they do not disturb its real business. In its furthest implications, *An Argument* is nothing less than a subversive inquiry into the general relations between spiritual and secular experience, advancing the most disturbing suggestions about people's efforts to seek institutional expression for their spiritual nature. The polemical Swift, to be sure, would define a healthy society as one that had met with some degree of honest success in discovering such a settlement. The satirical Swift sees in the effort only a prostitution—at best a compromise—of humanity's spiritual life, its first things. The mind that imagined nominal Christianity hated the Church, hated all churches, as mere instruments of nominality.[16]

———♦♦♦———

The special intensity of Swift's satiric art derives then from its unsettling movement toward possibilities whose radical and subversive character are out of kilter with the initially conservative pretensions of his didactic or polemical purpose. In this movement both Swift and his reader gain a kind of freedom, the freedom that distinguishes the poet from the rhetorician, the poet's reader from the rhetorician's audience. We move from a persuasive mode confident in its possession of utilitarian meaning to a mode that works to free meaning from any obligation to issue in action or decision. The only obligation of Swift's reader is to engage in the play against meaning now freed by his ironic art: we can surface from the *Proposal*, or the *Argument*, only as darkly delighted questioners, enjoying our freedom from certainty. Neither our assumptions about the humane and rational foundations of human community, nor an earlier audience's convictions about the Sacramental Test and the establishment that depends upon it, can have simply survived the play against meaning set loose in those pieces. This is the vexation Swift intends for the world, but in the freedom that accompanies it there is an increment of delight.

Swift's irony is both the agent and the effect of his shift from a didactic purpose to the satirical freedom that can trace down the fullest implications of such ideas as infanticide and nominal Christianity. But to take on the freedom of the ironic mode, though it yields its increment of delight, has costs of its own. One of these is the identity Swift loved to think of as his, the character of the Dean and patriot, the community leader, acknowledged as such as well beloved. "The Dean and his Merits we everyone know, / But this skip of a lawyer, where the De'il did he grow," he writes in an obscure broadside against a minor antagonist in some local affair.[17] But the broadside celebrates the pledge of some of his parishioners to protect him against his enemy, Sergeant-at-Law Richard Bettesworth, who had threatened to beat Swift for some lampoon the Dean had written against him. It is an obscure incident, played out in the dimness of Swift's last active years in Dublin, when his battles were mainly local, though consistent with those he had fought years earlier. But for all its obscurity, that Swift should occupy himself with a broadside celebrating a pledge of protection from a self-constituted neighborhood posse is noteworthy. "The Dean and his Merits we everyone know," he has them say of themselves. That is, he has them celebrate his own character, his well-established identity as Dean, with all its well-established merits. This portion of his identity, his public character, is sufficient authority for didactic and polemical address, even for furious invective. In *The Legion Club* for example— as furious an invective as any—Swift brings himself into the poem as a confidant of the keeper of the madhouse, Ireland's parliament, and as he releases a torrent of abuse, naming all his enemies, and directing the keeper to "Lash them daily, lash them duly"—he invokes, as the authority for his invective, his character as poet and patriotic philanthropist. The *Verses on the Death of Dr. Swift, D.S.P.D.* provides the best example of his cherishing that public character. To "One quite indiff'rent in the Cause" he assigns the job of summing it up; the details are familiar:

> "Fair liberty was all his Cry;
> For her he stood prepar'd to die;
> For her he boldly stood alone;
> For her he oft expos'd his Own.
> Two kingdoms, just as Factions led,
> Had set a price upon his Head;
> But, not a Traytor could be found
> To sell him for six hundred Pound."
> [2:347–354]

But there are inaccuracies in this well-deserved panegyric. They have to do with his career in satire and are an index to his awareness that that career stood in uneasy relation to the character he wished to claim as his identity:

> Yet Malice never was his Aim;
> He lash'd the Vice, but spar'd the Name . . .
> His Satyr points at no Defect,
> But what all Mortals may correct . . .
> [458–60, 463–464]

What, if not a universal malice, is the spur of Swift's most intriguing art? How many names did he spare, and which defects intrigued him more than those that were beyond correction—finally the smell and look of humanity itself?

In this very engagement with defects beyond correction Swift's cherished character fails him. Dealing with those matters upon which his thoughts were "allured to dwell," those matters "from which almost every other mind shrinks with disgust," was for him beyond the range of expression available to his public character. Invective, polemical rhetoric, didactic persuasion, the arts that assume a bond between audience and writer and are the expression of an integral and single self, knowing the strength of its own virtue, and reminding its audience of its own—these arts were insufficient to his allurement with ideas and feelings from which his did not, like "almost every other mind," shrink. His mind expanded into its greatest imaginative richness in its obsessive play beyond the frontiers of normal human concern.

Beyond those frontiers the force of character yields to the play of a personality whose stylistic agent is that vexatious irony we recognize as peculiarly Swift's and whose effect is the devastation, not, as in invective or persuasion, the assertion of utilitarian meaning. Everything that Swift so proudly claims in the signature, "D.S.P.D.," as in the verses on his own death and in his epitaph, becomes itself vulnerable to his personality's play. So *An Argument against Abolishing Christianity* releases those parts of his being which must have hated the church establishment he labored for in his public character—the establishment that depended upon occasional conformity and stood as the signature of political settlement. So *A Modest Proposal* releases as much hatred for the poor as labor for them—the brutalizers of their wives, the willing proprietors of butchers' stalls, which, we are reminded, "will not be wanting." All the interpretive difficulties these works create are a function of the play of personality against character, of passions released against meanings intended, of art's freedom against rhetoric's utility. Nor are these interpretive difficulties to be resolved: these works contain no "persona" whose consistent voice can be our key, only the constant play against one another of the author's character and his personalities, of that part of him that would speak in the single voice of virtue against those elements of his being all clamoring for recognition against it. For this reason the modest proposer can warn us against reminding him of virtuous alternatives: he knows them, for he is Swift, the statesman. But Swift the statesman is also the Swift who, in despair of virtuous statescraft, hated the race that proved itself incapable of it—the bestial poor and the unspeakable rich—and envisioned in that despair what every other mind shrinks from—the sight of human community in a butcher's stall, the sight that by itself denies the utilitarian meaning that alone can stand as an answer to the proposer's project. So it is that even the most furious of Swift's invective—which always issues from his character and assumes a bond with his audience—is not half so piercing as his irony, the agent and the sign of his break with all community and the release of all that was most peculiarly and most intensely his own.

The art that releases all that is most peculiarly and intensely Swift's own is tricky, playful, subtle. Its spring is in those elements of his being which played under the surface of his character and which his character would judge detestable. To the Dean and Drapier, this art of voices must have been as suspect as it was to Plato, who rejected the drama because its art speaks in a multiplicity of voices in which the playwright's own authentic and integral self is lost. Dr. Johnson's inability to integrate his sense of the most peculiar characteristic of Swift's mind—his obsession with disease, deformity, and filth—with his definition of the most distinctive quality of Swift's didactic style probably has a similar foundation. Johnson did not value art for its ability to offer surrogate experience for parts of our being we ordinarily deny; art's value, to him, was the help it could afford us in our efforts to recognize and energize our best self, the self of our moral consciousness. The Dean and Drapier sympathized with such attitudes. We can hear their ring throughout his work in a hatred of cleverness, subtlety, complication, and deviousness—in the admiration for the celebrative simplicity of the Houyhnhnms' poetry, in his approval of the minimal libraries of the giants, in his detestation of "the Free-Thinkers, the strong Reasoners, and Men of profound Learning." Much in Swift detests the playful intelligence that is a source of all irony and much art.

Our tendency today would be to attribute the virtue of authenticity to the art which releases the undersurface of Swift's consciousness; we can value his subtle play with his positives more readily than his assertion of them, play generally being more open to critical inquiry than assertion anyway. In the play of "Sweat, Dandriff, Powder, Lead and Hair" there may be more to consider than in the celebration of "Honor and Virtue, Sense and Wit" but it is still a real question why, and how, Swift ever managed to make this catalogue of the virtues resonate with the energies of his being in an art whose authenticity is as evident as the ironic brilliance of his subversive satire. This question seems to have intrigued Swift himself; he enjoyed toying with it, teasing with its implications. In the verses on his own death it leads him toward a not entirely accurate but still telling assertion of a positive literary identity, a celebrative assertion of a direct link between his public good works and his satiric manner. In the large body of poems he wrote to his intimates, he regularly raises the issue, apparently discovering in this kind of poem the opportunity to explore his literary identity, to explore it under conditions especially rich in opportunities for self-revelation.

The playfulness of his intimate poetry is obvious, but we should emphasize how regularly the character of that playfulness is determined by his aggressive insistence upon the mastery of his immediate audience. He creates this mastery by placing himself, as Dean, in a didactic situation, assuming his right to teach and his audience's interest in hearing him do so. In *An Epistle to a Lady, Who desir'd the Author to make Verses on Her, in the Heroick Stile,* Swift conceives of the poem as a response to Lady Acheson's request that he address her in a heroic style—that is, that his moral instruction ("You wou'd teach me to be wise; / Truth and Honour how to prize; . . . How to relish Notions high; / How to live, and how to die") be delivered with a dignity appropriate to its high positives, and a temperance in accord with some humane recognition of her virtues as well as of her faults ("'Tis but just, you shou'd produce, / With each Fault, each Fault's excuse: / Not to publish ev'ry Trifle, / And my few perfections stifle"). Swift succeeds in this peculiar poem in denying Lady Acheson's stylistic demand even as he acknowledges its aptness: "End, as it befits your Station; / Come to Use and Application" he has her say, linking her demand for stylistic and didactic dignity with his own sense that such dignity "befits" his station, that his character as Dean demands, or implies, a closer, more integral connection than he usually could manage between his high positives and his stylistic preferences. Those stylistic preferences are themselves a subject of the poem, and Swift uses the occasion to assert and demonstrate the didactic efficacy of his more violent manner even as he claims to be master of a gentler style. The poem's middle he gives over to a long invective digression against his political targets—a digression whose violence quite belies his assertion within the same poem that he "can easier scorn than hate" (2:634. 144):

> Let me, tho' the Smell be Noisom,
> Strip their Bums; let Caleb hoyse 'em;
> Then, apply Alecto's Whip,
> Till they wriggle, howl, and skip.
> [177–180]

To this image of his aggressive satiric violence Swift imagines Lady Acheson to reply, "Deuce is in you, Mr. Dean; / What can all this passion mean?"—crediting the lady for recognizing in him an intemperance not in accord with the Dean's effort to see himself more mildly. The lady's perception of the inner violence that energizes Swift's satiric manner calls forth her demand that he reapply his attention to her, that he end as it befits his station: that is, in dignified address, with "use and application." The poem continues, but does not develop from this point. Having acknowledged, through the lady, that he perceives a disjunction among his station, his character, his high positives, and the manner he continually discovers as most congenial, Swift proceeds to ignore this issue. He concludes the poem by asserting once more his preference for a raillery that he has demonstrated to be far more brutal in practice than his own description of it—"I encounter vice with Mirth" (142)—can acknowledge.

Even here, in a poem written to and for a friend, we can discover a tonal range whose effect is to produce that play with his audience, that intimate approach toward it and then that tricky withdrawal, which characterizes Swift's special achievement in ironic art. We should note here his own concern about the decorum of his undertaking, his own sense that the positive didactic enterprise he defines as his is not easily served by or embodied in the manner that most naturally expresses the negative energies of his personality. In his play with Lady Acheson's request for dignified address, Swift becomes elusive to her, and he imagines her to search for him, a search necessarily unsuccessful as he lets loose his invective, disfiguring his composure, drawing from her the puzzled recognition of the devil in him and, seeing this, the impossible demand—"End as it befits your Station." The demand is impossible because the devil in him and the Dean could be reconciled only under the rare and special circumstances he elsewhere created, and which he could create only from his connection with another.

These are the circumstances, at once intimate and celebrative, of Swift's connection with Esther Johnson, his dearest friend and sometimes close companion. Esther Johnson was a young child in Sir William Temple's household when Swift, then Temple's secretary, first came to know her and briefly to tutor her. She is, of course, the Stella of his poems and letters and *Journal*. Perhaps Swift's renaming of Esther Johnson tells us also that Stella is Swift's literary creation, but if so, she is a creation unlike any of his others. She is fashioned out of all that we would call positive in his imagination, yet fashioned so that she serves also to test this idealism. Even a casual reading of his various writings to and about her will strike us for their concentration of panegyrical topics—her beauty, her wit, her honor, her piety. Those topics, in short, which for Swift were generally unendurable as the subjects of simply celebrative rhetoric, became, with Stella as the vehicle for his celebration of them, fully and positively available to him. We may, then, when we examine his poems to her, be too easily prone to think of Stella as a creation of dubious authenticity, an inevitable alternative to the horrific female creations we know so well from the "unprintable" poems. But to think so about this unusual segment of Swift's work would be a mistake. Stella is undoubtedly a literary creation, but as such she demands of us a critical tact that acknowledges her actual identity before her literary one. For striking us first about her appearance in Swift's work—whether in poems, letters, or journals—should be his insistence upon her biographical actuality, to which he almost *offhandedly* engrafted his idealism. For him Stella was a personal fact as well as a literary necessity, and it is just this that seems to have continuously awakened his wonder and determined the character he would give her as his literary subject. In even the most intense of his celebrations of her we can hear his insistence upon her plain actuality: "Never was any of her sex born with better gifts of the mind, or more improved them by reading and conversation. . . . She had a gracefulness somewhat more than human in every motion, word and action." This report, for all its idealizing superlatives, still has a decorum that allows for such tempering and actualizing detail as that Stella was "looked upon as one of the most beautiful, graceful, and agreeable young women in London, only a little too fat."[18] Swift's characteristic practice, both in this piece, written under great emotional pressure at her death, and in the poems celebrating their friendship, is to make Stella into an idea with enough flesh on it to bear the inspection of just such irony as proves, without undercutting, the virtues she is made to embody and which she helps him to experience and to explore.

In his poems to Stella Swift regularly invokes the facts of their initial relationship: in life he was, and in these poems he remains, her tutor. The poems he addressed to her have at their center a didactic situation; they are teaching occasions of lesser or greater intensity. At their most moving, their didactic force is both generalized and particularized, generalized so that the lesson amounts to a celebration of the delivered doctrine, particularized so that its application develops from the personal substance of Swift's and Stella's connection, the mutual honoring, which is the proof, and the poignant acerbities, which are the test, of the positives these poems celebrate. The special circumstances of Swift's and Stella's personal relationship—that it developed into intimacy from their initially and literally didactic connection as tutor and tutee—Swift seems to have seized upon as rich with opportunities of extraordinary importance to him. Her actuality, her closeness, her willingness to acknowledge the shaping force of his influence, all seem to have come together to make her, in his imagination, just such an idea as could endure the strain of his obsession with the disjunctive antagonism between high and low, the ideal and the actual—the obsession, in short, that energizes his most intriguing and devastating art. But in the didactic art of the Stella poems the strain does not break the positive effort, the peculiar energies of Swift's personality do not overwhelm the effort of his character—nor are they yet denied.

In Stella Swift discovered an audience that eluded even his penchant for elusive trickery, an audience immune to his intriguing and devastating irony. As the addressee of his poems, as the single being he knew who grew for a time under his tutelage and would acknowledge it, she was, in her actuality, his ideal audience. His characteristic and vexatious irony, that irony in which he withdraws from his positives and from his audience as he makes them his target, was not necessary to him in the special circumstances he enjoyed as Stella's tutor in life and in verse. In writing to and for her, Swift could assume and maintain that direct contact with a good audience which is the condition of didactic address and which makes the didactic occasion also a celebrative one. We can hear these two strains together in lines such as these:

>   True Poets can depress and raise;
> Are Lords of Infamy and Praise:
> They are not scurrilous in Satire,
> Nor will in Panygyrick flatter.
> Unjustly poets we asperse;

> Truth shines the brighter, clad in Verse;
> And all the Fictions they pursue
> Do but insinuate what is true.
> [*To Stella, Who Collected and Transcribed His Poems*, 2:729.53–60]

The assertive and declarative manner of these lines is obvious in the diction: True Poets, Lords, Truth, shines. The thematic concern has to do with satire and panegyric, and asserts, aria-like, Swift's sense that the two kinds are not necessarily distinct or mutually exclusive: satire without scurrility, panegyric without flattery, are possible, but possible only where poets are true and when their matter is truth. These lines, which seem to reflect self-consciously on Swift's career in literature, mark the turn in the poem to which they belong. In asserting the possibility of an expression whose confident union with truth creates a manner free of both scurrility and flattery, their celebrative manner contrasts sharply with the poem's preceding section—a characteristically Swiftian obliteration of idealizing poets, though somewhat tempered in its scurrility—and introduces the tonal dignity required in the section to follow—a realistic assessment of Stella's character in which Swift demonstrates quite literally what a panegyric without flattery can be. The preceding section is typical of what Swift will ordinarily do when his matter permits him to dwell upon the polarities of the ideal and the actual:

> A Poet, starving in a Garret,
> Conning old Topicks like a Parrot,
> Invokes his Mistress and his Muse,
> And stays at home for want of Shoes:
> Should but his Muse descending drop
> A Slice of Bread, and Mutton-Chop,
> Or kindly when his Credit's out,
> Surprize him with a Pint of Stout,
> Or patch his broken Stocking Soals,
> Or send him in a Peck of Coals;
> Exalted in his mighty Mind
> He flies, and leaves the Stars behind,

> Counts all his Labours amply paid,
> Adores her for the timely Aid.
>
> [25–38]

Swift develops his game by intensifying the negative opportunities obvious in the conception, so that the starving poet's inspiration, his tattered mistress, can be represented as "Bright *Phillis* mending ragged Smocks, / And Radiant *Iris* in the Pox" (46–47). The line of argument sustaining Swift's play is that he, as Stella's friend, is saved from the idealizing foolishness of a poet whose sustenance, as well as inspiration, is his mistress. "With Friendship and Esteem possesst, / I ne'er admitted Love a guest"—this describes the nature of his connection with Stella, and also its enabling opportunity, for

> should my Praises owe their Truth
> To Beauty, Dress, or Paint or Youth,
> What Stoicks call *without our Power*,
> They could not be insur'd an Hour . . .
>
> [61–64]

What Swift does, then, is to attribute to the romantic coolness of his connection with Stella the opportunity for evading the (foolish) entrapment in the special dilemma his negative imagination revels in: the dilemma created in the antagonism of what was for him always a disjunct idealism and actuality.

But if Swift is honest enough to acknowledge that as Stella's friend he enjoys a freedom from one kind of poetic foolishness, he immediately complicates his task by assuming burdens the idealizing poet could never know: the burden of telling the whole truth about his subject:

> Your Virtues safely I commend,
> They on no Accidents depend:
> Let Malice look with all her Eyes,
> She dares not say the Poet lyes.
>
> *Stella*, when you these Lines transcribe,
> Lest you should take them for a Bribe,

> Resolv'd to mortify your Pride,
> I'll here expose your weaker Side.
>
> [79–86]

What follows is a remarkable achievement: the tonal dignity that Swift introduced as he moved away from his rougher manner now sustains his anatomy of Stella's "weaker side." The result can probably be considered Swift's demonstration of the work of the "true poet," who, he had written, can both "depress and raise."

> Your Spirits kindle to a Flame,
> Mov'd with the lightest Touch of Blame,
> And when a Friend in Kindness tries
> To shew you where your Error lies,
> Conviction does but more incense;
> Perverseness is your whole Defence:
> Truth, Judgment, Wit, give Place to Spite,
> Regardless both of Wrong and Right.
> Your Virtues, all suspended, wait
> Till Time hath open'd Reason's Gate:
> And what is worse, your Passion bends
> Its Force against your nearest Friends;
> Which Manners, Decency, and Pride,
> Have taught you from the World to hide:
> In vain; for see, your Friend hath brought
> To publick Light your only Fau't;
> And yet a Fault we often find
> Mix'd in a noble generous Mind;
> And may compare to *Ætna's* Fire,
> Which, tho' with Trembling, all admire;
> The Heat that makes the Summit glow,
> Enriching all the Vales below.
> Those who in warmer Climes complain
> From *Phoebus* Rays they suffer Pain,
> Must own, that Pain is largely paid
> By gen'rous Wines beneath a Shade.
> Yet when I find your Passions rise,
> And Anger sparkling in your Eyes,

> I grieve those Spirits should be spent,
> For nobler Ends by Nature meant.
> One Passion, with a diff'rent Turn,
> Makes Wit inflame, or Anger burn;
> So the Sun's Heat, with different Powers,
> Ripens the Grape, the Liquor sours.
> Thus *Ajax*, when with Rage possesst
> By *Pallas* breath'd into his Breast,
> His Valour would no more employ;
> Which might alone have conquer'd *Troy*;
> But Blinded by Resentment, seeks
> For Vengeance on his Friends the *Greeks*.
>
>   You think this Turbulence of Blood
> From stagnating preserves the Flood;
> Which thus fermenting, by Degrees
> Exalts the Spirits, sinks the Lees.
>
>   *Stella*, for once you reason wrong;
> For should this Ferment last too long,
> By time subsiding, you may find
> Nothing but Acid left behind.
> From Passion you may then be freed,
> When Peevishness and Spleen succeed.
>   [87–136]

In approaching this passage we should note that it answers to Swift's resolution to "mortify" Stella's pride, and we should recall the imaginative resources he could release elsewhere in the name of such a resolution: the Yahoos, the lady's dressing room, the Struldbruggs. Recognizing this, I find that the unusual achievement of these verses is their genuinely heroic manner, whose effect is to heighten their didactic intent, to affirm the positives according to which Stella is being scrutinized, and finally, to celebrate Stella in the very process of confronting her with her "weaker side." The heroic ring comes from the wholly serious use of mythological material (the references to Ajax, Pallas, and Troy) and from the quality of the reference to Aetna's fire ("Which, tho' with Trembling, all admire"). This kind of material

Swift more usually uses to produce sophisticated comedy—the mythological material in *Cadenus and Vanessa* sustains that poem's comedy through several hundred lines, for example. But here, though comedy is present, it is impossible to feel it as the dominant mode. The reason is that the mythological and heroic allusions are sustained by the didactic assertiveness of the passage, which is itself an effect of Swift's habit of cataloguing the very virtues that are the subject of the poem's teaching intent: "a noble generous Mind" is such an assertion, another is "Manners, Decency, and Pride," along with "Truth, Judgment, Wit." These positives are compacted in lists so that they literally occupy the space of the lines in which they appear, and accumulate assertive force by the nature of their physical presence in those lines. At the same time, these words are muted: either they occupy subordinate clauses, or they do not fall into rhyming position. This explains, perhaps, why the heroic and celebrative strain in the passage is felt as a coloring, not as a major mode. The major mode, in fact, is hard to pin down, but I would call it a kind of social ease, an offhandedness in keeping with the personal intimacy from which the passage springs and which it so successfully communicates. Moreover, Swift's offhandedness in asserting his positives is entirely right in this poem, for he has maneuvered it toward celebrative assertion after an earlier movement that had lampooned the easier celebrative manner of romantic idealizing. What he has aimed for here, and reached, is expression true to his claim of freedom from that idealizing manner. It is a heightening of plain truth that simultaneously asserts the reality of the virtues and the grandeur of the woman whose actual behavior is not always adequate to them. In the simultaneous presence of the heroic coloring and the social ease, Swift is able to contemplate the distinction between ideal and actual behavior without turning the one into proof against the other. This is a rare achievement for him and not something he has been remembered for.

Turning from its earlier manner which lampoons one form of celebration, the idealizing kind, the poem demonstrates the possibility of another celebrative style, one whose genuinely heroic coloring is still compatible with the realism Swift always insists upon. In his poem to Lady Acheson Swift had evaded her request to be instructed in a dignified and heroic strain and indeed, of that request, had made an occasion to let loose a torrent of invective abuse. We can attribute to

Stella—to Swift's experience of her grandeur and of her actuality—his success in devising a style that meets Lady Acheson's unmet demand: "But, I beg, suspend a While, / That same paltry Burlesque stile: / Drop, for once, your constant Rule, / Turning all to Ridicule . . ." (49–53). For in this poem, *To Stella, Who Collected and Transcribed His Poems*, Swift can express a thoroughly positive experience of his own best beliefs. The sign of this experience is that union of didactic intent and heroic tone with which he liked to credit himself despite the regularity with which it eluded him. Indeed, in this poem we can feel the peculiar intensity that the best Augustan poetry regularly discovers in didactic address. This intensity develops, I think, from the association of didactic and celebrative purpose, as if the teaching occasion were a kind of ritual experience of society's best beliefs, a firm acknowledgment of shared identity in shared belief.

This association of didactic and celebrative purpose, moreover, may help to illuminate a peculiarity of the poem's beginning and ending. For Swift frames the poem by addressing Stella as the collector and transcriber of his verses and therefore imagines her experience of the poem itself as a test of the efficacy of his instruction. To put it another way, he imagines her as the poem's audience and *as such*, in a special way, as its *creator*:

> As when a lofty Pile is rais'd,
> We never hear the Workmen prais'd,
> Who bring the Lime, or place the Stones;
> But all admire *Inigo Jones*;
> So if this Pile of scatter'd Rhymes
> Should be approv'd in After-times,
> If it both pleases and endures,
> The Merit and the Praise are yours.
> [1–8]

This puzzling assertion characterizes the poet as the poem's mechanic, its editor and transcriber as its shaping genius, apparently reversing the relationship we know to be the true one. But the puzzle clarifies when we look at the concluding lines, in which Swift addresses Stella, assuming that, in her editing, she has experienced the lesson of the poem's body, the exposure, that is, of her weaker side, her passionate pride:

> Say, *Stella*, when you copy next,
> Will you keep strictly to the Text?
> Dare you let these Reproaches stand,
> And to your Failing set your Hand?
> Or if these Lines your Anger fire,
> Shall they in baser Flames expire?
> Whene'er they burn, if burn they must,
> They'll prove my Accusation just.
>
> [137–144]

These lines in fact tell us that the poem's integrity and finally its survival depend upon its audience, the object of its didactic intent. And that, of course, is the point. The audience *is* the final maker of a didactic poem, the reason why it can rise to heroic and celebrative style. In responding positively to the doctrine, the audience acknowledges its possession of the doctrine, its understanding of manners, decency, pride, truth, judgment, wit. In the case of this poem, Swift has imagined Stella as just such an audience, like the audience he imagined for his didactic purpose in *The Drapier's Letters*, where his job was to remind his readership of what they already knew about virtuous community and patriotism. And, as in *The Drapier's Letters*, Swift in this poem can be arch, can be clever (as the "bite" in the last couplet demonstrates) without withdrawing from his audience and his positives in that characteristic irony of his, whose effect is to make his ideals dubious and his audience his victim, as in *An Argument* and *A Modest Proposal*. The opening and the end of this poem, along with the heroic and celebrative delivery of its doctrine in the middle, verify that bond that must exist between teacher and taught, poet and audience, if their best beliefs are to provide them the cognitive integrity that is the test and end of positive art. Swift's great negative art flourished in the absence of that cognitive integrity, which he could experience only rarely, and most intensely, as Stella's teacher and poet.

In Swift's writings for Stella readers have always felt a lyrical quality that is all the more moving for his general distrust of what he thought were the romantic sources of lyric expression. I want now to explore the nature and the sources of the special lyricism of these poems, a lyricism that I think is a function of their didactic movement. I call it a special lyricism because it arises from a didactic effort that we might more easily identify with Swift's public station rather than his private self. The achievement of these poems is to secure an integration of station and self that was difficult for Swift, whose satiric intensity elsewhere arises indeed in the very failure of that integration. In establishing Stella as the fit audience for the positive and celebrative assertion of his own best beliefs, Swift concentrates into one person the function and identity of the whole public audience whose goodness is the condition of the didactic address, the guarantor of its efficacy, the reason that the didactic occasion can be a celebrative one. But in these poems the lyric poignancy, which delicately evokes an unspoken intimacy, is surely a complex effect of Swift's awareness that his audience of one was a surrogate for that public community he knew did not exist. The intimacy we appreciate in these poems takes on much of its value for Swift precisely because he charges it with energies that could not find their proper public release—except in the satirical intensity not in keeping with his station. What he says to and for Stella communicates his poignant awareness that what he most owed her was the opportunity she provided him to stay in some kind of positive touch with the ideas he loved. The didactic movement of the best of these poems is, therefore, part of a larger mimetic intention—the representation, in the intimacy of two difficult people, of the reality, the value, the cost of virtue.

In *To Stella, Visiting Me in My Sickness*, what starts out as a discourse on honor becomes an imitation of gratitude, and in the movement from the one to the other the poem develops its lyric intensities. The discourse on honor begins aggressively:

> But (not in Wranglings to engage
> With such a stupid, vicious Age)
> If Honour I would here define,
> It answers Faith in Things divine.
>   [2:723.7–10]

The discussion of honor is initiated in the first place as a compliment to Stella, but Swift's lesson, his effort to define and illustrate, proceeds independently of any reference to Stella for some thirty lines. They strike me as remarkable lines, characterized in part by an epigrammatic wit that registers the speaker's comfortable familiarity with a set of ideas he possesses not simply as ideas but as heritage:

> As nat'ral Life the Body warms,
> And, Scholars teach, the Soul informs;
> So Honour animates the Whole,
> And is the Spirit of the Soul.
>   Those num'rous Virtues which the Tribe
> Of tedious Moralists describe,
> And by such various Titles call,
> True Honour comprehends them all.
> Let Melancholy rule supreme,
> Choler preside, or Blood, or Phlegm,
> It makes no Diff'rence in the Case,
> Nor is Complexion Honour's Place.
>   [11–22]

"Scholars teach" and "the Tribe of tedious Moralists" and "Those num'rous Virtues" (the demonstrative adjective does it here) all contribute to create our sense that the lesson is a kind of recital. But as the recital continues, the wit sharpens. The lesson, for all its familiarity—perhaps because of its familiarity, because it is a social as well as moral possession—can be easily misused. The wit of the following passage arises directly from the fact that moral knowledge *is* a social possession, and, as such, can be mere ornamentation or worse:

> But, lest we should for Honour take
> The Drunken quarrels of a Rake,
> Or think it seated in a Scar,
> Or on a proud triumphal Car,
> Or, in the Payment of a Debt
> We lose with Sharpers at Piquet. . . .
>   [23–28]

These lines help explain the aggressiveness of the lesson's beginning; these are the social uses of moral knowledge, the same graceful or complacent corruptions of doctrine which create the cognitive anarchy of *A Modest Proposal* and of nominal Christianity, the "dullness" of a "stupid, vicious Age." (We can easily see in these verses the salon of the Goddess Dullness.) Swift delineates here precisely the socialized viciousness that, in its complacent appropriation of doctrine, displays man's unfitness for doctrine. It is just this socialized viciousness that elsewhere and most memorably drives Swift into the satiric irony within which he withdraws from doctrine and from his audience, and in the simple additive intensification of the examples he adduces (there are four more lines and in them two more examples of stupid viciousness) we can see the anger that elsewhere generates his irony and motivates his withdrawal. Once again we are at the point where the ideal and the actual can break apart.

Here they do not, however. As the anger intensifies and the examples multiply, the passage comes to a sudden stop: to all these social corruptions of moral knowledge, there is an answer:

> Let *Stella's* fair Example preach
> A Lesson she alone can teach.
>
>   In Points of Honour to be try'd,
> All Passions must be laid aside:
> Ask no Advice, but think alone,
> Suppose the Question not your own:
> How shall I act? is not the Case,
> But how would *Brutus* in my Place?
> In such a Cause would *Cato* bleed?
> And how would *Socrates* proceed?
>   Drive all Objections from your Mind,
> Else you relapse to Human Kind:
> Ambition, Avarice, and Lust,
> And factious Rage, and Breach of Trust,
> And Flatt'ry tipt with nauseous Fleer,
> And guilty Shame, and servile Fear,
> Envy, and Cruelty, and Pride,
> Will in your tainted Heart preside.
>   [43–50]

Swift speaks for Stella here, but her example preaches. He, as speaker, acts as the vehicle for *her* doctrine in a collaboration that is a kind of marriage of her virtue and his intensity. In this remarkable union much is accomplished. We should note first the appeal to Brutus, Cato, and Socrates, that is, to the sternest, purest, most strenuous creators and exemplars of the moral heritage that Swift had invoked in the earlier lines. The effect of invoking these names is to remind us of the initial pure vigor of doctrine prior to its codification as heritage. Swift had celebrated doctrine codified as heritage in the ease and familiarity of his recital in lines 11–22, but it was heritage corrupted into social complacency which he had attacked in the section immediately following. Bringing Stella into the poem at this point has the effect of revivifying doctrine; it points to a living exemplar, an actual being whose life stands as reminder and proof of the original force of what has been so viciously and gracefully corrupted.

But if Stella can serve in this capacity, Swift still interprets her meaning, and his presence in these lines is clear in their doctrinal and tonal intensity. The lesson, lived by Stella, spoken by Swift, taken from Cato, Brutus, Socrates, is now not a definition of honor but a prescription for honorable behavior. The prescription is designed above all to prevent that "relapse to Human kind" in which actual behavior vitiates doctrine, and it is realized in a renunciation of self— "Suppose the Question not your own"—a conversion of personality into character—"How shall I act? is not the Case, / But how would *Brutus*, in my Place?" Stella thus enters the poem as an embodiment of the ideal, more precisely as one whose appropriation of the ideal does not strain against her experience of the actual. A sense of that strain, however, is not absent from these lines, the last six of which are an intense catalogue of the causes of that "relapse into Human kind" which Stella's example preaches against and Swift's words define. These six lines are at the edge of intense invective, a list of malicious passions which taken together shift the emotional emphasis of this moment in the poem from didactic celebration to satiric anger, precisely expressed in the force of the imputation, "your tainted Heart." Against the beauty of Stella's experience of the ideal, the verse expresses Swift's latent fury at the actual, and the poem at this point is emotionally uncertain, equally strong in its celebrative and invective energies.

This uncertainty does not, however, govern the poem's development toward its conclusion. Though we can recognize here the elements of an irreconcilable division similar to that in Gulliver's fourth voyage— irreconcilable because the alternative to virtuous conduct is a relapse into not evil only, but *Human Kind*—nevertheless Swift discovers a way out.

> Heroes and Heroins of old,
> By Honour only were enroll'd
> Among their Brethren of the Skies,
> To which (though late) shall *Stella* rise.
> Ten thousand Oaths upon Record,
> Are not so sacred as her Word:
> The World shall in its Atoms end,
> E'er *Stella* can deceive a Friend.
> By Honour seated in her Breast,
> She still determines what is best:
> What Indignation in her Mind
> Against Enslavers of Mankind!
> Base Kings and Ministers of State,
> Eternal Objects of her Hate.
>
> [51–64]

Here the force of the invective anger that had been building is retained, but its purpose is transformed. Swift does not exacerbate the strain between the ideal and the actual, and he does not withdraw from his didactic and celebrative intention. Instead, he smartly reapplies his attention to Stella in lines whose heroic tonality is unmistakable. Explicitly identifying Stella with "Heroes and Heroines of old," Swift converts the angry energy of the preceding section into heroically colored celebration: we feel this in the powerfully assertive effect of the third, fourth, and fifth couplets, two of which are hyperbolic in their particulars ("Ten thousand Oaths . . . The World shall in its Atoms end") while the third generalizes its praise from these grand exaggerations, confident in Stella's determination of "what is best." In the two concluding couplets of this section the transformation of anger into celebration is complete. The first is an open, plain expression of wonder: "What Indignation in her Mind / Against Enslavers of Mankind!" This is the rhetoric of wonder, wonder as the transfiguration of anger. The directness of "Enslavers of Mankind" is as far from corrosive irony as one can come: the words confidently define and declaim against a known and understood evil. Here Swift's confidence in Stella's knowledge of and her indignation against a clearly perceived evil makes it possible for him to experience and express his wonder at her capacity for proper indignation. The final couplet rises to boldly particular denunciation of those enslavers of mankind as "Base Kings and Ministers of State," and to a hyperbolic description of Stella's moral energy, a capacity to keep before her the "Eternal Objects of her Hate." The assertive grandeur of this passage is possible because Swift can free himself of the burden of hatred; he can do this by *attributing to Stella* a capacity for righteous hatred. Because Stella is now responsible for righteous indignation, Swift is free to value in her an experience which, in himself, would be corrosive. Stella gives him, then, the opportunity to celebrate in another a moral energy that, in himself, will find expression only in irony or invective. That moral energy can find positive, heroic, celebrative expression as praise for Stella, and this expression truly fits Swift's station.

These strong lines, in their heroic rhetoric, express fully Swift's own direct and healthy experience of his own best beliefs. The lines join the didactic and the celebrative in a moving, because rare, moment for Swift. The lesson on honor has not intensified in irony or invective, but in assertion; the strain between the ideal and the actual has not overwhelmed the initial commitment to the ideal. Instead, that commitment has found a local habitation and a name. And because the Stella of these lines is an indignant, angry Stella, the man who celebrates her does not endanger his authenticity. His movement into heroic praise involves no softening of, no blinking at, an actuality that more usually draws from him a meaner language. Because of Stella an occasion for irony or meanness becomes for Swift an occasion for a grander manner.

The poem's movement through several ranges of feeling as it continually adjusts its tonal coloring is at once a rhetorical and a poetic achievement. The progress from anger to wonder may be seen as the rhetorically persuasive accompaniment of the poem's didactic effort. Swift explicitly says as much:

> Her Hearers are amaz'd from whence
> Proceeds that Fund of Wit and Sense;
> Which though her Modesty would shroud,
> Breaks like the Sun behind a Cloud,

> While Gracefulness its Art Conceals,
> And yet through ev'ry Motion steals.
>
> [79–84]

The focus here is on the general audience who benefit directly from Stella's example, experiencing the same wonder—"Her Hearers are amaz'd"—we have seen in Swift's response to her, as well as the direct knowledge of a series of implicated positives: wit, sense, modesty, grace. But at the same time, the emotive movement from anger to wonder directly expresses the progress of a curve of private feeling, the inner experience of the poem's maker. For the final movement of the verse is distinctly personal; it brings us for the first time to the situation from which the poem springs, announced in the title: *To Stella, Visiting Me in My Sickness*.

This is a complex conclusion to the poem, intimate in its account of Swift's behavior and Stella's nursing. Its effect is to isolate the two from the audience, "the world," which had been to this point of the poem the addressee of its didactic and celebrative rhetoric.

> How would Ingratitude delight?
> And, how would Censure glut her Spight?
> If I should *Stella*'s Kindness hide
> In Silence, or forget with Pride.
> When on my sickly Couch I lay,
> Impatient both of Night and Day,
> Lamenting in unmanly Strains,
> Call'd ev'ry Pow'r to ease my Pains,
> Then *Stella* ran to my Relief
> With chearful Face, and inward Grief;
> And, though by Heaven's severe decree
> She suffers hourly more than me,
> No cruel Master could require
> From Slaves employ'd for daily Hire
> What *Stella* by her Friendship warm'd,
> With Vigour and Delight perform'd.
> My sinking Spirits now supplies
> With Cordials in her Hands, and Eyes.
> Now, with a soft and silent Tread,

> Unheard she moves about my Bed.
> I see her taste each nauseous Draught,
> And so obligingly am caught:
> I bless the Hand from whence they came,
> Nor dare distort my Face for shame.
>
> [92–116]

    This passage first is characteristically aggressive toward the larger audience outside the sickroom, seen as an armory of Censure, Ingratitude, Spite. But the aggression is absorbed by a more compelling feeling as Swift deftly gives the poem over entirely to Stella in a movement of praise which is at the same time a record of his gratitude toward her, and consequently a mimetic rendering finally of the full meaning of the poem's didactic subject—honor. This final movement completes that lesson in a mimesis of Stella's behavior to Swift, of Swift's full response to that moral beauty, and of his recognition of its costs.

    The lyrical intensity of this movement is an obvious consequence of the abrupt introduction of intimate detail. But we must not miss how finely this detail has been fitted to Swift's didactic material. The intimacy of "Then Stella ran to my Relief / With chearful Face, and inward Grief" concretely illustrates the earlier instruction, "How shall I act? is not the Case, / But how would *Brutus*, in my place?" transforming Stella from a pattern of stoic severity, with its subordination of personality to character, into an image of effective blessedness, fully revealing personality:

> I see her taste each nauseous Draught,
> And so obligingly am caught:
> I bless the Hand from which they came,
> Nor dare distort my Face for shame.

There is affectionate joking in this picture—a Swift on his best behavior, heroically taking his medicine—but the joking also is made from the didactic situation. The image of childish bravery—"Nor dare distort my Face"—is just right: yet another effect of Stella's virtue, it contributes to the intimacies portrayed, and sets off the earlier, harsher reflection of self Swift alludes to in "no cruel Master could require."

We are given a scene then, and the scene effectively lets us into the most private of details, the acerbities as well as delights of an often difficult, usually rewarding connection, the whole a mimetic rendering of honor in action, earning gratitude and a blessing, so that the didactic lesson, presented earlier in the most heroic of terms, can be felt now within the realistically diminished and very private sickroom.

By rendering this closing movement of the poem as a scene, Swift can make it fully responsive to the force of personal feeling. The didactic material—the lesson on honor—is assimilated to another purpose, the mimetic portrayal of the rewards of honor. These are simply the blessings Swift bestows, the signs of the gratitude honor earns. The personal, lyrical color now of the poem's mimesis of gratitude within the sickroom may be said to be the private, intimate transfiguration of the public experience of wonder the poem had earlier expressed at Stella's heroism. And as the poem narrows its focus onto the emotional communication between the two people, we can see the way in which the earlier portrayal of Stella as model yields to the celebration of Stella as person, the way, that is, Swift insists upon the real selfhood of the figure he had earlier pointed to as an example of stoic selflessness, one whose beliefs and behavior had been seen as proof against a "relapse to Human Kind." For the final didactic movement, coordinated now with the lyrical fullness of the poem's conclusion, is about the human costs of such virtue as Stella possesses:

> Best Pattern of true Friends, beware;
> You pay too dearly for your Care;
> If, while your Tenderness secures
> My Life, it must endanger yours.
> For such a Fool was never found,
> Who pull'd a Palace to the Ground,
> Only to have the Ruins made
> Materials for an House decay'd.
>
> [117–124]

Here Swift speaks directly to Stella imagining her as the recipient rather than the teacher of the lesson; this had been her role throughout the poem as its pattern of honor. Indeed, Swift uses that word as he directly addresses her in his thoughts—"Best Pattern of true Friends, beware"—but he can so address her because the other term that he applies to her in this small, lyric homily, the affectionate term "Fool," declares his poignant awareness of her real selfhood, just as the entire passage declares his recognition of the cost to that self of its virtue: "You pay too dearly for your Care." In full coordination with the poem's didactic material, these last lines complete the curve of personal feeling from invective anger to wonder to elegiac celebration, making the lesson in honor, which had celebrated Stella as pattern, now into a source of lyrical awareness, yielding the recognition of Stella as person, vulnerable to her virtues. The vehicle of this last movement is an almost Aesopian parable, simple in its didactic character: "For such a Fool was never found, / Who pull'd a Palace to the Ground . . ." The didactic character of this Aesopian homily, however, is clearly subordinate to the deeply lyrical feeling that informs the passage: indeed, it helps to create that feeling, as if Swift were invoking the public manner of the homily the more fully to show to Stella how intensely private this emotional moment is. More, the moment is made to carry a charge of self-revelation, also through the homiletic image Swift applies to himself: "an house decay'd." The poem completes its emotive curve in this self-revelation with its elegiac tonalities, fully expressive of the human actuality of its pattern of virtue and of the intensities of two people, whose human experience of suffering and sacrifice becomes the poem's final subject, the vehicle for its fullest demonstration of the meaning of honor, its didactic subject. As pattern yields to person, honor is shown to be the costly virtue whose effects are finally known only in suffering and sacrifice.[19]

The finest, and the last, of Swift's celebrations of Stella marks the fullest integration he achieves of didactic and lyric expression. *Stella's Birthday, March 13, 1726/7* is a dramatic poem, entirely conceived as a mimesis of an inner action, and as such, dominated throughout by its charge of lyric feeling. To that feeling the didactic movement is grafted, quite unlike the previous poem which traces its emotive curve through several stages of public address toward a moment of private self-revelation. Now the private focus and intensity are immediately revealed in the opening lines, which set a scene toward which the previous poem had worked as its conclusion:

> This day, whate'er the Fates decree,
> Shall still be kept with Joy by me:
> This Day then, let us not be told,
> That you are sick, and I grown old
> Nor think on our approaching Ills,
> And talk of Spectacles and Pills;
> To morrow will be Time enough
> To hear such mortifying Stuff.
> [2:763.1–8]

We hardly need to point out how precisely and plainly the unadorned language defines the intimate privacy of this occasion and also its solemnity. Although Swift speaks of his intention to mark the occasion with joy, and despite the witty offhandedness of the detail, there is an almost ceremonial decorum to the moment. Stella's day is a day he "keeps," and in just a few lines he will show that "keeping" this day means, among other things, delivering some "serious Lines." Moreover, keeping this day with joy requires that he arrange its circumstances: for the proper observance of the occasion he will exclude all that "the Fates decree"; "Let us not be told / That you are sick, and I grown old" is a poignant yet willful self-assertion, a necessary condition for the didactic meditation on virtue which is to compose the poem's body and be the celebrative commemoration of Stella's life. Yet if we look ahead to the poem's conclusion we can see that the poise of this first movement will give way to more complex and difficult feelings:

> O then, whatever Heav'n intends,
> Take Pity on your pitying Friends;
> Nor let your Ills affect your Mind,
> To fancy they can be unkind.
> Me, surely me, you ought to spare,
> Who gladly would your Suff'rings share;
> Or give my Scrap of Life to you,

>   And think it far beneath your Due;
>   You, to whose Care so oft I owe,
>   That I'm alive to tell you so.
>
>   [79–88]

The plaintive urgency of these final lines, in language as unadorned as the poem's opening, clearly reveals the difficulty of maintaining the ceremonial poise of that opening. What had begun in poise ends in pleading. In the distinctly different tonal coloring of these framing sections of the poem we can sense the direction of the poem's movement, the inner emotional action it imitates.

The final lines, perhaps the most personal Swift ever wrote, are addressed to a difficult woman. Swift joins their personal urgency—"Me, surely me, you ought to spare"—to an elegiac acknowledgment of that woman's lifelong virtue—"You, to whose Care so oft I owe, / That I'm alive to tell you so." The plea of these lines is that Stella demonstrate, now when such a test is most difficult, that her life of virtue is not vitiated by the strain of her final crisis, that at this most difficult moment she sustain her moral biography so that its author may be vindicated. The personal urgency of the poem's conclusion expresses not only a poignant and realistic description of Stella's impatience now toward the beneficiary of her former selflessness, but also Swift's full awareness that the authenticity of his celebration of her, and of virtue, is at the stake. This poem is as much a test of all he has written about Stella as it is of her, and it is no surprise that in its final lines it should record his sense that his moral and imaginative life is an adjunct of hers. Here he pleads for the value of his own life.

Of the results of that plea we can know nothing. The tact in this refusal to conclude and to assert is itself a moving acknowledgment of Stella's existential actuality, indeed of her physical being, now in its last painful illness. This final scene of Swift's final poem for Stella is brutally realistic in its presentation of a strained experience charged with retrospective significance, demanding of the sufferer that in her suffering she prove out the force of that virtue Swift had attributed to her throughout her life, the life that has provided the measure of the value of Swift's own. And yet, the poem is in no significant sense inconclusive. This intensely elegiacal final movement, for all of its contrast with the more poised and assertive opening, still develops naturally from the poem's body, that is, from those "serious Lines" that Swift delivers as his birthday gift, the sign of the joy with which he means to keep this day.

Those earlier lines are a didactic meditation on the efficacy of virtue, offered to Stella now as support for her effort to endure her present crisis, and their argument, simply, is that a life of virtue should "leave behind / Some lasting pleasure in the Mind, / Which by Remembrance will assuage, / Grief, Sickness, Poverty, and Age . . ." Swift announces this as a wisdom in keeping with his station: "From not the gravest of Divines / Accept for once some serious Lines?" (13–14). We should notice his invoking his station here as against Stella's more intimate knowledge of his personality, his identity as "not the gravest of Divines." The delivery of the doctrine that is to follow, then, is a special effort to realize for Stella the force of his character as against the more private energies of a personality that pulls against it. To be adequate to Stella now means to realize the identity he most fully experiences as her poet.

What then is the quality of the didactic movement that follows? Its substance, as I have said, is that virtue's force will sustain in the mind the moral identity now being assaulted by grief, sickness, poverty, old age.

> Were future Happiness and Pain,
> A mere Contrivance of the Brain,
> As Atheists argue, to entice,
> And fit their Proselytes for Vice;
> (The only Comfort they propose,
> To have Companions in their Woes.)
> Grant this the Case, yet sure 'tis hard,
> That Virtue, stil'd its own Reward,
> And by all Sages understood
> To be the chief of human Good,
> Should acting, die, nor leave behind
> Some lasting Pleasure in the Mind,
> Which by Remembrance will assuage,
> Grief, Sickness, Poverty, and Age;

> And strongly shoot a radiant Dart,
> To shine through Life's declining Part.
>
> [19–34]

We must not miss here the blend of assertion and tentativeness, the organization of the lesson as a concession first to the other party, imagined here as "Atheists," and then as a response to them. But this response is muted in its strictly argumentative character. That is, it arises not from personal certainty but from personal need. Grant the atheists their rejection of future happiness and pain, "yet sure 'tis hard, / That Virtue, stil'd its own Reward . . . Should acting, die . . ." The word "stil'd" is peculiarly active here; it contributes to the passage's argumentative tentativeness, and seems a choice appropriate to the special impetus of the thought, the feeling that the other alternative—virtue as ineffective—were "hard" (not, we should note, "untrue").

Swift had earlier introduced these "serious lines" as "A better and more pleasing Thought" (10). This better thought, however, he develops with a full sense of its willed character, its responsiveness to a compelling need, not its doctrinal certainty. It is an effect of that rational will that seeks to be adequate to the plain experience of such moral beauty as Stella's life has demonstrated. The didactic body of this poem, in fact, develops its "argument" in accord with this prompting of the rational will, and the lyric intensity toward which the poem builds is in great part created by our sense that the didactic argument is wholly shaped and tested by the private knowledge of Stella's worth that Swift brings to the occasion. His lesson, as lesson then, seeks to activate Stella's own moral being to fit itself to what Swift imagines, or hopes, are similar inner promptings. "Say, Stella, feel you no Content, / Reflecting on a Life well spent?" (35–36).

Organizing the poem's didactic matter in this way opens an opportunity for celebration, and the next movement is emphatically celebrative, a rehearsal of Stella's conduct (37–50). But this celebrative movement, after all, is introduced by the question just put to Stella, the answer to which we never do hear. It leads to the next step in the meditation, in which the personal urgency and lyric intensity become unmistakable:

> Must these like empty Shadows pass,
> Or Forms reflected from a Glass?

> Or mere Chimaera's in the Mind,
> That fly and leave no Marks behind?
> Does not the Body thrive and grow
> By Food of twenty Years ago?
> And, had it not been still supply'd
> It must a thousand Times have dy'd.
> Then, who with Reason can maintain,
> That no Effects of Food remain?
> And, is not Virtue in Mankind
> The Nutriment that feeds the Mind?
> Upheld by each good Action past,
> And still continued by the last:
> Then, who with Reason can pretend,
> That all Effects of Virtue end?
>
> [51–66]

I emphasize again the unadorned language in which this poem is delivered. In this passage the plainest homiletic similes are the vehicle of its didactic movement: shadows, forms reflected in a glass, the body and its food. These may be said to be the rhetorical adornment of the lesson. But the poetry here is to be found and felt in the form of the statements, all of which are presented as questions. Rhetorically an argument is presented and illustrated; poetically that argument is vindicated. For the poetic meaning of the passage is not that the argument is true; rather, it is that the rational will requires that the argument be made, and be insisted upon, even as its certainty is left in doubt, doubt acknowledged by the very questions in the form of which the argument is advanced. Poetically, however, the passage imitates the intensifying force of the speaker's need for this doctrine, and this we can feel only in the rhythms and repetitions of the questions within which it is shaped. The reader feels these insistent rhythms built into the progress from the "medial" summary ("Then, who with Reason can maintain . . .") toward the conclusion ("Then, who with Reason can pretend . . ."), the shift from "maintain" to "pretend" reflecting the intensifiication of Swift's inner commitment to a doctrine whose truth he feels as rational need, not rational certainty.

This delicate blend of assertion and skepticism, of belief and doubt, develops sufficient force to generate the assertiveness of the application as the poem returns its attention to the difficult woman whose pain and impatience are, as we have seen, its final subject. We hear this in the address of the next section—"Believe me, Stella"—and the next—"O then, whatever Heav'n intends." But by this time we have come to understand this assertiveness as an expression of need and love, of the fully charged rational will, which is all this poem will vindicate. Furthermore, we can recognize this strained style of assertion as entirely appropriate to the emotional character of the poem's conclusion, that is, its character as Swift's plea to Stella that she find her substantial identity and acknowledge his in his words to her, in his need for her. If we feel in this poem the lyric intensity I have claimed for it, we feel this intensity in the poem's joining of its didactic content to its personal urgency. These come together in a poetic mimesis of the inner movement of the rational will seeking to realize itself, in the most difficult of circumstances, with reference to its best beliefs. In representing fully both the forces against which that will must strive, and the resources it possesses, the poem provides Swift the opportunity for self-revelation that makes his embrace of his own positives always a lyric occasion.[20]

───── ♦♦♦ ─────

In Swift's poems for his friend we see the opportunities for self-discovery inherent in the didactic stance, the opportunities for introspection inherent in the fulfillment of a public charge. My line of argument has sought to account for the intensely moving success Swift achieves in this respect when we consider his poems to Stella against the achievements of his career in satire. In his satire the didactic stance is the platform for attack, the occasion for irony, for the feigned commitment to beliefs and to an audience from which he subsequently withdraws. He withdraws in these circumstances into the subversive experience of a personality whose energies cannot be contained by the commitment to culture presupposed in the purposes of a moralist. But in Swift's poems to Stella he succeeds in realizing those purposes, and in a manner fully responsive, though not vulnerable, to the impulses of his anarchic energy. The characteristic movement of these poems is from public toward intimate address, tracing a curve of feeling expressive of the moralist's inner experience as he strives to understand and to value his positive commitments. This curve of feeling creates the lyric charge of the poetry; it is the sign of the poetry's developing adequacy as a mimetic representation of the inner meaning of its initial didactic commitment. As the poetry intensifies, its readers, responsive to its emotive line, are no longer the object of its public address, but the overhearers of its inner music. We read a lyric poem.

We overhear the poignant melody that sustains and accompanies the speaker's commitment to his high station. In that poignancy we discover a language whose oblique dignity, whose truth to the love and to the strain Swift's best beliefs generated within him, still survive the anarchic energy he elsewhere directed against those beliefs. The oblique dignity of this language mirrors the manner in which the great Augustans experienced their best beliefs: with reverence and doubt. And this blend of reverence and doubt is the explanation for the inherent lyricism of their work, that tension of the personal against the public which so movingly expresses the strain they felt in maintaining their fidelity to what they loved best. When we speak, as we sometimes do, of the decline of lyric expression in Augustan art, we are missing its presence in works whose shape, though not nominally lyrical, is yet ultimately adequate to the impress of such personal pressure as writers could know in devoting their minds, hearts, and skills to the celebration and to the scrutiny of moral commitments they represented as essential to them even as they recognized their vulnerability and their cost. Dr. Johnson, the most responsible spokesman for Augustan culture, said it best in a prayer he composed near the end of his life: ". . . give me Grace always to remember that thy thoughts are not my thoughts, nor thy ways my ways. And while it shall please thee to continue me in this world where much is to be done and little to be known, teach me by thy Holy Spirit to withdraw my Mind from unprofitable and dangerous enquiries, from difficulties vainly curious, and doubts impossible to be solved."[21] The Swift who wrote the poems to Stella merited, though he did not receive, the praise of the critic who could compose his own reverence and doubt into the poise of such a prayer.

3

Teaching and Pleasing: Johnson's Lyric of Reason

IN SAMUEL JOHNSON'S CRITICISM the insistent didacticism of the humanist tradition becomes a vexing problem. Especially today, working in a very sophisticated critical climate, we are likely to take Johnson's more notorious judgments as evidence of a crisis in that tradition, for in them we feel most strongly the strain between literary and ethical value. Judgments that we might ignore, or perhaps interpret positively in other writers, in Johnson become baffling, because of both their special bluntness and the power of his insistence upon them. Good critics have managed to demonstrate, of course, that in the vast body of Johnson's work we can find and patch together a substantial set of insights that show him to be capable of a critical sophistication at least as discerning as ours: these are insights into the peculiarly aesthetic character of aesthetic objects, into the distinction between objects of art and actual experience, into the insufficiencies of works that otherwise satisfy Johnson's didactic preferences. If we wish to, we can join (and have joined) Johnson to us by constructing such a patchwork and discovering enough consistency within it to credit him with the sophistication we value.[1]

This effort is useful; without it, surely, no adequate estimate of Johnson's stature as a critic can be made. Nevertheless, it risks missing what is most Johnsonian about Johnson, and most puzzling: the blunt literalness of so fine a mind on those important occasions when, as a judicial critic, he expressed judgments that can find no accord with ours, as, for example and perhaps most notably, his preference for

Nahum Tate's decidedly untragic *King Lear* over Shakespeare's. This preference is not to be explained away; moreover, it is a consequence of Johnson's deliberations on another topic which among us will not generate much interest: poetic justice. Johnson wants to know whether *in principle* a tragic drama that parcels out rewards and punishments according to the deserts of the characters and the desires of the audience, could not be fully as pleasurable as one that does not. His approach to the problem is anything but naive: "A play in which the wicked prosper and the virtuous miscarry, may doubtless be good," he writes, "because it is a just representation of the common events of human life, but since all reasonable beings naturally love justice, I cannot easily be persuaded, that the observation of justice makes a play worse, or that if other excellencies are equal, the audience will not always rise better pleased from the final triumph of persecuted virtue."[2]

Clearly, Johnson is distinguishing here between the aesthetic merit of a faithful and valuable realism and something higher, something of which art alone, with its liberating prerogative to shape actuality, is capable. To apprehend the character of Johnson's demand upon *King Lear* requires that we take in the full force of the words "all reasonable beings naturally love justice": beings (not merely mortals), *reasonable* beings love (with the adverbial force of "naturally") justice. Reason, nature, justice come together here in a statement of powerful generalizing force. Johnson has in mind here not merely spectators at a play, but spectators raised to the height of transcendent self-awareness—the special self-awareness of *all* reasonable beings when *as* reasonable beings, they are experiencing the *natural* love of justice. This statement, empowered by the concentration in it of what F. R. Leavis might have called all the Augustan positives, defines the auditor's response to a play's observation of justice as the experience, not of a vicious sentimentality but of the pleasure arising from the satisfied desire of an erected mind, a mind heightened into reason simultaneous with love, knowing itself in its capacity to know the natural love of justice, and pleased in this instruction.[3]

Now obviously in Johnson's argument here there is no conflict between pleasure and morality; equally obviously the pleasure he imagines to be consistent with Cordelia's survival is not the pleasure of tragedy. Our own better understanding of the nature and sources of *Lear*'s tragic pleasure is rooted in our readiness to discover in the design of the play the necessity for its almost unbearable and inexorable conclusion. To us, the demands of art which Shakespeare satisfies as he relentlessly fills out the design of his play imply in their satisfaction their own manner of instruction and provide their own yield of pleasure. We can hypothesize the nature of that instruction and pleasure in something like the following argument: with Aristotle we may notice that "tragedy is an imitation not only of a complete action, but of events inspiring fear or pity. Such an effect is best produced when the events come upon us by surprise; and the effect is heightened when, at the same time, they follow as cause and effect. The tragic wonder will then be greater than if they happened by themselves or by accident; for even coincidences are most striking when they have an air of design."[4] We could then go on to point out that the sufferings of the just in the design of *Lear* are both shocking and inevitable (therefore pleasing) and that as the fortunes of the just decline in instance after instance of savage cruelty—until we wonder at the playwright's strength to tell such things—the symmetry of the design tightens. If we read for the values of John Keats's negative capability, we may discover the play's instruction to inhere in that integrity of design which does not yield to our impatient seeking for deliverance. Or, if we read with the Platonic inclinations of Sir Philip Sidney, we might discover in the tightening design the intimations of a golden world whose presence is known and felt in a structure that can accommodate, order, and thus make moral experience from the brutal facts of this brazen nature.

But Johnson's preference for Tate's ending to *Lear* is a sign of his unwillingness to judge in any of these ways. It demonstrates his unwillingness to perceive moral value in aesthetic closure, a refusal to see in structure and design the determinants of either utility or pleasure. Unable to acknowledge that art may teach by the very integrity of its formal perfection, its closure upon itself, he is forced to demand those explicit lessons that seem to us naive or bluntly perverse, blind to the distinctions between art and life. Our modern formalisms all depend on that distinction, discovering as we do the source of art's autonomous existence and autotelic function only in the life of the imagination. Our imitations of actuality are products or representations of that mental activity—hence the integrity and autonomy possible in them. But Johnson insisted that art inquired into actuality external to the mind. Most strange to him, for example, was Shakespeare's indifference to the Lear chronicles in which *actual history* gave to Cordelia's story a happy ending, at least temporarily. Johnson's insistence on the viability of Cordelia's survival is both a rejection of the particular design of a play that demanded her death in contradiction of historical fact, and a desire for an explicit stimulation of mental and moral processes not in accord with that design—the mental and moral processes whose workings Johnson thought we could recognize in our natural and rational love for justice. For the sake of that recognition he is willing to allow Shakespeare's design to be wrenched apart. In approving Tate's ending he approves what he must have thought of as an act of the rational will imposing itself on materials whose own inner force and logic pulled in another direction. To submit to that force and logic, to Johnson, was not a sign of aesthetic and moral integrity but rather of carelessness: Shakespeare "carries his personages indifferently through right and wrong and at the end dismisses them without further care, and leaves their examples to operate by chance."[5] To this charge we would be correct to answer that Shakespeare's examples do not operate by chance at all, but entirely by design. Still, this would be to talk past the point.

In presenting Johnson in this way, I am not unaware of the numerous instances that can be cited from his work to qualify my argument. Perhaps this is precisely the important point: that the didactic urgency of Johnson's judgments drives him into corners so that on several points of special importance to him his judgments can be violently contradictory. It would be easy enough, for example, to draw up a catalogue of observations that show his alertness to the values of structure and design.[6] But this effort would merely show how recalcitrant these matters were to his efforts as a judicial critic, one who would "superintend the Taste and Morals of Mankind"—which is, after all, for him a definition of criticism's preeminent function.

Undoubtedly his difficulties reflect his uneasy position in the history of criticism. Johnson is a great humanist critic in the classical tradition, but in his thought the didacticism intrinsic to that tradition clearly was a source of special difficulty. It is no accident that the next great step in critical thought was in part a response to the didacticism of the older system; the great achievement of romantic criticism was to offer a new way of assimilating art's didactic obligations to its own proper power. Samuel Taylor Coleridge's idea of organic form, along with his blunt definition of poetry as a species of composition whose first object is pleasure not instruction, were aimed at problems that had become elusive to the categories of judgment Johnson inherited and liberally reinterpreted. Johnson too exercised his liberal and humane empiricism more in defense of Shakespeare than in attack, and he too felt the need to justify Shakespeare's practice against a censure based upon what Coleridge was to call the principles of a merely mechanical regularity. But here again we must emphasize that Johnson was not impelled to base his liberal defense of Shakespeare's mixed drama, for example, upon new definitions of generic or structural integrity. Defending Shakespeare's mixture of genres, Johnson tells us that we get twice the instruction from tragicomedy than from tragedy or comedy alone, and twice the delight, for "upon the whole, all pleasure consists in variety."[7] Murray Krieger has shrewdly observed that Johnson's sudden shift in emphasis here to the pleasure inherent in variety contrasts sharply with the traditional value placed upon the virtue of unity; in this Krieger has seen a movement by Johnson in the direction of what was to come.[8] Nevertheless, what is striking here is the breeziness of Johnson's discussion of the generic decorums. Coleridge was to see that the real question was not the mingling of kings and clowns in general, but the mingling of specific kings with specific clowns—Hamlet and the grave digger, Lear and Lear's fool—each demanded by the other within the decorums each play generates of itself. But Johnson was not impelled to search for such a line of argument. Though he recognized that the old formal prescriptions had lost their justification, a new formal defense of Shakespeare's practice was of little interest to him. Matters of structure, design, and form simply were never crucial to Johnson in what mattered most to him—art's obligation to instruct—and I can think of no instance where he appeals to the values of structure and design in order to vindicate a practice he understands to be morally lax, vicious, or insignificant. Whatever we may explain about Johnson in terms of his place in the history of criticism, therefore, there remains his stubbornly personal imperative that between art and moral knowledge all distinctions must be finally be overcome. This is very much a personal imperative, and the resistance to fictionalizing which it implies and which lies at the heart of his peculiarly blunt didacticism tells us more about Johnson himself than about the history of criticism. It points us to his biography and his imaginative writing; only there can we fully see the meaning of Johnson's criticism.

❖❖❖

Without an adequate theory about how and what art teaches, Johnson was still quite clear, then, about how it does not: meaning in art does not inhere in the logic or the force of structure of design. His well-recognized and liberal empiricism on matters of generic decorum seems directly in line with this position and may be seen as a consequence or corollary of the same didacticism that in other respects can be so frustrating to us. No individual work for Johnson inherits a curve of meaning simply by virtue of its membership in an identifiable class of the literary kinds. His desire for Cordelia's triumph precedes any concern for the tragic logic of a play demanding her death. In that tragic logic itself he sees no moral significance. Similarly, a pastoral means nothing implicitly by being a pastoral: the best way to think about it is as a poem about the country, the best way to judge it is to ask whether it escapes absurdity when it loads its rural material with other significance.[9] A poem inherits no system of meaning anterior to its own achievement; its closure upon its conventional or generic design constitutes no claim for its didactic value, nor, for this reason, can it be an interesting question for the critic of a work to pursue. Johnson's lack of interest in questions of genre, of *inherited design*, is only a special case of his more general disinclination to consider the values of structure and design as very pertinent to literature's didactic obligations, its moral meaning.

And yet, despite Johnson's disinclination to accept the inherited designs as authoritative ways of seeing, neither his criticism nor his art has the feel of a "polemic against historical continuity." Irving Howe has used this expression to characterize the art and the consciousness that, taken together, define the cultural condition he understands as "modernism."[10] Howe was responding to Lionel Trilling's own exploration in *Sincerity and Authenticity* of the influence upon art of our culture's valuation of authenticity, that personal condition "possible only to those who have discarded the delusion of wholeness, and in whom the relation between me and myself is not harmonious. This relation must also be, for the program of authenticity, close to self-contained, so that the inner, fragmented struggle for definition or re-creation is uncontaminated by social constraints."

In Trilling's account of the literary values implied in this "self-contained" program of personal authenticity, the individual artifact

> is itself authentic by reason of its entire self-definition: it is understood to exist wholly by the laws of its own being, which include the right to embody painful, ignoble, or socially unacceptable subject-matters. Similarly the artist seeks his personal authenticity in his entire autonomousness—his goal is to be as self-defining as the art-object he creates. . . . When, in Sartre's *La Nausée*, the protagonist Roquentin . . . permits himself to entertain a single hope, it is that he may write a story which will be "beautiful and hard as steel and make people ashamed of their existence."[11]

The value placed upon the autonomy and self-definition possible only in personal activity freed from social constraint is reflected in this modern rationale for an aesthetic of structure and design. By its own similar freedom from "social constraint" art is able to figure forth a model of authentic being: completed and self-enclosed, design itself mirrors the inwardness that is the only possible condition of authentic being. It is no wonder, then, that Jean-Paul Sartre's protagonist desires to produce a work that demonstrates its artistic authenticity by its power to make people ashamed, authenticity in life, as Trilling describes it, being a certainly harrowing and possibly humiliating way of experiencing one's self.

A work of art that might make people ashamed of their existence—this wish contrasts strikingly with Johnson's declaration that writing is useless if it fails to support either our enjoyment of life, or our endurance of it. The contrast shows why Johnson, though he rejected the older conflation of form with instruction, still maintained a strong sense of the outward push, the social reference, which was to him central to art's moral significance. Johnson always demonstrates a sense of the meaningfulness of the past in the present, of the continuity between one person's experience and another's, of the wholeness possible in one's existence when, instead of freeing himself from social constraints, he willfully seeks them. Put in another way, Johnson's skepticism about the power of inherited form either to see into or to order properly the facts of general nature could no more lead him toward an aesthetic of (deracinated) structure and design than it could draw him back toward a classical one. For Johnson's didacticism, seeking no support from the authority of inherited forms and their inherited ways of seeing, still derives its force from the fact of "historical continuity" which he understood as a field of human experience wholly open to empirical and teachable inquiry. We therefore do not learn the truths that Johnson tells as heritable meanings coming to us in heritable forms. They are instead the personally discovered and perhaps the willed wisdoms of Johnson's own experience. To be instructed and moved by Johnson's art is to know the outwardness of its sympathies as the expression of the strength of his own inner being. The revelation of that inner authenticity in an art of deep social sympathy gives Johnson's work its special character: his didactic purpose is a sign of a social sympathy that grows outward still from his own monumental self, revealing it fully. And in that self-revelation is the characteristic charge of lyrical feeling in which the inherent pleasure of Johnson's work has its source. His lyricism is the accompaniment to the truths he teaches, the sign of their origin, not solely in tradition nor solely in himself, but in the test to which he subjected tradition in the laboratory of his own mind and feelings. Considered this way, the lyricism of his work and the insistent empiricism that is the distinguishing excellence of his mind may each have their roots in his often painfully idiosyncratic being. As we know, his mind and feelings often swept him toward the painful idiosyncrasy that was for him both opportunity and torment. This strain between self and other is registered in the lyrical tonalities that he joins to his didactic intention to create a mix marking his work off so precisely from any other; what is a source of vexation in his criticism becomes a cause of pleasure in his art. In the remainder of this chapter I shall consider the many reasons for this.

Authenticity is one of our words, and as Trilling defines it, then, it describes an exigent condition of personal being, one painfully at odds with social constraint. To this condition, Johnson, despite the turbulence and idiosyncrasy of his own inner life, was not willing to allow himself to be led. Yet, the strain between his inner turbulence and his social sympathy was powerful and often disruptive, and his effort to be true to both must indeed be seen as a struggle for authenticity of being, if authenticity of being can be understood to be compatible with a willing and conscious acceptance of social bonds.[12] Certainly Johnson's struggle for authenticity of this brand attracted James Boswell to him, awakening repeatedly in Boswell the admiration and reverence that, as Ralph Rader has shown, are the experiences designing and structuring his monumental celebration of his hero. Rader has sensitively interpreted Johnson's life as a heroically successful effort to live both bound and free, "free to express his own deepest passions . . . [yet] bound by the ties of morality and convention that link him to other men in love and respect."[13] The wonder we feel as we contemplate Johnson's effort must come from our awareness of the turbulence and antisocial qualities his own deepest passions could have. We see this everywhere in Boswell's *Life of Samuel Johnson,* and no doubt we all have our own favorite anecdotes: my own comes from that supper with Dr. Adams very late in Johnson's life, suddenly shocked out of pleasant sociability by the look of horror on Johnson's face as he acknowledges his fear of death. "I am afraid I may be one of those who shall be damned." When Dr. Adams (Boswell pointedly labels him the "amiable Dr. Adams") proposes a question about the meaning of damnation, Johnson's response is vehement: "Sent to Hell, Sir, and punished everlastingly!" The exclamation point and the stage directions—"passionately and loudly"—are Boswell's.[14]

The contrast is between Dr. Adams's amiability and Johnson's pain—between a liberal cleric and the strangely liberating assertiveness of Johnson's literal-mindedness. The orthodoxy in Johnson's outburst is authenticated by its vehemence, and the vehemence tells us that he understands perfectly well that reasonable and pious and blameless men could think the subject through toward more amiable conclusions than he could ever know. Our own joy in his passionate assertion of a comfortless truth perhaps parallels some joy of his own in his ability to define and distinguish himself so boldly among a company that he enjoyed and admired. (For the person of Dr. Adams, whom he had known since his Oxford days and had once even consulted about abandoning literature for a try at the law, Johnson had the highest respect, and for his learning, reverence.[15]) But in the whole of the dialogue there is no comfort at all of the kind Johnson most deeply desired. Most wondrous about it is the chain of reasoning leading toward and then proceeding from Johnson's outburst, a chain which Johnson tightens around the arguments offered first by Dr. Adams for the infinite goodness of God and then by the doctor's wife for the merits of the Redeemer. "Madam, I do not forget the merits of my Redeemer; but my Redeemer has said that he will set some on his right hand and some on his left." And earlier, to Dr. Adams's suggestion that God was infinitely good: "That he is infinitely good, as far as the perfection of his nature will allow, I certainly believe; but it is necessary for good upon the whole, that individuals should be punished. As to an *individual*, therefore, he is not infinitely good; and as I cannot be *sure* that I have fulfilled the conditions on which salvation is granted, I am afraid I may be one of those who shall be damned." Then comes Adams's query about Johnson's definition of damnation, then Johnson's outburst, and Adam's response: "I don't believe that doctrine." *Johnson:* "'Hold, Sir; do you believe that some will be punished at all?' *Dr. Adams:* 'Being excluded from Heaven will be a punishment, yet there may be no great positive suffering.' *Johnson:* 'Well, Sir; but if you admit any degree of punishment, there is an end of your argument for infinite goodness, simply considered; for infinite goodness would inflict no punishment whatever. There is not infinite goodness physically considered; morally there is.'" When Boswell suggests that in hope there may be some relief from the fear of death, Johnson points to the very vehemence of his talk as the symptom of his persistent anxiety, and only then adds, "but I do not despair."

The reasoning—that there is reasoning at all in the presence of the terror—first strikes us. The conversation is almost a disputation, but it is colored entirely by the vehement and literal-minded definition of damnation upon which Johnson insists, and it is therefore pushed toward the two comfortless conclusions he insists upon facing: to individuals, God's behavior is not infinitely good, because God inflicts pain; therefore, physically considered, there is no infinite goodness, though morally there is. But "physically considered," after all, means "in nature," on the ends of our nerves. If in Johnson we find bark and steel, as Boswell did, we discover it in the authenticity of this personally felt and comfortless orthodoxy—in the reasoning away from comfort, and simply in the sheer fact of such reasoning itself, reasoning generated by and enlightening the passionate assertiveness that thus becomes the liberating gesture it always was for Johnson: the supremely honest and sudden revelation of self. Johnson is indeed bound as he is free—bound by those parts of his being upon which the comfortless orthodoxies were proved into viscerally compelling truths, and free simultaneously by the monumental revelations of self by which he made those truths known to others. His brand of authenticity therefore could not, almost by definition, be merely self-contained or uncontaminated by social constraints—they are part of its very substance. Nor could it, on the other hand—by virtue of its nervous empiricism, its awareness of the absolute distinction between physical and moral experience, between an individual's experience of the general system and that system looked at from a loftier perspective—seek much cognitive or emotional sustenance from heritable ways of seeing or saying.

This moving anecdote reveals Johnson's power to define and distinguish himself fully in the very process of affirming the connection between the deepest impulses of his being and doctrinal orthodoxy. The acerbic idiosyncrasy of his being surfaces here, saved from mere idiosyncrasy by the connection he establishes between his inwardness and doctrinal orthodoxy. But Johnson's power to bind himself to the general experience of the race has its milder and no less significant modes. There is another wonderful encounter in the *Life*, and Boswell's management of it demonstrates the keenness of his appreciation for this quality of his hero: the chance meeting between Johnson and Oliver Edwards, the most ordinary of men.[16] In the forty years since the two men had last seen each other as college students at Oxford, Johnson had achieved his literary fame, while Edwards's life passed into the successful obscurity of a London law practice. To Boswell the meeting was "one of the most curious incidents in Johnson's life," and Boswell succeeded in prolonging it, making of it one of those experiments he delighted in, like setting up Johnson to meet John Wilkes at a dinner party in order to see whether Johnson could delight in that charming, unscrupulous man, and so score a triumph for civility, despite the force of his enmity against Wilkes's politics. In the meeting between Johnson and Oliver Edwards, the experiment was about genius and mediocrity, fame and obscurity, and the wonder of it—the wonder of Boswell's understanding of Johnson—is that the obscure and ordinary

Edwards is allowed to develop as the measure, momentarily, of the extraordinary Johnson.

The two men talk about supper:

> *Edwards*: "How do you live, Sir? For my part, I must have my regular meals and a glass of good wine. I find I require it."
>
> *Johnson*: "I now drink no wine, Sir . . . And as to regular meals, I have fasted from the Sunday's dinner to the Tuesday's dinner without any inconvenience. I believe it is best to eat just as one is hungry: but a man who is in business, or a man who has a family, must have stated meals. I am a straggler. I may leave the town and go to Grand Cairo without being missed here or observed there."
>
> *Edwards*: "Don't you eat supper, Sir?"
>
> *Johnson*: "No, Sir."
>
> *Edwards*: "For my part now, I consider supper as a turnpike through which one must pass, in order to go to bed."

Here Johnson speaks to Edwards's obscurity, acknowledging for Edwards the distinction between them, emphasizing his perception of his own "bohemian" existence. As readers of the *Life* we know about the unhappy sources of Johnson's abstemiousness as well as of his unscheduled days and nights—the religious melancholy and desperate discipline, the sometimes exhilarating and sometimes desperate London nights and early mornings, Johnson sought by or seeking company, at all events evading solitude. Here with Edwards he calls himself a straggler, and sees in his own extraordinary life-pattern an obscurity of its own kind, the obscurity of fame. He may go to Cairo without being noticed or missed, for he is a man not in business and without a family. Johnson pushes this: "You are a lawyer, Mr. Edwards. Lawyers know life practically. A bookish man should always have them to converse with. They have what he wants."

Johnson handles this encounter movingly; he satisfies Edwards's simple wonder at the differences between their lives, and at the same time takes the edge off the contrast, honoring Edwards's useful obscurity. Edwards's next comment is simply: "'I am grown old; I am sixty-five.'" To which Johnson answers also simply: "'I am sixty-eight next birth-day. Come, Sir, drink water and put in for a hundred.'" It is an utterly affectionate response, joining the two men as mortals, and referring to Johnson's abstemiousness, which a moment earlier had been a point of contrast between two styles of life, making it now the occasion for a gentle joke of the kind two old men might make when they talk about their diet and digestion.

For Boswell the incident confirmed his opinion of Johnson's "most humane and benevolent heart," but Boswell very shrewdly saw that the meeting disturbed Johnson: his remarks about lawyers and the practical life were the hint, and Boswell's follow-up develops it. Johnson and Edwards having parted, Boswell addresses the reader, recalling that Edwards had remarked to him in an aside that Dr. Johnson should have been of a profession. Boswell then repeats the remark to Johnson, and Johnson agrees. He agrees, and, quite specifically, adds that he ought to have been a lawyer. Boswell wants Johnson to say more about this: he points out to him that we would not then have had the *Dictionary of the English Language*. True, had Johnson been Lord Chancellor he "'would have delivered opinions with more extent of mind . . . than perhaps any Chancellor ever did, or ever will do. But, I believe, causes have been judiciously decided as you could have done.' *Johnson:* 'Yes, Sir, Property, has been as well settled.'" And then, just at this point in the narration, Boswell tells us of a conversation *in the past* between Johnson and the chancellor of the University of Oxford who had remarked to Johnson what a pity it was that he had not followed the law: "'You might have been Lord Chancellor of Great Britain' . . . Johnson, upon this seemed much agitated; and, in an angry tone, exclaimed, 'Why will you vex me by suggesting this, when it is too late?'"

This outburst of Johnson's in a conversation many years prior to the meeting with Oliver Edwards is, in the disposition of Boswell's art, the actual conclusion to the Edwards incident. This marvelous and moving art has made that encounter between genius and mediocrity an occasion for the revelation of one of the profoundest of Boswell's insights into Johnson's meaning. Boswell preserves the distinction between Johnson and Edwards, of course, but he simultaneously raises the obscure lawyer into a measure of Johnson, a measure Johnson himself has acknowledged in his own conversation with Edwards and in his praise for the usefulness of Edwards's profession. For Edwards the incident had ended by his departing "seemingly highly pleased with the honor of having been thus noticed by Dr. Johnson." But for us the incident ends only with the contrasting image of a vexed Johnson; though he had experienced that vexation in an incident some years earlier, it is, by Boswell's art, the final expression we have of Johnson vis-à-vis Edwards—the smaller man pleased, the great man vexed, vexed after all by his recognition that Edwards's obscure success could nevertheless serve as an appropriate, if momentary, measure of his own life. Johnson found Edwards deeply meaningful to him—another sign of his extraordinary ability to discover only among all kinds of other men the fullness of his own humanity. The meeting with Edwards shows Johnson, more gently than in his behavior to Dr. Adams, still taking the risks of self-revelation by which simultaneously he made himself known to others as he bound himself to them. But also Johnson sent on to Edwards a complete set of his periodical, *The Rambler*, which Edwards had never before read. The gift was a kindness to the lawyer and at the same time a way of getting in the last word, a gentle self-assertion of the lawyer manqué: as he explained to Boswell, "I was unwilling that he should leave the world in total darkness, and sent him a set."

———◆◆◆———

There are no discontinuities between Johnson's life and his work. His criticism and his imaginative writing, and the didacticism of each, have their source in a moral being who discovered himself most fully among other men. As these two anecdotes show, Johnson's way among other men was marked by that willingness for risks of self-revelation, bold or gentle, by which an extraordinary individual vitalizes the social constraints making human intercourse and human moral knowledge possible. His art is a similar social act—a teaching, sharing, and asserting of what is known and of what he knows. As such it too proves out its authenticity more by the risk taking characteristic of his daily social behavior than by the construction of formal integrities designed to stand as evidence of his hold upon the truths he means to tell.

Criticism of Johnson's poetry and fiction, of course, has not ignored their formal characteristics. We have had important studies of the structure of *The History of Rasselas*, and of its generic type. His long poem, *The Vanity of Human Wishes* has been judged, with reference to its generic classification, a failure by one, by another, a success.

Such discussions can provide useful background, of course, but they do not provide or lead to useful explanations of the poem's own peculiar life. One critic, judging the poem a failure because its tonal diversity deviates from Juvenal's angry consistency, is answered by another who seeks a definition of satire which would permit what he perceives as Johnson's richer practice.[17] Yet it is difficult to imagine that Johnson himself, seeking to deal in his art with the questions urged upon him by the anxieties of his moral and religious experience, would in the first place look to generic convention for useful tools of inquiry. As the "satire" of *The Vanity of Human Wishes* reveals, Johnson will more likely convert what he finds in a familiar form to some new one whose rhetoric will be likely to stimulate unexpected responses—sympathy, for example, rather than scorn. Anyone aware of Johnson's insistence that art help us to endure life will not be unpleased then by *The Vanity of Human Wishes* because its elegiac and lyrical pessimism is inconsistent with the angry pretensions of satirical form. It is perhaps tactless to see in Johnson's refusal to maintain the stance of "hypothetical anger" generically demanded by Juvenalian satire a symptom of the poem's inadequacy, a sign of its failure to please or instruct.[18]

F. R. Leavis hits it most correctly in his approach to Johnson's formal excellences:

> His sense of form was a sense of a traditional morality of his craft, enjoining an artistic and intellectual discipline. If we call it a literary sense, "literary" must be allowed to convey no suggestion of "superficial"; it was inseparable from a profound moral sense in the ordinary meaning of "morality." . . . Both the professional and the moralist are felt in the characteristic weight that makes his verse so unmistakable for Pope's. This weight is partly a matter of the declamatory deliberation of tone—the tone of formal public utterance; Johnson writing does not feel within close range a polite, conversing society. But his warrant for public utterance is a deep moral seriousness, a weight—a human centrality—of theme.[19]

Discussions of form in Johnson's art, that is, will be useful to the extent that they recognize the immediacy of the reference to life which that art contains. This art, above all, was used. Boswell makes numerous references to a habit of reading which seeks the direct application, the search for the moral "in the ordinary meaning of morality." So Boswell says of *The Vanity of Human Wishes* that "the instances of variety of disappointment are chosen so judiciously and painted so strongly, that, the moment they are read, they bring conviction to every mind. That of the scholar must have depressed the too sanguine expectations of many an ambitious student."[20] In a letter to Johnson, Boswell, weary and depressed, speaks of the benefit to him of regular conversation with Johnson on "a day fixed every week, to meet by ourselves and talk freely." He begs in the letter for "a few lines merely of kindness, as a *viaticum* till I see you again. In your *Vanity of Human Wishes*, and in Parnell's *Contentment*, I find the only sure means of enjoying happiness; or at least the hopes of happiness."[21] Boswell is not concerned to distinguish immediately among a letter from Johnson, some conversation with him, and the reading of his poem—each is a social occasion of moral import "in the ordinary meaning of morality," an opportunity for relief and improvement. Boswell shows us that Johnson's reading public discovered pleasure in the process of drawing a moral. We need only think for a moment that people *subscribed* to *The Rambler*, paid a certain sum for twice-weekly discussions of such topics as procrastination or the endurance of pain. Boswell writes that

> *The Rambler* furnishes such an assemblage of discourses on practical religion and moral duty, or critical investigations, and allegorical and oriental tales, that no mind can be thought very deficient that has, *by constant study and meditation* [emphasis added] assimilated to itself all that can be found there. . . . I will venture to say, that in no writings whatsoever, can there be found *more bark and steel for the mind* . . . more that can brace and invigorate every manly and moral sentiment.[22]

He goes on to cite a sentence from *Rambler* 32 that he reads over regularly, always "feeling my frame thrill." Of *Rasselas* he says that "Every sentence may furnish a subject of long meditation. I am not satisfied if a year passes without my having read it through . . ."[23]

Johnson's art has the character of a public declamation which is at the same time an address to the private reader alone with the book. More precisely, he was a private reader who, Johnson would know, was likely to "practice" with the poem or the essay or the tale, as Boswell shows in his remark about the meditative utility of *Rasselas* and by his acknowledgment of his own yearly rereading of the tale. But again one hesitates to discover explanations for Johnson's way in any assumptions he may have been handed, either about the implicit meanings of literary forms or the habits of his readers. What Johnson did know most vividly about people who staged private encounters with themselves was that the process could be dangerous. Rasselas's guide, Imlac, speaks at one point about the dread a man feels for the moment "when solitude should deliver him to the tyranny of reflection."[24] The immediate reference of this observation is to foolish men who, in society, feign a happiness they do not possess and who therefore dread the bleak honesty solitude imposes upon them. But this for Johnson was a fact of life, for the wise as well as the foolish, "for who is pleased with himself?" In defining the pathology of solitude as a "tyranny of reflection," Johnson evokes the obsessive and delusive character reflection can assume when the encounter even with truth takes place in moral isolation. Even truth, when so experienced, can grow into madness and delusion of its own.

So it is that as an artist and a moralist, Johnson would develop a rhetoric whose effect would be to deliver the practicing reader from the tyranny of moral solitude into the liberation truth can be when the experience of it is at the same time shared and personal. Johnson, then, does not so much rely upon a reader who enjoys seeing a moral drawn; rather, he understands the social basis of that pleasure and creates an art in which the need to escape the tyranny of the self—a bondage which Johnson saw could tyrannize even over truth—is satisfied by giving to private reflection a public character. Perhaps we could say that the tyranny of reflection is broken in Johnson's art by the liberation it brings through meditation. I understand meditation to combine, with the idea of reflection, the full force of its etymological relation to ideas of curing and caring, and to signify a process that has always had an outward aim or guide, though its physical occasion is almost always private. Meditation is an inner speech that still presupposes a real reference point outside the speaker. "Let the words of my mouth and the meditations of my heart be acceptable in thy sight" the psalm says (19:14), a prayer that could serve as a fine epigraph for *The Vanity of Human Wishes*.

———◆◆◆———

Johnson showed in his poem *London*, his imitation of Juvenal's third satire, that he understood well enough the formal demand for anger that a satire can make, though even here it is doubtful that his anger was of the hypothetical kind. James Clifford has shown that Johnson's frustrating life in the city during his first years there provoked within him contempt real enough to explain his inclination for such a poem.[25] Juvenal's tenth satire, however, which Johnson would imitate as *The Vanity of Human Wishes*, must have struck him, as it must strike us, as a very different kind of poem—if we forget for a moment the anger that is supposed to mark this kind of satire. Juvenal's poem becomes scornful soon enough, but there is an elegiac quality to the opening movement which is never entirely lost. It is created partly by the inclusion of the virtuous, like Seneca, under the general doom proclaimed for those who live under the mist of error, and partly by the poet's similar inclusion of his reader, and perhaps even himself. "Few remove the mist of error—and when does our reason / Govern our hope or fear. In your own case, what did you ever / Plan with the omens so good that you never thereafter repented / Making the try, or never repented the wish come true?"[26] It is an important point that the poet addresses those who already have seen and are now ready to know. He seems to be asking for, or perhaps providing opportunities for, the acknowledgments that should come appropriately from the wise or those willing to be wise.

Johnson appears to have recognized this immediately. His own imitation of Juvenal's tenth satire enlarges for the reader this opportunity for making the acknowledgments of wisdom:

> Let observation with extensive View
> Survey mankind, from *China* to *Peru*;
> Remark each anxious toil, each eager strife,
> And watch the busy scenes of crouded life;
> Then say how hope, and fear, desire and hate,
> O'erspread with snares the clouded maze of fate . . .[27]

Here are the same lines in William Gifford's translation of Juvenal (1802); in their differences from Johnson's opening, they help underscore my point:

> In every clime, from Ganges' distant stream
> To Gades, gilded by the western beam,

> Few, from the clouds of mental error free,
> In its true light or good or evil see.
> For what, with reason, do we seek or shun?
> What plan, how happily soe'er begun,
> But finished, we our own success lament,
> And rue the pains, so fatally misspent?—
> To headlong ruin see whole houses driven,
> Cursed with their prayers, by too indulgent heaven![28]

What Johnson emphasizes—in an emphasis created by the dominant and parallel positions of the verbs, all imperatives—is a process of seeing and then saying. "Let observation . . . Survey . . . Remark . . . And watch; Then say . . ." This imperative to see and to say constantly recurs in the poem, and seems to me to be a special intensification of a didactic effect implied but considerably muted in both the original and Gifford's translation. Thus, following Johnson's lines on Democritus, we have:

> Such was the scorn that fill'd the sage's mind,
> Renew'd at ev'ry glance on human kind;
> How just that scorn ere yet thy voice declare,
> Search every state, and canvass ev'ry pray'r.
>   [69–72]

Neither Juvenal nor Gifford parallel this invitation to consider and then respond to Democritus. It is an exhortation to declare after seeing which, in fact, gives Johnson's poem its shape, whatever the apparent reference to Juvenal's satiric form may appear to be. Each of the poem's various sections is an imperative to see resulting in something to be said, an immediate application to oneself.[29] And its final movement is a prescription for the most proper saying of all—proper prayer.

This patterning is so insistent that documentation becomes cumbersome: "Let hist'ry tell . . ." (29), "But will not Britain hear . . ." (91), "In full blown dignity, see Wolsey stand" (99), "Speak thou, whose thoughts at humble peace repine . . ." (121), "For why did Wolsey . . . Why but to sink . . . ?" (125, 127), "What gave great Villiers to th' assassin's knife . . . What murder'd Wentworth . . . What but their wish indulg'd . . . (129, 131, 133), "See when the vulgar 'scape . . ."

(168), "But hear his death . . ." (174), "Deign on the passing world to turn thine eyes . . . There mark . . . See nations . . . Hear Lydiat's life" (157, 159, 161, 164).[30]

About midway through the poem, however, there is a shift in manner; the imperative mood virtually disappears, and the narration itself accomplishes the saying attendant upon seeing. The rhetorical shift registers the joining of reader and narrator which has occurred in the course of the poem's first half, a joining effected by the narrator's repeated demonstrations and his demands for concurrence. The reader's acts of seeing and saying have become the joint exercise of two minds that have met each other now in the narrative. That meeting seems to be a major objective of the poem, the larger social outcome of each of the private acts of meditation by which it has been earned.

This effect is achieved by an art answering to our need or desire to make acknowledgments of what we are and what we know. Acknowledging is a quiet form of celebrating, a social act done in private by which we affirm what is shared in our moral experience. The art promoting it delivers us from the tyranny of reflection to that state of meditation which is private and at the same time guided outward, an experience of self in a social direction. This involves, of course, the drawing of a moral, and the pleasure of the process is surely enhanced, as it was for Boswell, by our knowledge that the poem's narrator is Samuel Johnson himself. It is difficult to read his poem as though it were anonymously written, or hypothetically spoken, or presented as a fiction.[31]

We feel the pleasure of acknowledgment as Johnson's long verse paragraphs close in on their concluding epigrams. Rader has discussed the pleasure of the statement in these epigrams, showing how it arises from our confidence that we are being directly addressed.[32] Leavis puts it somewhat differently in his characterization of the quality of Johnson's wit: "wit in general as Johnson exhibits it might be defined as conscious neatness and precision of statement tending towards epigram. It means a constant presence of critical intelligence . . ." Leavis calls this a wit "that informs the declamatory weight."[33] These two ways of accounting for the inherent pleasure of Johnson's verse easily merge to explain why that verse is so compelling: it gives us constant evidence of the critical intelligence of a man we seem to know; yet, at the same time, it engages us in the acknowledgment of familiar sentiments, which,

114 ♦ Chapter Three

without the critical wit, would be merely clichés (what vitiated acknowledgments are). The following section of the poem is exemplary:

> But few there are whom hours like these await,
> Who set unclouded in the gulphs of fate.
> From Lydia's monarch should the search descend,
> By *Solon* caution'd to regard his end,
> In life's last scene what prodigies surprise,
> Fears of the brave, and follies of the wise?
> From *Marlb'rough*'s eyes the streams of dotage flow,
> And *Swift* expires a driv'ler and a show.
> [311–318]

The rhetorical wit of the concluding couplet is in its expansion of the paralleled antitheses in "Fears of the Brave, and Follies of the Wise": Marlborough, the brave, and Swift, the wise—each is given a line built out of the pertaining but more generally stated half line preceding the couplet. But a deeper wit justifies the rhetorical neatness: the pervasive intelligence that perceives the irony wisdom imposes upon history (a major thematic statement of the poem), making of those two enemies in life, Swift and Marlborough, strange companions in their now exemplary dotage. There is delight in recognizing the wit that brings the legendary figures of Solon and Croesus together with the almost intimate contemporaneity of Swift and Marlborough, whose mutual animosity in life makes the irony of their exemplary union in the epigram a deft illustration of the wisdom of the legend. This kind of wit arises from and celebrates the cultural matrix—past, present, legend, history—out of which the moral life is formed and then demonstrates that the familiar material of that culture can be surprisingly presented even in the process of affirming one of wisdom's most familiar lessons. To acknowledge these lessons, in this case and throughout the poem, is simultaneously to acknowledge membership in the culture they create. Such acknowledgments, again, are at once private and social acts. The wit that is so obvious in the concluding couplet has thus been informing the preceding lines as well, which contain, in one version or another, all the material to be compacted finally in the contemporaneity of the examples of Swift and Marlborough. Here, incidentally, is a good example of Johnson's own definition of wit as the fusing of the new and the familiar—a definition that is an especially apt account of our experience when we make an acknowledgment.[34]

The pattern of seeing and saying which informs the didactic movement of the poem is capable of subtle development. The portrait of Thomas Wolsey, for example, opens with the imperative "In full-blown dignity, see Wolsey stand" and concludes, with reference to the acknowledging reader, only in the two sections immediately following. The first opens with a directive and a question: "Speak thou, whose thoughts at humble peace repine, / Shall Wolsey's wealth, with Wolsey's end be thine?" It proceeds to another question—"For why did Wolsey . . . raise th'enormous weight" and then offers the opportunity for the acknowledgment: "Why but to sink beneath misfortune's blow . . ." This answer is the act of saying now possible for the meditating reader. The repeated questions and demanded responses in the next section are in the same form: "What gave great *Villiers* to th' assassin's Knife . . . What murdered Wentworth, and what exil'd Hyde? . . . What but their wish indulg'd in courts to shine . . ." The process itself is an explicit recording of the political history that is the reader's possession, and fine evidence, as was the lesson drawn from Marlborough and Swift, of the meaningfulness of the past in the present, an idea against which the pursuit of modern authenticity, as it were, polemicizes.

This evocation of acknowledgments can be seen moreover in Johnson's development of the nominally satiric exempla themselves. All of them are variations on the proper pattern of seeing and saying, generally examples of mistaken seeing and foolish saying. Johnson develops them to produce the pathetic tonalities whose lyric intensity distinguishes his poem from Juvenal's, tonalities created by his demands upon his reader's own sight and speech. The treatment of Wolsey is a fine case in point: Wolsey sees nothing, but instead is seen ("Thro' him the rays of regal bounty shine"). Not seeing, and deluded into imagining himself the proper object of sight, no wonder Wolsey is mistaken in his own speech after his fall: ". . . his last Sighs reproach the Faith of Kings." Not the faith of kings, but the mistake of supposing that kings were the proper object of his sight was his downfall. Initially mistaking the king as the proper object of his sight, Wolsey next deludes himself by supposing that he is something more than the medium through which others can see the king (it is, again, only *through* Wolsey that the rays of regal bounty shine).[35] The reader, however, is made to see the most; his vision includes the fickle courtiers. They themselves can perceive better than Wolsey, but still with narrow sight: they "Mark the keen glance, and watch the sign to hate." Wherever Wolsey looks, "he meets a stranger's eye." Bringing the courtiers into the passage to emphasize their own pitiless yet foolish gaze permits Johnson to deflect the satiric focus from Wolsey onto the court as well, and thus to enlarge our feelings for Wolsey. Thus even as our own more comprehensive sight prepares us for our own proper speech (to be immediately demanded from us in the next two sections), we are still able to pity Wolsey. In this way the figure who had separated himself in his power from other mortals in imagining himself the focus of their sight still is allowed to make a claim upon our fullest human feelings. The proper speech we utter as we judge his life is able to express with elegiac tonality our feeling understanding of Wolsey's moral confusion. Similar effects are achieved in the passages about Charles Albert of Bavaria and the senile old man. Charles Albert is first the bold Bavarian who *sees* defenseless realms receive his sway, sees incompletely, and ends up as "the baffled prince." The treatment of the dotard begins by pointing first to the deluded suppliant, who in praying for long life, refuses to see: he "hides from himself his state, and shuns to know . . ." Willful moral ignorance in time conspires with physical incapacity: having wished for pleasures, "He views, and wonders that they please no more." Not able to see properly he is therefore compelled into foolish saying: ". . . everlasting dictates croud his tongue, / Perversely grave, or positively wrong." The dotard is an image not so much of physical horror as of moral incapacity. His physical incapacities in Johnson's poem do not provoke the disgust and scorn we feel for Juvenal's dotards. Rather, the physical incapacities signify the entirely enclosed self, a being whose sayings therefore, though familiarly wise, are void of any real social reference, and draw upon him only justified contempt. Yet even here, as in the treatment of Wolsey's downfall, there is room for the reader's full human response, as Johnson deflects some of our attention to the dotard's heirs, whose behavior is similar to that of Wolsey's courtiers.

The pity that Johnson evokes in his responding reader is a sign of his willingness to permit life to impinge upon art. At every point where we feel Johnson's peculiar personal pressure most strongly he seems to demand the responsiveness of a rational understanding in full consciousness of its own full powers of awareness. He addresses us in the height of our awareness in an art that seeks to join us to the community of consciousness which authenticates, and is authenticated by, our individual rational participation. So that when he writes about Charles of Sweden, and concludes by wondering at the life that now serves only to point a moral or adorn a tale, he is himself acknowledging that something about that life eludes even his appropriation of it within his poem, and he expects us, as moral and rational beings to see this—to see that even our experience of Charles as an exemplum within the poem is not wholly sufficient to the final bewilderment and bafflement of that life itself. Even our acknowledgments of the wisdoms we hear can thus be acknowledged for what they are—the limited, though very useful, experiences of life only momentarily ordered by art. Johnson makes us suddenly realize that we are, after all, only reading a poem about Charles.

He is willing to take this kind of risk as a poet—to pause awhile from letters to be wise—even in the midst of his poem. Johnson's is an art whose content, to paraphrase Northrop Frye, is always too oppressively real to permit self-enclosure in a merely formal integrity (another way of describing its readiness for risk). Earlier in the poem Johnson had asked the reader to withhold for awhile his assent to Democritus's scorn. The poem's subsequent development—and it is really difficult to guess whether this was intended—eliminates scorn as a proper response. Instead, the pathos we hear and with which we respond works in *The Vanity of Human Wishes* as the lyrical accompaniment to the admonitions and the judgments with which we join throughout; the pathos is the poem's acknowledgment of the limits of admonition and judgment themselves, entirely necessary as they are, as ways of understanding the force and the immediacy of deluded human desire. Again, we are made to see properly and to say properly, but as fully rational and feeling beings.[36] In the pathos evoked by the poem, we acknowledge the powerful inwardness of human experience, inwardness that eludes, even as it is vulnerable to, the judgments demanded by the poem's didactic movement. Johnson wanted this effect, even at the risk of disrupting the decorums of satiric form. The pathos is joined to the didactic lesson, the satiric judgments, as a sign of a feeling rationality to which Johnson wanted those judgments assimilated. Moreover, as we respond with pity to exempla we negatively judge, we reveal ourselves to ourselves; we come to acknowledge our own vulnerability to our own better judgments even as we recognize Wolsey's, and we experience this enlightenment with the lyric force of self-discovery. In Wolsey we "overhear" ourselves. We should remember here that the poem's author himself was said to have wept when he read aloud his own lines on the scholar's life.[37]

The proper saying with which the poem concludes is a prescription for prayer, a kind of saying going beyond the socially directed judgments and acknowledgments the poem has so far evoked. In stating these prescriptions the poem returns to the imperative mood because the prescriptions for prayer are now Johnson's statements alone, presented as answers to questions that arise in the mind of the meditating reader, questions urged by the pity the poem calls forth for the "satiric" exempla. Prayer as Johnson understands it here is a personal release from dilemma, the totally honest supplication of a being who has acknowledged in the poem's various movements the need for repressing what is foolish or mistaken and has understood in pity the compulsive force of the deluded desire that rational humanity must repress. This difficult final section recognizes what the poem's evocation of pity has all along responded to: the inner immediacy and power of the will's energy in desire. Proper prayer itself, therefore, must arise almost in desperation from the same forces of the personality that can propel us into delusion. "Where then shall Hope and Fear their Objects find?" It must have at least their energy. Johnson understands the personal cry that prayer must be as wholly appropriate: prayer dare not be "specious" and it may ask for things, just as Wolsey asked for things, so long as the petitioner (as the suppliant is conceived in the first part of the closing section) recognizes, as Wolsey did not, in whose hands the dispensations rest and by whose measure they are deemed appropriate:

>   Enquirer cease, petitions yet remain,
>   Which heav'n may hear, nor deem religion vain.
>   Still raise for good the supplicating voice,
>   But leave to heav'n the measure and the choice.
>   Safe in his pow'r, whose eyes discern afar
>   The secret ambush of a specious pray'r.

> Implore his aid, in his decisions rest,
> Secure what'e'er he gives, he gives the best.
> [349–356]

But as the poem moves on to its conclusion, Johnson describes an even more intense kind of prayer: it is prayer not for things, but for qualities, the qualities that can direct a rational will. This prayer Johnson imagines as the most fervent and personal kind of human utterance:

> Yet when the sense of sacred presence fires,
> And strong devotion to the skies aspires,
> Pour forth thy fervours for a healthful mind,
> Obedient passions, and a will resign'd:
> For love, which scarce collective man can fill;
> For patience sov'reign o'er transmuted ill;
> For faith, that panting for a happier seat,
> Counts death kind nature's signal of retreat:
> These goods for man the laws of heav'n ordain,
> These goods he grants, who grants the pow'r to gain;
> With these celestial wisdom calms the mind,
> And makes the happiness she does not find.
> [357–368]

This final prescription is for prayer that unites personal urgency with fervent devotion to ask for those goods that liberate the personality. Its fervor comes from those very forces of the self, hope and desire, which can energize a rational will (or propel a deluded one). And the poem's conclusion is a definition of an act of the rational will: the making of a happiness not to be found. In the fervors of devotion one begins to discover oneself as a being whose freedom from the delusions of the self is signified still by an assertion of self whereby the mind, if not in possession of celestial wisdom, is at least calmed in the pursuit of it.[38] This prescription for and account of prayer earns whatever authority it has from the wit that makes the final epigram with its play upon the distinction between "make" and "find" yet another example of the critical intelligence that has all along joined with and guided the reader in meditations that convince as well as they console.[39]

––––––◆◆◆––––––

In his discussion of poetic justice in the commentary on *King Lear*, Johnson described that state of self-awareness to which we can be brought by art. It is an awareness of ourselves as rational beings with a natural love of justice—hence the grounds at least for a theoretical consideration of the reasons why the triumphs of the good might be as pleasing to us in art as they are in life. The implicit demand he made upon the playwright, therefore, was for an act of the will which could overcome the recalcitrant realities of sublunary nature and assert in art that triumph of the just which should evoke pleasure from the rational mind in its full emotional self-awareness of its natural love of justice.

In his own poem Johnson teaches how one comes to experience oneself as a fervent and a rational being, discovering oneself fully in an act of proper supplication for the moral qualities that liberate the will in action. This rational will he demands of the playwright is, in his poem, seen as the best possession of the properly enlarged and enlightened self. It acts in life as Johnson asked the playwright to act in his art—it makes the happiness it does not find. Johnson's didacticism can be thought of as a demand for an art that parallels this assertion in life of the rational will, an assertion he understands as possible only for a being at the height of self-awareness. His own poem in its doctrine and procedure stands as an example of the art emanating from this condition of being. Its lyricism is an effect of our movement toward self-awareness as we feel in sympathy the similarity between our own inner energies and those of the nominally satirical exempla.

The difficulties we can define in Johnson's argument for poetic justice in *King Lear* are dissipated when we consider *The Vanity of Human Wishes*. For Johnson's poem, unlike the play, is built out of a radical artlessness. There are no fictions in it, and it seeks no closure upon its own internal logic of design. What design it has works toward that concluding moment in which the poem guides the reader outward toward an act he can perform only in life. The poem presents the reader with opportunities for making a series of moral and social acknowledgements, but it concludes with a set of prescriptions for prayer. The prescriptions end the poem, describing but not feigning the experience of proper prayer. Uttering that prayer is an act belonging to life, beyond the realm of art. It is impossible to say, therefore, that the poem *becomes* its own doctrine. It does not have that kind of life. It feigns nothing, nor does it permit the reader to join in a feigning. Its assumption about the reader is consistent with Johnson's description of an audience at a play: "The truth is, that the spectators are always in their senses, and know, from the first act to the last, that the stage is only a stage, and that the players are always players."[40] Whether or not this is true about spectators at a play, it seems to describe what Johnson aims for in his own poem: its art points directly outward, it is not self-enclosed; it is a saying, not a figuring forth; it is about life, not about itself. The experiences it offers are acknowledgments that might lead to actions, but they are not fantasized or fictionalized surrogates for those actions. The doctrine it teaches is to be lived subsequent to one's experience of the poem; the experience of the poem is not in itself the doctrine, it is only consistent with it.

Ian Watt has called this "the literature of experience," and has noted how elusive it has been to our familiar critical procedures.[41] His suggestion that we think of Johnson's writings as "wisdom literature" lends some support to the argument I am making here about their artlessness, by which I mean only that they do not promulgate, or achieve their effects by the promulgation of fictions or the sculpting of fictional form. Johnson as a critic had a sophisticated understanding of fictionality and could discourse upon it as well as anybody, but the peculiar judgments he makes of individual works demonstrate the strain he experienced as a judicial critic—one who would "superintend the Taste or Morals of Mankind" (*Rambler* 158)—when he tried to reconcile the self-enclosing dynamics of fictions with what he thought were their didactic function. It is only as an artist of a very special kind, therefore, that he may be said to complete his criticism, complete it in poems, essays, and an apologue that do not function as self-enclosed fictions, but rather as utterances that continue into experience itself.

Plato's understanding of the nature of fictions also is as striking as his distrust of them. The acknowledgment Socrates makes of the powers of the tribe of "pantomimic gentlemen" is eloquent evidence:

> But there is another sort of character who will narrate anything, and, the worse he is, the more unscrupulous he will

> be; nothing will be too bad for him: and he will be ready to imitate anything, in right good earnest, and before a large company . . . he will attempt to represent the roll of thunder, the noise of wind and hail, or the creaking of wheels, and pulleys, and the various sounds of flutes, pipes, trumpets, and all sorts of instruments: he will bark like a dog, bleat like a sheep, or crow like a cock; his entire art will consist in imitation of voice and gesture, or will be but slightly blended with narration. . . . And therefore when any one of these pantomimic gentlemen, who are so clever that they can imitate anything, comes to us and makes a proposal to exhibit himself and his poetry, we will fall down and worship him as a sacred, marvelous, and delightful being; but we must also inform him that in our state such as he are not permitted to exist; the law will not allow them.[42]

The context of these thoughts is the discussion of the epideictic narration that Socrates will allow as the only art appropriate to his commonwealth. This is an art without voices, only a voice; it does not imitate roles, it is the actual expression of the real being of the poet. Unlike the pantomimic gentleman, who can discover in himself surrogates for anything, this epideictic artist is only and always fully himself, a monolithic integration of private personality and public character, and his only voice is the voice of virtue. We might playfully imagine the ideal Augustan poem: it will have been created by just such an artist, and it will be an utterance celebrative in nature, spoken by one in whom the distinction between private personality and public character has been overcome. And then we must immediately say that the peculiar life of real Augustan poems is in their rich deviations from the hypothetical ideal, deviations that open them to the play of private personality against public character, being against role, doubt against knowledge, man against houyhnhnm, Pope-Scriblerus against Pope-Virgil, Swift-Jack against Swift-Dean.

The Vanity of Human Wishes has a closer affinity to the hypothetical ideal. It is not, of course, a song such as the houyhnhnms might sing, but it does value that integrity of will and desire which might make their song. What is wonderful about the poem is its insistence that in the fusion of will and desire (which man knows in prayer, not song), the energies of the private personality are of paramount importance, and that the forces of hope and desire, after we recognize them, drive us to the proper prayer through which we may achieve the integrity of being we experience as rational will. Moreover, the private personality demands and responds to the elegiac tonalities, the expressions of pity, without which the public acknowledgments evoked by the poem would be barren. The private personality, its power acknowledged and indeed shaped to the didactic movement of the poem, gives the poem a lyricism we cannot imagine in the song the houyhnhnms or Plato's good artist might make. This union of didacticism and lyricism is the sign that the poem's lessons are valuable only in their assimilation to the reader's full, sympathetic humanity.

But if the achievement of a full humanity demands directing the sympathies of the private self outward, it necessarily demands also the repression of the useless and dangerous energies of that private self. For Johnson repression is a necessary and even healthy act. Boswell's well-known sketch of Johnson's monumental capabilities of repression is an especially apt account of the process as Johnson himself knew it. We can never forget the image of Johnson the gladiator in the midst of an arena beating back the beasts into their dens: in setting Johnson this way, Boswell dramatizes the public significance of his repression, along with his totally conscious awareness of it. Johnson's own accounts of repression are less spectacular, but thoroughly consistent with Boswell's picture. In *Rambler* 71 Johnson speaks of the mild mania of procrastination, which in one of its forms is produced by an irrational desire to gather together before acting "all the Requisites which Imagination can suggest." "Where our Design terminates only in our own Satisfaction the Mistake is of no great importance," he continues; but when our purpose is a public one, when the interests of many are involved, "nothing is more unworthy of Wisdom or Benevolence than to delay it from Time to Time . . . [until] an idle Purpose to do an Action sinks into a mournful Wish that it had once been done."[43] Again, the distinction between the private and public self is crucial here, and the discussion assumes that this distinction is always present to our consciousness. Johnson even allows considerable latitude to the play of private mania, so long as it is recognized as such, but he assumes that that play can be stopped when we recognize the demands made upon our social beings: only with reference to our social beings can our recognition of regret become pathological; only then does it "sink into a mournful Wish." As a self-indulgence of private life a fantasy is trivial and recognizable—a mild mania to be repressed when it needs to be, enjoyed when it can be.[44]

A more dramatic discussion of repression is the case of the astronomer in *Rasselas*. We recognize his symptoms today as psychotic, as is clear from his own self-analysis and a portion of Imlac's advice to him:

> The sage confessed to Imlac, that since he had mingled in the gay tumults of life, and divided his hours by a succession of amusements, he found the conviction of his authority over the skies fade gradually from his mind, and began to trust less to an opinion which he never could prove to others, and which he now found subject to variation from causes in which reason had no part. "If I am accidentally left alone for a few hours, said he, my inveterate persuasion rushes upon my soul, and my thoughts are chained down by some irresistible violence, but they are soon disentangled by the prince's conversation, and instantaneously released at the entrance of Pekuah. I am like a man habitually afraid of spectres, who is set at ease by a lamp, and wonders at the dread which harassed him in the dark, yet, if his lamp be extinguished, feels again the terrours which he knows that when it is light he shall feel no more."

This is the latter part of Imlac's response:

> "But do not let the suggestions of timidity overpower your better reason: the danger of neglect can be but as the probability of the obligation, which when you consider it with freedom, you find very little, and that little growing every day less. Open your heart to the influence of the light, which from time to time, breaks in upon you: when scruples importune you, which you in your lucid moments know to be vain, do not stand to parley, but fly to business or to Pekuah, and keep this thought always prevalent, that you are only one atom of the mass of humanity, and have neither such virtue nor vice, as that you should be singled out for supernatural favors or afflictions."[45]

In each of these instances—Boswell's picture of Johnson in the arena, Johnson's discussion of the delusive dynamics of procrastination, the astronomer's self-analysis, and Imlac's "cure"—the sufferer understands that he must manage his mental life with reference to two dimensions of his being, the public and the private. He understands himself, furthermore, knowing *that* he represses and *what* he represses. The consistent image is of a man whose mental life is entirely open to his consciousness and then to the direction of his will. In Boswell's picture of Johnson-gladiator, Johnson sees what he beats back; in *Rasselas* the astronomer comes to know his mania for a mania. To cure it is not to eradicate it, but to recognize and repress its stubborn reappearances: "Fly to business or to Pekuah." Consciousness, will, and society all come together in our continuous creation of our sanity, the creation of a being who can know himself as fully free though vulnerable to the "chains of some irresistible violence" in his delusive solitudes. The astronomer is able to out-reason his disorder, and Imlac speaks here of reason as "considering with freedom."

What his notions about repression suggest for Johnson's thinking about fictions is not that he distrusted the imagination as a species of insanity (the section in *Rasselas* on the dangers of the imagination is immediately followed by the meeting with the unillusioned, and very depressing old man) but that he did not value the power of the imagination's *fictional* creations to liberate in surrogate experience one or another of the delusive obsessions or desires we repress in actual life as conditions of our social existence. In the first place, Johnson saw the demands our public character makes upon our private personality as in themselves liberating, even if costly. Second, and most important, he did not think that the mental life was largely determined by energies not always available to the common sight of consciousness. We do not require of art whatever temporary therapy it may provide by allowing for the surrogate play of those parts of our being of which we are not consciously aware and which we would not value if we were. Instead, and quite to the contrary, we require art to clarify that condition of the self we experience when our rational will directs our mental and moral life. As J. W. Krutch interestingly showed, Johnson's literal-minded interpretation of Aristotle's conception of catharsis shows how firmly he resisted the idea that art benefits us in the ritual release it provides for parts of the self that play under the surface of our awareness.[46]

For Johnson there need be no undersurface to our self-awareness.

His conception of the mental life is like Sartre's, who objected to Sigmund Freud's model of the mind because of the powerful and determining role Freud assigned to forces unavailable to the common sight of the consciousness. For Sartre, such a model of the mind precluded any possibility of authentic existence as a moral being. Johnson too insists, as does Sartre, that a man can know what he is by keenly examining the phenomenological pattern of his behavior. ("The behavior studied by [existential] psychoanalysis will include not only dreams, failures, obsessions, and neuroses," Sartre writes, "but also and especially the thoughts of waking life, successfully adjusted acts, style, etc."[47]) Again, it is a matter of seeing properly and then saying properly. Thus, Johnson could value the imagination as an agent of the ego, recognizing that it can express itself in other modes than the fictive, as *The Vanity of Human Wishes* demonstrates.

John Traugott has described Swift as a repressive personality, and certainly so is Johnson. But for Swift the creation of fictions was an act enabling him to free and value the play of those parts of his being which he may well have ordinarily detested; his kind of imagination may be said to have functioned as an agent of the subconscious. But for imagination so to function was foreign to Johnson, and threatening to him, as we can see in his bafflement at Swift's obsessive and minute representation of the disgusting. Johnson could not conceive of this as serious and liberating play and was ready to admit that he could not understand it at all. To state the point another way, the impulse to make fictions, as Plato knew, reveals a high degree of sympathetic capaciousness in the personality of the maker. These sympathies, however, are inward in their direction, often embracing those parts of his being he normally does not value. He has *too much personality* and in his fictions only does he have the opportunity to value all of it in subliminal and surrogate acts that release, but do not disclose, the repressed dimensions of the self. Johnson's emphasis, on the other hand, is on acts of social sympathy which become possible only as we disclose to ourselves what we necessarily repress. We do not seek surrogate experience from art, but rather the direct disclosure of what is repressed. Beings with social sympathies repress their aberrations and know it. Art is one way of knowing what we repress, not a way of valuing it. Interestingly, Plato coupled his distrust of the pantomimic gentlemen with a willingness, rather more than Johnson shows, to acknowledge the capaciousness of the sympathies their feigning demonstrates. But again, these were internal sympathies, better repressed than allowed their play, for their play could only disrupt the establishment of that monolithic integrity of character Plato deemed desirable, whatever its cost to the personality.

What then saves Johnson's own epideictic from the barrenness we must imagine is the quality of the houyhnhnm-like singing in the *Republic?* I have already answered this question but I can enlarge upon it here. For repression did not mean simple denial to Johnson. Repression, since it was seen, done and adjusted by our powers of consciousness, was tantamount to an enlargement of those powers. We grow in our knowledge of ourselves and in our sympathies for others by seeing the necessity for repression even as we acknowledge, in pity, its strain. The experience of pity is registered in the poem's lyrical charge; it authenticates the inner growth that *The Vanity of Human Wishes* describes and that is the point of the seeing and saying we do as we read it. Our growth through rational and sympathetic seeing and saying explains, moreover, why certain devices of Johnson's art strike us as authentic when in other writers they seem lame. An example is the personification: Johnson did not simply find this figure suitable to the expression of general and shared ideas which he easily possessed. Rather, the personification as he uses it is often a precise description of a repressed quality drawn out into the vision of the consciousness, where it can be plainly scrutinized ("Then say how Hope, and Fear, Desire and Hate, / O'erspread with Snares the clouded Maze of Fate . . ."). Hope, fear, desire, and hate are those passions of the mind the poem insists we can examine if we will only draw them out. The personification is precisely that drawing out, an image, a thing to be seen.[48] It moves us as Johnson employs it because he personally discovered it to be a figure appropriate to the things he wanted to say about the mental life—about our power to repress, to know what we repress, and to evaluate the emotional strain of the process. The personification is therefore one cause of our rational and real sight of the passions of the mind; as a thing to be seen, it functions to disclose rather than to release an inner and aberrant energy. Hence its appropriateness within Johnson's poem and its power to move that reader who is, as Johnson's reader should be, always in his senses.

My discussion has been emphasizing the lyrical tonalities in which Johnson registers the experience of the self as it grows in feeling awareness toward its fullest apprehension of his didactic lesson and toward its fullest acknowledgment of the power of the rational will. But Johnson's lyrical range is not limited to the scale of pathos; Johnson's teachings about the power of the will often have a peculiar grandeur in them, touching a range of feeling that can properly be called heroic. Johnson's evocation of heroic feeling is a complex achievement of his rhetoric functioning in accord with his doctrine to demonstrate man's capacity for knowledge and for happiness, his very real limitations in these respects, and his inherent adequacy for moral living even within these limitations. This demonstration of adequacy and limitation is always felt as heroic in Johnson; and, because it always involves the reader in, and reflects in the author, an inward movement toward self-recognition, its tonal character is strongly lyrical. This is the sentence that Boswell said he never read without feeling his frame thrill:

> I think there is some reason for questioning whether the body and mind are not so proportioned that the one can bear all which can be inflicted on the other, whether virtue cannot stand its ground as long as life, and whether a soul well-principled will not be sooner separated than subdued.   (*Rambler* 32)

There is a tact in this sentence which suits its somber doctrine and helps to shape its beauty—I mean the decision Johnson made to put the assertion in the form of a probability, a topic for serious consideration. On the other hand, the sentence's strange force is in the incremental repetition of its doctrine: we hurry to embrace it. Along with its tentativeness, we feel its assertiveness as it repeats itself in three "whether" constructions and closes in a perfectly cadenced antithesis. The sentence is moving, first, because of the grandeur of the sentiment, the power it ascribes to us; second, because the rhetoric so deftly encompasses the sentiment, tentative or not; third, because the tentativeness is evidence of the critical intelligence of the author. Both the tentativeness and the assertive grandeur are real in a union of mind and will entirely characteristic of Johnson.

The rhetoric is a progressive consideration of the categories body and mind, virtue and life, and finally, soul. The thought in each section of the sentence, with reference to the central topic, endurance, is disposed into a pattern typical of Johnson's prose, the paralleled or antithetical doublet: body and mind—bear and inflict; virtue—stand—life; soul—separated or subdued. The theme, the tact, and the pattern of this sentence recur in many others. In its largest sense, the theme enunciates a principle of measure, and the essay as a whole is about the heroic effort possible to the rational will that seeks an accord between itself and that principle. The essay on procrastination (*Rambler* 71) moves toward its conclusions in a similar fashion by observing that "the duties of life are commensurate with its duration," a statement of measure similar in theme, different as it is in intensity from the thought on endurance. And almost all of *Rasselas* is an exploration of the kind of fit humanity makes with reality, an exploration that begins in Rasselas's discovery of the immeasurable capacities of desire to exceed fulfillment. The essay on procrastination enlarges upon all the variety of thinking disorders, pleasurable fantasies, and foolish delusions that sustain our uneasy delight in delaying—and that show that if some principle of measure might validate the rhetorical design of the neatly parallel "duties" and "duration," it may be inherent in life at large, but it is not easily apparent in individual people, whose favorite fantasy is to possess measureless spaces of time commensurate only with their desires, not their duties. The sentence Boswell admired expresses a principle of measure that refers to man's capacities for endurance, not for happiness. Yet the essay concludes with a gentle exhortation to maintain "a settled conviction of the Tendency of everything to our Good, and of the Possibility of turning Miseries into Happiness." This demand upon the will is the source of the grandeur of Johnson's rhetoric, and the rhetoric's authenticity is in its expression of an act of will of the author's, very much like the one he counsels for his readers. The doublets are not facile, but forged together. Boswell must have sensed this quality in them, seeing them as very real impressions of Johnson's habits of mind and above all of his character.

These antithetical and paralleled doublets are especially marked features of the prose in *Rasselas*, appearing so frequently that discussion of that work must involve an interpretation of the doublet itself. Here is a typical instance:

> The world, which you figure to yourself smooth and quiet as the lake in the valley, you will find a sea foaming with tempests, and boiling with whirlpools: you will be sometimes overwhelmed by the waves of violence, and sometimes dashed against the rocks of treachery. Amidst wrongs and frauds, competitions and anxieties, you will wish a thousand times for these seats of quiet, and willingly quit hope to be free from fear.[49]

In rhetorical patterning, this description of the world of experience is very similar to the description of the world of innocence in the Happy Valley, and also very much like the description of the "real world" in the *Preface to Shakespeare*, where the ordered doublets express the chaotic simultaneity of morally antithetical events.[50] Furthermore, the larger patterns of *Rasselas* seem to accord with these smaller designs: the movement from city to hermit's cave, from court to country; the investigations now of marriage, now of celibacy; of childless couples and of families; of marriages entered into early, and marriages made later; of the dangers of the imagination, and of the barrenness of the unillusioned existence. In what ways are these large and small structural patterns to be understood? What does the artful ordering of the description of chaos and violence mean? Is the ordering itself an imitation of some principle of measure which makes such chaos and violence intelligible? Is the craft of *Rasselas* ultimately to be interpreted as an intimation of that intelligibility of things which eludes the characters throughout their lives? Are we to search finally for an integrity of fictional design which itself bodies forth that intelligibility? Is *Rasselas* a mimetic structure, figuring forth one or another vision of what experience is or is not?

We can seek answers to these questions in the paragraph quoted above. That paragraph is governed by an informing distinction between the world as we figure it to ourselves and the world as we find it. It elaborates from this doublet into many others: the fantasized lake and the real sea compose a major subsidiary pair, each of whose terms generates still other pairs. Thus, the lake is smooth *and* quiet, the sea foaming *and* boiling: foaming and boiling refer again to tempests and whirlpools. After the colon, the sentence describes human experience in the actual world in doublets that proliferate to distinguish between "overwhelmed by" and "dashed against," each bearing reference to its own doubled agent or object—the waves of violence, the rocks of treachery; waves are to rocks as violence is to treachery as being overwhelmed is to being dashed against. The final sentence is a veritable explosion of doubled structures—wrongs and frauds, competitions and anxieties—all gathered together in the movement toward a statement of epigrammatic force like the conclusions to the verse paragraphs in *The Vanity of Human Wishes*: you will "quit hope to be free from fear."

What creates these doublets? If we think mainly in terms of imitative fictions, embodiments either of form or fantasy, our interpretive tendency will be to construe the doubleness as an imitation of some apprehensible and operative design outside the fiction or as a figuring forth of some subliminal event or fantasy of the author's mind. But a close look at the context of the passage shows that Imlac is supplying a corrective to an illusion that has hold of Rasselas's mind: Imlac supposes that the prince has been figuring (imaging) the world to be smooth and quiet as a lake. Imlac then presents an alternative image in order to challenge the first. This has the potential effect of releasing the mind from the hold of a single beguiling and obsessive commitment. But it is more. For supplying the alternative is a way of making inquiry into Rasselas's idea possible in the first place, as if inquiry itself depended upon and were managed by the presentation to the mind of a doubled perspective—as if, indeed, the condition of knowing anything at all were this very presentation of an alternative to it (not necessarily an opposite). This accords well with Johnson's justification of Shakespeare's mixed drama and his description, also in doublets, of the field of inquiry—sublunary nature—which that mixed drama explores. The mixed drama is a good vehicle of instruction because as a continuous presentation of alternatives it is a powerful instrument of inquiry. It is not surprising then that the epigrammatic statements on which Johnson's verse and prose paragraphs close in are characteristically composed of compacted alternatives: happiness is to be understood with reference to making and finding, the soul with reference to virtue and life, hope with reference to fear, duration with duty, Marlborough with Swift. These doublets are not imitations of operative designs external to the work or of fantasies inside the mind of the author; they express instead the intellectual will of that mind itself, which, in presenting the alternative, creates the focused field within which alone inquiry is possible. The style is an agent of inquiry, not a figuring forth of what is discovered or what is released.[51]

Compacted doublets and neat antitheses or parallels are rhetorical devices that do not by themselves reveal the feeling an author has for their significance. To present an alternative is in the first place to expand the possibilities for our understanding anything; but it necessarily involves a contraction of those possibilities as well. When we read *An Essay on Man*, we feel that the rhetoric tends to support the sense of Pope's expansive vision: he thinks in rhetorical doublets because his very topics are, in fact, ordered for such understanding (for example, "self-love and social") and his style is fictive in one sense in which I have been using the term—it is a figuring forth itself of a design he apprehends as operative in the nature of things. But in Johnson the rhetoric means something quite different. I would characterize it by saying that in his wit we sense how much the presentation of an alternative depends upon the exclusion of others. If in Pope we feel how much his couplet rhetoric is able to include, in Johnson we feel the pressure of much that it must exclude.[52] Johnson proceeds toward epigrammatic discriminations that are possible only because he initially limits the scope and character of the doublet expressing them. We understand happiness with reference to the discrimination between "making" and "finding"—but he has not allowed, say, for "demanding." We understand "hope" with reference to "fear," but not also "joy." The lake and the sea in the long passage I have quoted are necessarily limited to certain immediately illustrative characteristics—if the lake is quiet, the sea is determined to be a tempest; its waves are necessarily the waves of "violence," not also "opportunity," its rocks, the rocks of treachery, not "rescue." Undoubtedly this has a stagey, framed, perhaps even histrionic character. And undoubtedly there is an arbitrariness in these precisely illustrative figures. But this is just the point, and Johnson recognizes it fully. In the *Life of Pope* he describes the character of figurative language in didactic poetry: "In didactic poetry, of which the great purpose is instruction, a simile may be praised which illustrates, though it does not ennoble . . ." He had just previously, however, defined a perfect simile as one that "must both illustrate and ennoble the subject."[53] His choice, then, is to enlighten the understanding rather than to stimulate the fancy. Again the style accords with the conditions of our knowing anything at all. Not only must we present alternatives to the mind, we must exclude others. "Ennobling" seems to have suggested "fictionalizing," introducing fuller possibilities for emotive response and thus unfocusing the field.

There is a moment in *Rasselas* when the inquiry stops and its method is considered. Interestingly, this is the only moment of quarrel between Rasselas and his sister, Nekayah. The prince has been displeased with Nekayah's gloomy conclusions about the possibilities for happiness in private life (he himself has just reached similarly gloomy conclusions about high life) and he chides her for logical slippage: "You seem to forget, replied Rasselas, that you have, even now, represented celibacy as less happy than marriage. Both conditions may be bad, but they cannot both be worst. Thus it happens when wrong opinions are entertained, that they mutually destroy each other, and leave the mind open to truth." Her whole reply needs to be quoted:

> I did not expect, answered the princess, to hear that imputed to falsehood which is the consequence only of frailty. To the mind, as to the eye, it is difficult to compare with exactness objects vast in their extent, and various in their parts. Where we see or conceive the whole at once we readily note the discriminations and decide the preference: but of two systems, of which neither can be surveyed by any human being in its full compass of magnitude and multiplicity of complication, where is the wonder, that judging of the whole by parts, I am alternatively affected by one and the other as either presses on my memory or fancy? We differ from ourselves just as we differ from each other, when we see only part of the question, as in the multifarious relations of politicks and morality: but when we perceive the whole at once, as in numerical computations, all agree in one judgment, and none ever varies his opinion.[54]

Most important is Nekayah's insistence upon the frailty of the inquiring instrument, the mind. It simply cannot, in affairs of politics or morality, perceive the whole: it must judge the whole by parts (precisely just what Pope derided), and humanity must be ready to accept this condition of its knowledge. But this limitation implies a method that is true to our dependence upon the available evidence, and to the frailty of the scrutinizing instrument. In accepting our restriction to the knowledge of parts, we therefore aim for the greatest possible clarity in our knowledge of each part. The properly managed inquiry then would seem to be one in which only the most pertinent parts are, in proper order, set up against others, properly chosen. To know *at a given moment* the most we can know about hope means scrutinizing it within some limited and focused field, with reference, say, to fear. Other contexts are certainly possible, but they imply other choices, other exclusions, and these are urged by the needs of other moments. (This recalls *Rambler* 4, where Johnson emphasizes selecting rather than synthesizing as the process of artistic creation.)

These choices and exclusions are certainly also creative acts of imagination and of will—and if they do not leave the mind open to truth, as Rasselas demands, they do at least direct it toward truths. Johnson's rhetoric is a cognitively powerful instrument; it is created by acts of profound imaginative perception, but his style of imaginative perception is above all true to his sense of the limits and procedures of human knowing. It accords with the will of an inquirer who is ready to make order of what can be ordered, but it makes no claim for the more comprehensive power of figuring forth and enclosing in structures of completed integrity whole realms of moral knowledge apprehended in their shaped entirety. In this sense again of what a fiction is, it seems that Johnson's most characteristic rhetoric, in either its smaller or larger designs, is not fictive; his structural tropes are not implicit metaphors, his poems and narrations are not about themselves. We might call this the rhetoric of empiricism.[55]

Earlier I said that a principle of measure underlies Johnson's moral thought, but that he enunciates this principle only after he has searched fully into the unmeasured desires and fantasies with reference to which we tend to think of happiness. If then Johnson insists upon a principle of measure which ought to be the proper reference point for the happiness of a rational and feeling being, he certainly does not ignore the existential immediacy of our irrational and fantastic energies and desires. Nor does he promise that our discovery of an accord between ourselves and a proper principle of measure is a discovery that refers in a simple way to our longing for happiness. "All that virtue can afford is quietness of conscience, a steady prospect of a happier state; this may enable us to endure calamity with patience; but remember that patience must suppose pain" (*Rasselas*, chap. 27). A very similar sentiment concludes *Rambler* 32: "A settled Conviction of the Tendency of everything to our Good, and of the Possibility of turning Miseries into Happiness, by receiving them rightly, will incline us to bless the Name of the Lord, whether he gives or takes away." In this same essay the sentence Boswell most admired offered a consideration of the measure between our minds and bodies, our will and our nerves. Its bracing and somber assertion was that we need not yield, because our faculties are so proportioned as to permit us to lose consciousness before we yield, to die before we are subdued. And now this concluding sentence explains how we may think of happiness with proper reference to so somber a measurement of virtue against life: we may maintain settled convictions of the possibilities of turning miseries into happiness by receiving them rightly; maintaining these settled convictions, itself an exercise of will, inclines us to bless the name of the Lord. This is important. Proper cheerfulness does not promise happiness, yet it does certainly direct one toward prayer. Again, what we see here is similar to the conclusion of *The Vanity of Human Wishes*, and in the largest sense, similar to what we see in the pattern of Johnson's life: the simultaneous presence of a will asserting itself, and a man humbling himself. The will that asserts itself in settled convictions in doing so discovers the inclination toward prayer. Self-assertion discovers its proper accord with an outward-reaching humility.

The quarrel Rasselas has with his sister seems to me to express his frustration at those findings of hers which deny his desire for a simpler kind of accord between the self and reality. He wishes to deny dilemma: "Both conditions may be bad, but they cannot both be worst." And he wishes to discover a more cheerful measure than Johnson ever could see between what an individual feels and what reality demands: "The good of the whole, says Rasselas, is the same with the good of its parts. If marriage be best for mankind, it must be evidently best for individuals . . ." In this quarrel, Nekayah has the last word before Imlac insists upon changing the subject: "Those conditions which flatter hope and attract desire, are so constituted that, as we approach one, we recede from another. These are goods so opposed that we cannot seize both, but, by too much prudence, may pass between them at too great a distance to reach either. . . . Of the blessings set before you make your choice, and be content. No man can taste the fruits of autumn while he is delighting his scent with the flowers of the spring: no man can, at the same time, fill his cup from the source and from the mouth of the Nile."[56]

In Nekayah's statement we see the acceptance of the dilemma of human action, as in Johnson's doublets generally we see the acceptance of the limitations of human thought. But the elaborated doublets of her thinking, in their definition of dilemma, do not express bafflement any more than the precise discriminations in Johnson's thinking do. We see here a full and positive response to the limited conditions of human life, even as in Johnson's doublets we see a positive response to the limits of our minds. This is no anxiety at the irreconcilability of antinomies. It is rather an exhortation to action based precisely upon the perception that to try to reconcile antinomies—to try to seize two goods each of which is opposed to the other—is to chance passing "between them at too great a distance to reach either." "Flatter not yourself with contrarieties of pleasure," she says to Rasselas in this same exchange. Rasselas had been seeking that simplicity of understanding which seeks closure, structural integrities, parts understood from our antecedent apprehension of wholes. Nekayah describes instead that substantiality of experience still possible in a life that does not yield to the first of our fantasies, complete intelligibility, and does not need to reconcile antinomies in order to endure meaningfully.[57]

The action of the narrative is not yet complete at this exchange, of course; much is to come which darkens the melancholy optimism Nekayah expresses here, and, significantly, near the end it is Rasselas who, emerging from the catacombs, feels the need for choosing and acting while Nekayah, at that same point later on, finds herself more concerned with the choice of eternity than with the choice of life. For, after all, even Nekayah's earlier optimism had no direct reference to happiness; it only expressed her sense of the real possibilities for acting. The experiences that follow necessarily temper the optimism of this moment as they release in Nekayah those aberrant forces of the personality which delude her with false valuations of Pekuah and drive her to hypochondriacal excesses and vanities, primarily desires for seclusion and withdrawal. But Nekayah's experience is in keeping with the process Johnson usually perceives as necessary before we can define and reach toward a rational desire. We retire first into pathological privacy, and then only meditate and see our way out. This is the seeing we must do before we are capable of the most proper saying. The figures who emerge from the catacombs, neither baffled nor humiliated, but humbled and clear-sighted, have reached this readiness. "The whole assembly stood a while silent and collected." This is the silence and stability that indicate a rational being's readiness for proper speech.[58] As in *The Vanity of Human Wishes*, which concluded only with the prescription for that proper speech, this narrative also stops short of acting out its own doctrine. We never do hear that speech. It is the reader's own to make.

For the reader the experience has probably been consoling. Sheldon Sacks's classification of the book as an apologue helps explain why.[59] If an apologue proceeds as a gradual uncovering of some theme, so that the reader's instruction and pleasure involve his conscious and constant communication with the book as he searches for a moral and an application, then this is a good description of *Rasselas*, as it is of *The Vanity of Human Wishes* and many of the *Rambler* essays. Beyond this, *Rasselas* has the mark of the unique experience and pleasure Johnson can give: we feel it in the authenticity, the humanity and the closeness of the voice we communicate with. We feel it in the kinds of truths Johnson tells and in the artless way he tells them. The episode of the flying machine is an example—the long build-up, the sudden fall, all done in a recognizably comic (even slapstick) pattern, yet we do not produce the laugh that the comic shape of the narrated incident seems to require. We cannot laugh because we cannot miss the dignity, the humane decency, the knowledge and the intelligence Johnson has given to the inventor, drawn by the prince from the lake, not humiliated, but "half dead with terrour and vexation."[60] This is a small instance of Johnson's refusal to permit the curve of fictional form to determine our responses to what he is showing us, as is apparent also in the larger procedure that takes a theme so tragic in its literary possibilities—the discordance between all desire and any fulfillment—and still resists enlarging the dimensions of the characters and the style to anything resembling tragic grandeur. Nor do the larger structural resemblances to comic form overshadow the dignity, courtesy, and decency of the figures who make the book's comic journey back upon itself. Johnson does not lean upon the power of fiction, either as form or as fantasy, in order to achieve his purpose. This purpose is to permit us to know our best, our see-able selves, so that we may respond with our fullest, most free humanity, as we respond to the terrified aviator and as Rasselas responds with his humane silence to the foolish but pitiable stoic.[61] These are the proper responses of beings risen to the height of rational and sympathetic self-awareness, fully in possession of their limited, vulnerable, but entirely adequate powers. These responses, undetermined by the curve of familiar fictional form, arising only in the rational and sympathetic capacity of the imagined character or the actual reader, responses measured when spoken, and when silent charged with understanding and restraint—these are Johnson's lessons. They mark moments of high accord between our best and our usual selves. In their intensity and their quiet Johnson would have us recognize ourselves in our capacity for understanding, sympathy, and control. There are few moments like these in any other art, and no other art quite like theirs in its risky freedom from art itself.

4

The Deserted Village
and Lyric Discovery

IN A CURIOUS PASSAGE following his adverse judgment of the Emperor Julian's savage and vindictive destruction of a Persian city, Edward Gibbon pauses to reflect: "Yet these wanton ravages need not excite in our breasts any vehement emotions of pity or resentment. A simple, naked, statue, finished by the hand of a Grecian artist, is of more genuine value than all these rude and costly monuments of barbaric labour: and, if we are more deeply affected by the ruin of a palace, than by the conflagration of a cottage, our humanity must have formed a very erroneous estimate of the miseries of human life." In making this judgment, Gibbon alters the rhetorical line he had been pursuing: in the previous sentence he had characterized Julian's behavior as "ignorant or careless, of the laws of civility which the prudence and refinement of polished ages have established between hostile princes," and, as if to evoke in his reader precisely those feelings of pity and resentment he now calls in question, he had detailed an elaborate catalogue of the ruin done in Julian's "undistinguishing massacre" of the city's monuments and its people.[1] But now it is neither Julian's behavior, nor the ruined splendors of the city that Gibbon focuses on; nor is it prudence, refinement or polish that he appeals to. Instead, the passage finds its true vehicle in the contrast between a ruined palace and a gutted cottage, its true purpose in a test of the reader's habits of judgment and his capacity for sympathy, its true subject in his humanity, his way of estimating the "miseries of human life." This turn, which I would characterize as marking a momentary shift in focus from event to response, from history to feeling, Gibbon richly complicates by the peculiar connection he makes between our ability to value correctly the work of the Grecian artist—his simple, naked, and finished statue—and our ability to respond to the obscure human suffering emblematized by the gutted cottage. Not the high events of Roman history, nor the monuments of Oriental civilization, but classic Greek art and the ruined cottage, high culture and rustic pathos, join to form a standard of civility and feeling which is a test of our humanity.

Abruptly breaking the rhetorical line that he had been shaping into a judgment against Julian, Gibbon wins a momentary release from the bond with the reader that had been established by that rhetorical line, with its preference for irony and its assumptions about the reader's urbanity. Gibbon's reflection on the cottage and the palace has no clear or immediate reference to Julian at all. It introduces another subject entirely, one that Gibbon does not pursue, and it momentarily disrupts the urbane irony that conducts the reader through the continuous act of judgment demanded by the history. Neither the emperor nor the destroyed city, but instead a mixed image of rural devastation and classical art occupies the reader's attention, along with an invitation to turn inward and discover in response to that image the resources of sympathy necessary to one's full apprehension of the obscure suffering entailed in history's great events. This accomplished, the narrative immediately reassumes its focus upon the movers of great events and resumes also the urbane irony that is Gibbon's expressive medium for that subject. But the momentary relief from urbanity was necessary, for both writer and reader, so that the full human import of the history could be acknowledged by each in terms other than those provided by the literary union between the two the work itself creates and depends upon. Urbane irony was insufficient to express all the writer felt about this instance of urban devastation.

Quickly over, the moment is nevertheless revealing. It interrupts the narrative and disrupts the assumptions that help to conduct the reader through the myriad judgmental occasions the writer presents. The moment illuminates the ground shared by reader and writer: their intelligence, social perspective, education, all of which make urbane irony possible. Disrupting the social and literary relationship by making its conditions explicit, Gibbon frees himself to assert, and frees the reader to recognize, values and feelings necessary to the fullest apprehension of the literary material, but which elude the expressive range of its central style. The moment passes, the style can be reassumed; it need no longer be a barrier to the writer's fullest communication of all his feelings about his material. This is possible, however, because the limitations of the style have been acknowledged. Put differently, the tacitness underlying all literary strategy, the gradually developing effect of style, is opened to conscious recognition. And to open in this way what had been tacit is to interrupt literary procedure and literary response, in this case to test their limitations and to deepen or extend the range of mental and sympathetic response to the material of the narrative.

It is as if the writer has felt the excluding tendencies of literary procedure with its self-enclosing dynamics, as if in the enveloping tacitness of literary procedure itself he has felt expressive range insufficient to the urgency of a momentary and significant impulse. How could the urbane reader—trained by Gibbon's urbane irony to respond with familiar regret to that familiar image of urbane regret, a ruined city—be made to respond adequately to the writer's perception of the obscure but intense suffering the large event hides? The writer seems to seek something more immediate and direct than his art permits in his effort to meet the reader and to express a meaning outside the range of the style he has chosen. Something that might have been edited out of the manuscript as inappropriate to its style and its range of meaning is permitted to remain; committed to the page is a feeling or perception that might have been only overheard, a private murmur of the writer. Committing it to his page, he breaks one kind of bond with his reader in the name of another more personal one.

Such a moment, now recorded, has a lyrical cast to it, lyrical in the sense that it records an inner movement or a personal discovery of some urgency. Quite apart from the formal generic structures within which such a discovery might seek to express itself, this "natural" lyric occasion may be behind such interruptive devices as Henry Fielding's direct address to the reader, or even such odd ideas as Laurence Sterne's conception of the French count in A *Sentimental Journey*, charming and even thrilling us strangely with his confused delight in the possibility that Yorick is *the* Yorick. Fielding's narrator and Sterne's lover of Shakespeare both seem to seek some more immediate link between literature and actual life than merely literary experience or procedure can yield. What if Yorick *really were* Yorick? What if Shakespeare were not *merely* an artist?

The writer's assertion of, the reader's longing for, some direct and immediate link with each other seem to me characteristic of a period in which lyrical utterance is often frustrated by public, rhetorical, declamatory obligations understood to be inherent in a writer's duty, in accord with his special authority and involved in his very identity. An interruption in his duty, a relaxation of his authority, a revelation of some new aspect of his identity will then make for a moment of inner, personal, or, as I have used the word, lyric discovery. Such a moment can be extraordinarily intense even if artistically disruptive; concentrated into it are some of the deepest impulses of lyric expression.

◆◆◆

The preceding considerations are important to my subject in this chapter, the lyric character of *The Deserted Village* by Oliver Goldsmith. This deeply evocative and urgently didactic poem in its dual nature seems to epitomize the achievements and the strains in eighteenth-century lyric expression, its impulses and inhibitions. The poem is a complex and disrupted mixture of intentions and modes, and its very real success is perhaps more evident in our responses than explicable in the craft that evokes them. The poem's didactic force is rooted in its charge of personal emotion—feelings of loss, abandonment, isolation, and violation—and its procedure is a search for a resolution of feeling and teaching, of lyricism and didacticism, of personal and public address. But this procedure is difficult because it involves the poet in a search for a stance, that is, a search for identity, which can be adequate to his obligations as an authoritative public speaker at the same time as it fulfills the personal demands of his inner situation. The search for a stance in fact becomes a subject of the poem, perhaps its major subject, and the success of the search, to the degree that it is successful, seems founded in the discoveries the poet makes about his identity, about his relation to his material, and about his relation to his audience. The very process of the poem yields to the poet a recognition of the lyric character of his initially didactic enterprise, and this recognition, this lyric discovery, is itself a cause of the poem's evocative power and finally the source of its didactic authority. The poem's evocative success, its gift of pleasure, comes from its *developing* adequacy in personal expressiveness and from its successful representation of the poet's *developing awareness* that he is in a lyric situation and must be, in fact, a lyric poet. A curve of feeling, therefore, informs the poem and gives to it a dramatic character quite different from and problematically aligned with its progress as a declamatory demonstration of its didactic theme. Whatever declamatory success the poem has is a function of its lyric development, and this too is a discovery that the poem itself records, a discovery with profound implications for the identity of the poet, his duty, and his authority.

The poem is a composition of stances and modes, of rural pathos and didactic utterance, of declamation and inner speech. This variety of compositional material surrounds a central situation that is essentially a drama of consciousness made out of the encounter between sophistication and simplicity. This encounter in its progress produces a shifting set of relationships among the poet-speaker, his rural material, and his audience of readers. The drama is completed in the poet's concluding demonstration that the exile of Auburn's villagers is the exile of Poetry itself. Authenticating that demonstration is the work of the poet's sight, memory, and imagination as he stands in the desolated landscape negotiating between his feelings and his obligations, his sight and his memory, his subjects and his audience. The demonstration of Poetry's identity with the villagers is finally charged with the poet's own recognition that his personal identity is merged with theirs, that the perspective he shares with the sophisticated reader is less significant, both to him and to his capacity for speech, than the identity he claims with the villagers. In this recognition he discovers to his readers and for himself the lyric capacity that *is* the poem's point and the source of the poet's authority.

———◆◆◆———

In *The Deserted Village* the poor are crucial to the poem's lyric development; their story, their plight, and their image carry the weight of, provide the "objective correlative" to, the poet's inner situation, with its peculiar charge of personal feeling. But because of his bond with the reader, the poet cannot easily release that charge or recognize this significant identity with the poor. In a strained passage central in the poem's development we can see the inhibitions to full lyric discovery defined even as they begin to yield to it.

> Yes! let the rich deride, the proud disdain,
> These simple blessings of the lowly train;
> To me more dear, congenial to my heart,
> One native charm, than all the gloss of art;
> Spontaneous joys, where Nature has its play,
> The soul adopts, and owns their first born sway;
> Lightly they frolic o'er the vacant mind,
> Unenvied, unmolested, unconfined.[2]

This passage makes explicit and breaks the bond of consciousness that had been shared by poet and reader to this point in the poem. If we take the whole poem seriously and believe that Goldsmith did, we must come to accept fully what he says of himself here in breaking that bond. Like Gibbon's sudden focus on the ruined cottage, Goldsmith's sudden acceptance of the "lowly train" is a challenge to the sophisticated reader and to the poet himself. It calls in question the procedure and social perspective his poem had assumed. The suddenness and the assertiveness of the declaration—"Yes! let the righ deride, the proud disdain, / These simple blessings of the lowly train"—mark a tonal shift and, doing so, open the line of development the poem will take toward its final demonstration that the poor are indeed worthy subjects for the most serious contemplation of the rich and the proud. This is the concluding demonstration that the exile of the poor is also the exile of poetry. This assertion of the identity between culture and the suffering poor—much like Gibbon's linking the Grecian statue with the gutted cottage—is authenticated by the strength of Goldsmith's recognition that large issues, the matters of history, politics, culture, may be seriously concentrated in small subjects: great things and small coalesce without condescension, are shown to be the same, in a demonstration that is at once a discovery. Like the similar moment in Gibbon, this one in Goldsmith's poem radically alters the perspective within which great things are viewed: a standard of sympathy and feeling is imposed upon history and politics, which then yield new dimensions of meaning. This resolution is not easily earned, and the assertiveness of the quoted section in its bold tonal contrast with the poem's preceding manner, provides the direction and the strength for it.

The preceding sections of the poem are variously rendered: they are contemplative, declamatory, elegiac, humorous. Though he varies his manner, Goldsmith does not, however, vary his point of view. What he sees and says in the poem's first half about Auburn as he regrets the opportunities of retirement now denied him expresses his own complex consciousness and thus unites him attitudinally with his reader rather than with his rural subject. He stands in Auburn's desolation rather like a minister of culture, pondering his (ruined) intention to tell the folk of all he saw and all he felt, his (supposed) authority for such speech in retirement residing in his distance from the people he would speak to. We are familiar with his portrait of the schoolmaster, for example. However we judge it or value it, that portrait could not possibly provide the poem with the force it requires to move toward its final demonstration that culture itself is now inextricably identified with the poor. The reason is plain: Goldsmith himself underscores it in a couplet on the village inn just preceding the passage quoted: "Imagination fondly stoops to trace / The parlour splendours of that festive place" (225–226). How we weight the word "splendours" depends entirely upon Goldsmith's definition of the consciousness choosing that word: this consciousness "fondly stoops" and therefore precisely limits the range of our responses to its discovery of splendor in the village inn. But very soon the idea reappears:

> Ye friends to truth, ye statesmen who survey
> The rich man's joys encrease, the poor's decay,
> 'Tis yours to judge, how wide the limits stand
> Between a splendid and a happy land.
> [265–268]

and again,

> . . . While thus the land adorned for pleasure, all
> In barren splendour feebly waits the fall.
> [285–286]

Between these usages—small splendors positively judged by a condescending imagination, large splendors negatively judged within a satirical assertion—is the passage quoted above (251–258). Its effect simply is to remove all reason for condescension to the parlor splendors of the village inn and to assert the emotional history of the speaker as the authority for his adverse judgment of those larger splendors standing in necessary opposition to happiness. Because the proper measure of splendor *is* happiness, the parlor splendors ought to be real *and* sufficient; implied in this perception is the speaker's recognition that there is no need to stoop fondly in order to perceive the poor properly. Indeed, he will later see that proper perception demands instead that the poor be raised in his sight. Defining the meaning and the source of this recognition is, of course, implied in the poem's lyric achievement.

But what is actually recorded in this central passage? The tonal shift to direct assertion away from the more complex attitudinal stances Goldsmith had been employing is a surprise, the expression of a sudden realization. It does not in itself record the writer's fullest understanding of his return to Auburn, however. The shift in tone *does* disrupt the bond between writer and reader, and is evidence of the writer's inner movement toward his rural material. But it is assertion, not demonstration, and as assertion it reflects an effort of the will more than an achieved realignment of sympathy and point of view. In these lines we can notice a strong charge of sentimentality, the desire for a valued state of feeling, rather than the authentic experience of it. Yet the passage demands from us something more than an adverse judgment on these grounds. We do not read it adequately unless we recognize that the poet's willingness to risk sentimentality expresses a real though not fully understood inner movement on his part. This inner movement has been generated by his fond though condescending memories of the village, and the passage records a moment of considerable psychological complexity. The fond memories have released feelings the speaker cannot fully articulate, though he can sense their value to him, and the language of the passage precisely illuminates the inner strain and psychological complexity of this experience. The adequate reader will find more than sentimentality at work.

> To me more dear, congenial to my heart,
> One native charm, than all the gloss of art;

> Spontaneous joys, where Nature has its play,
> The soul adopts, and owns their first born sway . . .
> [253–256]

Aware that the complex consciousness that could produce the fond but condescending portrait of the schoolmaster is not really adequate even to that schoolmaster, Goldsmith does not trivialize this recognition. We should notice that the simple and almost formulaic assertion of the first couplet gives way to the subtlety of its amplification in the second. What is more "dear," "congenial," and natural nevertheless must be *adopted*—that is, is not available without some significant conscious effort. The activity here is in "adopts," a precise and complex choice in its contrast with the words that apparently carry the thematic and assertive weight of the passage: "dear," "congenial," "native," "first born." By turning on the word "adopts," the passage counters the simple sentimentality of the thematic burden with its conventional and easy expression of preference for nature over art. "Adopts" denotes the poet's intellectual recognition of his difficulty, as writer and man, when he feels that preference. The word acknowledges also the act of will the whole passage springs from: that is, by an act of will, the soul must adopt—and only then can acknowledge the firstborn (natural) sway of—feelings, spontaneous joys, which are compelling yet not easily valued in the soul's maturity. It is then an act of maturity to adopt what once was spontaneous; having adopted it, one possesses it by recognizing it—"owning" it—in its firstborn sway. Spontaneous joys must be understood if they are to be properly valued and finally repossessed, adopted before they can be understood, willed before they can be had. The passage in its complexity, far from expressing a simple sentimentality, evaluates it. The evaluation is positive: it records the action of a mature consciousness in its effort to open itself to feelings whose force is real though not easily assimilated to one's maturity. But it is an act of maturity to make the effort. To adequate readers the disruption this whole passage creates in their bond of sophistication with the writer will be welcome, and as necessary to an apprehension of the poem's lyric impulses as it was to the writer's effort to free those impulses.

That effort is defined rather than achieved in this central passage, which works from feelings generated by the poem's idyllic image of the village and toward those evoked by the heroic image of the village that is to come. The passage is anything but simpleminded in its positive evaluation of simplicity; it records the action of a poet's complex consciousness as his response to his memories and his recognition of his present situation begin to deepen. The thrust of the passage is to make explicit, for both reader and writer, the elements in conflict in the drama of consciousness which underlies the poem's lyricism: they are sophistication and simplicity, maturity and childhood, urbanity and rusticity, knowing and feeling, art and nature, culture and countryside. Insofar as the poet's initial assumptions about his purpose and his authority align him with the first of each of these paired terms, the passage tends to ease the rigidity of that alignment, to create opportunities for the poet to question those assumptions and to redefine his own connection with culture and with the village. The concluding line is crucial here in the precision of its three adjectives ("Unenvied, unmolested, unconfined" [258]), which together and at the same time define the idyllic village and the depredations of culture when culture is seen in terms of its effects upon the landscape of the poem's present: that is, as a predatory economics, an envying and confining molestation. The poem's didactic purpose in revealing the violence culture contains begins to merge with its lyric force as the poet obliquely recognizes his own connection with culture at the same time as he asserts his emotional link with the countryside.

The poem's didactic intention, which from the start had involved an adverse judgment of the larger world from which the poet returns, begins to deepen as it is associated with lyric impulse. The didactic import remains the same, but the process of internalizing it begins. As the poet opens himself to the force of feelings he values but does not entirely command, the adequacy of his initial stance in the landscape becomes a question. That stance had limited his commitment to the landscape; it had demanded a style of speech which could simultaneously praise the village and record the poet's distance from it—hence the portrait of the schoolmaster and, more generally, the idealization, in idyllic terms, of the village itself. This style of speech is adroit; its sign is irony, its source is intelligence, and its prerequisite is perspective. But when Goldsmith shifts from adroit address to the simple assertiveness of this passage, he is enabled to conjure, release, and value feelings with which intelligence is not always at ease. As with Gibbon's reflection on the palace and the cottage, the poet's subject here calls for a new alignment of his faculties of sympathy and judgment—faculties now felt to be more pertinent to each other than had been supposed, like the ruined cottage and the Grecian sculpture. Put differently, one mode of intelligence begins to yield to another, one set of ironies becomes less important than another. Goldsmith's shift to assertive address reveals the larger personal ironies informing the poem rather than the ironies the poet, as a visitor from the city, imports to the countryside. The poet's immediate situation, standing silently within the *real* landscape of the poem's moment, becomes now fully active as the determinant of his feelings and judgments, and the ironies involved in that situation begin to dominate the poem and shape the poet's responses. These are the ironies inherent in the situation of a man who returns to discover epiphanies, having intended to return as a sage; of a man who now must tell the world of a village, having intended to tell the village of the world; of a man who, having hoped to return with a poet's authority, will discover instead that the authority of poetry resides, mysteriously, in the vanished villagers he had intended to please and to teach. In a word, the poem begins to realize its own lyric nature as the record of a poet's discovery that the village of his memory is real, that it is not a refuge from history—the events of the great world—but, like Gibbon's gutted cottage, history's scene and its victim. These ironies, created by history and suffering and perceived by the sympathetic self, are the significant ironies of the poem. They are its cognitive material, the true burden of its didactic intention. Deeply involved with the inner experience of the poet in the moment of the poem as he ponders the ruined landscape, they are the discoveries of its lyric movement. Next to them the shallow and simpler ironies of posture and perspective dwindle, those that made the condescending portrait of the schoolmaster possible before they are seen to be inadequate even to him. When Goldsmith risks the assertion, "Yes! let the rich deride," he, in fact, acknowledges his recognition of these larger ironies, discovering richer work for his judgment by the action of his sympathy, sensing that his willed embrace of the village values is an authentic response to his deepening perception of the human complexity of his situation and that of the violated villagers.

Consider the initial situation: a man returns to his birthplace. Had Auburn still stood, there would, of course, have been no "deserted village," but the refugee would not have been mute. Auburn, after all, was to present him with the opportunities of retirement and tale-telling:

> I still had hopes, for pride attends us still,
> Amidst the swains to shew my book-learned skill,
> Around my fire an evening groupe to draw,
> And tell of all I felt, and all I saw . . .
> [89–92]

Precisely naming the vice that taints this fantasy of virtue, Goldsmith complexly defines a talker's dream. In miniature he constructs the virtuous domain that merits such a retired poet at its center—a little princedom of virtue and a little poet, reduced in size, but not in kind, from that community Pope would celebrate if only Burlington would build it. Here, though, the situation is turned around: the village is not the subject of the poet's tales, as the city would be of Pope's song; rather, the village will *listen* to tales of the city and of the poet. The greater world will become song and story, the village, strangely, their domain. Nothing actual happens in the village—this freedom from history is both a condition of its innocence and the reason for its desirability. But Goldsmith will come to recognize this freedom from history as a fantasy and will name the source of that fantasy as "Pride," the pride that accompanies the characteristic desire of a tale-teller, a man of words amid a community of play.

Considered in this context, the actual return of the poet to his village is a return to verbal desolation. The community of listeners that was to welcome his talk has vanished in fact, and it is fitting that he should perceive its ruin at this point in the poem as a silence: "But now the sounds of population fail" (125). Indeed, the special intensity engendering the inner speech that is *The Deserted Village* comes from this recognition of ruined Auburn as a scene of silence. It was a place to whose concord of sounds the poet was to have contributed. It was the domain of harmonized sound. Now, literally nothing, it is the occasion not for speech but for thought and feeling only. We see here in a desolation the discovery of space for thought and feeling only, and the filling of that space with the poem we have. Facing a desolation, the poet fills it, gives it meaning, shapes it into his poem, which can now be only the silent record of his own interior response to this experience. The opportunity for his discovery of his lyric impulse quite literally comes then with the poet's discovery that there is nobody to tell tales to. Encountering nothing but himself, he makes a poem *about* the village he was to make poems for. This is at the same time a poem about himself.[3]

Yet the deserted village is an actual place. "Near yonder copse," "beside yon straggling fence," "there," "here," "now"—these adverbs of place and time stud the poem, connecting the poet's utterance to the moment and to the palpable objects that stimulate it. Between the stimulus and the response, however, is the action of memory, and memory's idyllic manner contrasts markedly with the poem's way of apprehending its immediate present. Critics have always recognized the pastoral character of Goldsmith's poem but have more usually seized upon it as an interpretive handle than puzzled over it as a source of interpretive difficulties.[4] We need to note immediately that the poem's pastoral character is felt most strongly in the poet's memory of the village, not in his final understanding of it. In the lines on the village noises, for example, we can recognize in their construction something of the paratactic quality of pastoral verse which Thomas Rosenmeyer points to as the pastoral poet's way of rendering his own immersion in what Rosenmeyer calls "the democracy of the bower."[5]

>   Sweet was the sound when oft at evening's close,
> Up yonder hill the village murmur rose;
> There as I past with careless steps and slow,
> The mingling notes came softened from below;
> The swain responsive as the milk-maid sung,
> The sober herd that lowed to meet their young,
> The noisy geese that gabbled o'er the pool,
> They playful children just let loose from school,
> The watch-dog's voice that bayed the whispering wind,
> And the loud laugh that spoke the vacant mind,
> These all in sweet confusion sought the shade,
> And filled each pause the nightingale had made.
> But now the sounds of population fail,
> No chearful murmurs fluctuate in the gale,

> No busy steps the grass-grown foot-way tread,
> For all the bloomy flush of life is fled.
>
> [113–128]

The democracy of the bower is that charmed state of equality in which all the pastoral characters exist, not vying for significant distinction but valued as they are. We see this in Goldsmith's lines as they record the indiscriminate mingling of the village sounds by indiscriminately mingling people and animals. These lines are made problematical, however, by the poet's relation to the scene. He is not in it, not even in his memory's picture. His "careless steps and slow" are appropriate to the figure he remembers himself to have been—carelessness and leisure being proper pastoral conditions—yet even in his memory he was not himself a participant in the village's pastoral equality, but somehow outside it. These lines, whose paratactic arrangement does not quite survive the wit binding the couplets into small pictures and directing them pointedly to the neat summary—"These all in sweet confusion sought the shade, / And filled each pause the nightingale had made"—these lines indicate the limits of the poet's ability to extend his identity fully into the life of the village. Not themselves the paratactic utterance of a simple consciousness, the lines merely imitate such utterance. They are the work of memory, of intelligence, and of affection, but they lower the villagers and distance the poet from them. Recording the democracy of the bower from without, the passage condescends to it by the very perspective it provides. What seems like parataxis functions as parallel, and the lines serve to join the speaker with his reader rather than with his subjects. The passage all-in-all is an act of judgment, not sympathy.

The village that Goldsmith idealizes is, as we have always known, sentimentally rendered. This means that the feelings that are available to this material, both the poet's and the reader's, are restrained from their full play. Before they can be realized as the vehicle for the poet's and reader's more complete identification with the material, these feelings are limited by the self-consciousness the idyllic passage proceeds from and induces. Therefore nostalgia and not pity is the experience the poem's idyllic movement gives us. To pity is to give oneself without irony to the object of one's feelings, to enter into it with some significant part of oneself. Plainly, the idealized village is too thoroughly diminished to permit that. The most obvious example is the portrait of the schoolmaster, but we see it even in the more imposing parson, perhaps the most interesting of the village portraits precisely because it itself is about the play of sympathy and judgment within a figure of embowered intelligence.

The figure of the parson stands almost as an alter ego of the poet: his active duties as teacher and guide parallel the leisure work of tale-telling the poet had defined for himself in his retirement. And like the poet he commands some perspective on the village; he too understands the schoolmaster with affectionate condescension: "In arguing too, the parson owned his skill, / For even tho' vanquished, he could argue still . . ." (211–212). Most interesting in his portrait, then, is Goldsmith's effort to understand through it the functioning of a relatively complex consciousness in a pastoral environment. Considered in this respect, the most salient feature of the parson is that he appears not as a figure of authority and judgment mainly, but of sympathy. Goldsmith represents him so by placing the parson at the center of the village's incessant storytelling, but as a listener, identifying his listening somehow with his pastoral care.

> The broken soldier, kindly bade to stay,
> Sate by his fire, and talked the night away;
> Wept o'er his wounds, or tales of sorrow done,
> Shouldered his crutch, and shewed how fields were won.
> Pleased with his guests, the good man learned to glow,
> And quite forgot their vices in their woe;
> Careless their merits, or their faults to scan,
> His pity gave ere charity began.
> [155–162]

These important lines define the special innocence of the idyllic village and also the special innocence available to consciousness within it. For in this place action is transformed into story, judgment into response. The ruined spendthrift, for example, claims kindred by virtue of his sorrow and his story, not of his deeds. By means of their stories and their sorrow, such figures as the spendthrift and the soldier contribute to the moral economy of the place, in an exchange whose currency is pity. In such transactions the world of experience outside the village is reduced and tamed, action converted into feeling, as in the case of the soldier, whose wounds are what the village can contain of war, whose weeping is the village equivalent of action. This is a good example of the economy that makes innocence the final quality of experience by removing from experience the taint of real action. To this transformation and purification the parson contributes his own capacities of sympathy, tempering his own proper authority as judge by an inner capacity for pleasure and sympathy. The pastoral overtones here are unmistakable: "pleased" and "careless" are the key words modifying and transforming the actions of intelligence—"learned," "to scan"—of which he is capable. Thus his "pride" is "to relieve," his duty is to watch, weep, pray, and feel. Just as the actions of the villagers are transformed into story, the actions of the parson are converted into responses. This is the moral economy of Auburn's pastoral life, and despite the seriously heroic suggestiveness in Goldsmith's presentation of the parson ("the reverend champion," "some tall cliff") that figure does not loom larger than his environment. Even his acts of admonition and reproof are decorously diminished to suit a pastoral climate:

> And, as a bird each fond endearment tries,
> To tempt its new fledged offspring to the skies;
> He tried each art, reproved each dull delay,
> Allured to brighter worlds, and led the way.
> [167–170]

But all of this is a construction of the poet's memory and desire. His parson embodies an idealized alignment of sympathy and judgment defining the opportunities of intelligence within a pleasance. Thus, although the parson is the poet's closest kindred spirit within Auburn, his portrait is, strangely, a product of the poet's uneasy self-scrutiny, a measure of the distance between the poet's present identity and the village life he is trying to value. As a kind of surrogate for the poet, the parson is his study of an inner condition he would like to attain. This point is important because it helps to define the shape of the whole poem and to explain why Goldsmith radically alters the manner of his address as the poem proceeds. To be like the parson but more, a being whose coordinated sympathy and judgment function within the world of experience as well as of story, the poet must fully come to terms with knowledge and suffering the parson cannot have had. Unable to preside like the parson over the village's ideal innocence, the poet must negotiate between his memories and his knowledge, between nostalgia and pity, making this effort itself the occasion for aligning his faculties of sympathy and judgment.[6] The idyllic and ideal village must give way in his mind to the real village, the human desolation he beholds. This turns out to be a rich process, one culminating in a heightened sense of the villagers and a deeper understanding of self. Irony and self-consciousness do their part—they help to define the poet's inner task as he faces the desolation. This task is to recognize the new identity that the desolation has forged between him and the villagers, to understand the meaning of both his and their involvement with a world of experience which cannot be tamed into a tale. In a word, his business now is to see and feel Auburn's history as an actual place, to connect with its people as real people. Memory and desire and the ironies of perspective they induce are put aside. Replacing these faculties, the richness of the poet's sympathy repopulates the desolation with a humanity it never before contained.

For, in its memoried innocence, Auburn is a scene of reduced human agency. In keeping with its idyllic status, we only hear of its work, but we see its play. Indeed, Goldsmith's pastoral memory reduces even this scene of play, so that when he mourns the dispersal of the community, not people but "charms" and "sports" are the objects of his vision:

> These were thy charms, sweet village, sports like these,
> With sweet succession, taught even toil to please;
> These round thy bowers their chearful influence shed,
> These were thy charms—but all these charms are fled.
> [31–34]

These lines fittingly conclude a passage whose verbal habit is to substitute action for agent: "while many a pastime circled in the shade," "many a gambol frolicked o'er the ground," "slights of art and feats of strength went round," "[as] each repeated pleasure tired / Succeeding sports the mirthful band inspired." Defining the villagers in terms of their pleasures, the passage diminishes them as human agents; not people but their activities are the subjects of the verbs. "Far, far away, thy children leave the land"—"children" is a precise and self-conscious choice here, thoroughly in keeping with the diminished human agency by means of which the idyll of Auburn is rendered, and perfectly appropriate to the poet's construct of Auburn as a place where story substitutes for deed, art for life.

This is the mode of memory; its yield is nostalgia. In almost complete contrast to it is the mode of sight, the poet's apprehension of the present moment. Its yield is pity:

> . . . For all the bloomy flush of life is fled.
> All but yon widowed, solitary thing
> That feebly bends beside the plashy spring;
> She, wretched matron, forced, in age, for bread,
> To strip the brook with mantling cresses spread,
> To pick her wintry faggot from the thorn,
> To seek her nightly shed, and weep till morn;
> She only left of all the harmless train,
> The sad historian of the pensive plan.
> [128–136]

Unlike the passage on the village sports, this presentation of the solitary widow focuses upon and is dominated by a single figure. A "solitary thing," she stands as an emblem of lost identity. But at the same time she is more poetically active than any of the villagers who were presented as incarnations of sport. Unlike them, she is the active subject of a series of verbals: to strip, to pick, to seek, to weep. Barely alive physically, she powerfully dominates a landscape of feeling, and her presentation progressively intensifies her significance, which builds toward the final line, where Goldsmith names her "the sad historian of the pensive plain." "Historian" is crucial here; concentrated into that word are much of the poem's internal dynamic. This important word attributes to the suffering figure a measure of consciousness and authority not given to the pastoral villagers. For the solitary woman stands in the poem along with the parson as a surrogate for the poet, a vehicle of self-discovery.[7] But whereas the parson embodies a kind of ideal identity, a perfectly coordinated system of feeling and intelligence, representing the opportunities of intelligence within the poet's fantasy of the village's pastoral life, the ruined figure of the widow reflects the poet's relationship with the landscape of the poem's present:

both poet and woman are historians, a word investing them with authority of a different kind from the parson's. Theirs is the authority that inheres in the sufferer, not the listener; considered in this respect, Goldsmith's choice of the word "historian" enlarges the widow, creates opportunities for identifying the poet and widow as sufferers, instead of distinguishing between them in terms of status or intelligence. Both have suffered a loss of their pasts, both have discovered in the desolation of Auburn that lyric landscape—the pensive plain—the experience of which is inward, not social. So the poet can say of himself that "Remembrance wakes with all her busy train, / Swells at my breast, and turns the past to pain" and, at the same time, can describe the old woman as "forced, in age . . . / To seek her nightly shed, and weep till morn." Each is a figure violated by events, similarly diminished by them, denied the social identity the village could have provided, left only with the inner experience of pain but with all its lyric opportunities. Thus robbed and diminished, they gain only in the consciousness suffering brings, and the authority that suffering implies. Their identity as sufferers merges them in the character of historians, a word that raises the village figure in relation to the poet by suggesting that her silent suffering is not merely a subject for literature but a kind of equivalent of it. The distinction between the literary and rustic intelligence is no longer crucial: to suffer and to speak are similar acts. From the poet's point of view sympathy for another accompanies the definition of his own plight in a process that reduces in significance the considerations of intelligence and status, which in turn create the perspective for the poet's idyllic but reduced rendering of Auburn's remembered life. The figure of the old woman answers to feelings within the poet too immediate and too strong to be contained in or reflected by the pleasance. These feelings of loss, abandonment, isolation, and violation demand for their expression connection with an image of the village as suffering in history, not as a charmed sanctuary from it.

It is the village as a charmed sanctuary, a "green cabinet," however, which the poet will present to us as the immediate response to his sight of the ruined solitary. Not until the final movement of the poem, with its picture of the villagers departing into exile and its assertion that with them depart Poetry and the Virtues themselves, does the poem fully achieve the expressive manner and the charged vision adequate to the feelings generated by the image of the ruined widow, with its resonant connection to the personal plight of the poet. This last movement is a product neither of sight—like the image of the widow—nor of memory—like the village idyll; it is a record of neither present nor past. It is, rather, a vision: a product of imagination, of poetic power fully adequate now to the personal intensity of the poet's experience, fully responding to his own understanding of the meaning, personal and political, of his return to Auburn. Memory, sight, imagination—these are the faculties composing the poem, linked to each other in a process recording the poet's own inner movement toward an understanding of the meaning of his return home.[8] The indirection of this movement reflects the variety of stances available to him as a poet confronting an experience rich in personal and public meaning. Sight is stimulus, memory and imagination, responses. Memory, yielding the idyllic village, is the faculty most in accord with the poet's desire to speak publicly, to share the perspective of the reader, statesman, and judge. Memory works by distancing the poet from the villagers, permitting him to function as an authority in their behalf, his intelligence and sophistication defining their attractiveness but limiting their interest. Sight, however, presents the compelling immediacy of the desolation, the empty landscape, inviting the poet to fill it with his feelings. Sight reveals lyric opportunities, demands personal responses. Memory, stimulated by these opportunities, backs away from them, forms perspectives; it creates distance between the poet and his subject, and joins him with his reader. Memory creates the parson and the schoolmaster; sight presents the figure of the widow, rich in half-understood resonances with the poet's own inner situation: a ruined, solitary thing, the only human figure actually present to the poet as he broods over the ruined landscape. Between sight and memory the poem pursues, separately, lyric and didactic impulses. But these impulses finally merge in imagination and vision.

In what I have called the poem's central passage (251–258) this resolution begins to take shape. This passage—abandoning the ironic manner of the village idyll with its distance, perspective, and affectionate condescension, all linking the poet to his reader rather than to the villagers—asserts that the village virtues are indeed important *personal* realities even to the sophisticated consciousness. Moreover, the passage defines as an act of intelligent maturity the effort to value virtues and feelings with which maturity, intelligence, and sophistication are not easily in accord. Thus the passage works positively from the nostalgic feelings developed in the village idyll, yet expresses the poet's desire to abandon the distance and perspective necessary to the presentation of the idyll. The central passage works back through the idyll to the powerfully personal charge of feeling known by the poet as he stands before the desolation, with the personally resonant figure of the ruined solitary in his sight. The passage thus draws upon the energies of sight and of memory, of lyric feeling and didactic intention, of true sympathy and nostalgia, in order to turn the poem in the direction of its fullest power, the imaginative power that can fuse the poet's two sources of emotional energy and therefore its two styles of expressive form. But as part of this process this central passage is more important in its manner than its content; this strong and assertive manner expresses the value of only the remembered, idealized villagers and their innocent lives. It remains for the poet to extend his sympathies to their fuller identity in history, their experiences in the present as sufferers. And this extension of sympathy produces the act of *imagination* which concludes the poem.

It is crucial that we recognize what happens to the poem's didactic progress subsequent to the central passage. Simply, the poet denies himself the rhetorical stature and privilege from which didactic utterance may be expected to come, but simultaneously makes didactic pronouncements with a satiric and bitter vigor as yet unheard in the poem:

> Ye friends to truth, ye statesmen who survey
> The rich man's joys encrease, the poor's decay.
> 'Tis yours to judge, how wide the limits stand
> Between a splendid and an happy land.
> Proud swells the tide with loads of freighted ore,
> And shouting Folly hails them from her shore;
> Hoards, even beyond the miser's wish abound,
> And rich men flock from all the world around.
> Yet count our gains. This wealth is but a name
> That leaves our useful products till the same.
> Not so the loss. The man of wealth and pride,

> Takes up a space that many poor supplied;
> Space for his lake, his park's extended bounds,
> Space for his horses, equipage, and hounds;
> The robe that wraps his limbs in silken sloth,
> Has robbed the neighboring fields of half their growth;
> His seat, where solitary sports are seen,
> Indignant spurns the cottage from the green;
> Around the world each needful product flies,
> For all the luxuries the world supplies.
> While thus the land adorned for pleasure, all
> In barren splendour feebly waits the fall.
> [265–286]

Rhetorically giving over the task of judgment to the statesman, the poet nevertheless proceeds to judge. The active word here is "survey." It defines the inadequacy of the statesman even as it describes the condition of his authority. That is, the surveyor—removed, personally distant, a figure entirely of judgment, and entirely devoid of sympathy—emerges in this passage as strangely inert despite his authority and because of his perspective. It is the judge whom the poet judges here, seeing him inactively surveying "the rich man's joys encrease, the poor's decay." The passage creates a contrast between the furiously active energies of a mindless commerce—

> Proud swells the tide with loads of freighted ore,
> An shouting Folly hails them from her shore;
> Hoards, even beyond the miser's wish abound,
> And rich men flock from all the world around.

—and the curious inertia of the surveying statesman. And this contrast is its point. In this passage the poet severs his own commitment to politics in an act of anger and of understanding. Politics is surveying; it is the sphere of the judge. Sympathy is the power of the poet. No ordinary politics can intervene in a situation whose meaning is available only to intelligent sympathy. It is sympathy which can distinguish between "parlour splendours" and "barren splendour," between a "splendid and an happy land," because only sympathy penetrates to the inside of a village inn, and to the "political" essence of that place, whose whole meaning *is* its function to "impart / An hour's importance to the poor man's heart." Proper judgment is literally a question of sight—not the ranging sight of the surveying statesman but the sympathetic sight of the poet specifically focused on so small a space as the inside of an inn, and once there, on the poor man's heart. It is again the distinction between the sight of judgment and the sight of sympathy. When he addresses the statesman at this point in the poem, then, Goldsmith quite forcefully delivers over to him all the privileges of perspective and authority—"'Tis yours to judge"—which, for the poet's purposes, revised now by the lyric opportunities of his situation pondering the desolation that was Auburn, are useless to him. Between the inert figure of the surveying statesman and the emotional intelligence of the sympathetic poet (at this point in the poem still struggling to understand the value of his feelings), the poem's drama of sympathy and judgment finds its opening toward a resolution. In this moment when the poet breaks his connection with the world of the statesman, however, we should not miss the heightened anger, the emotional authority with which he delivers his judgments. Giving over the perspective and privileges of the judge, he judges more confidently, more intensely, more angrily than at any previous point in the poem. The poem's drama of sympathy and judgment does not therefore lead toward a choice between two faculties never heathily apart, but rather to an understanding of the true nature of poetry's authority to unite them. Here a poet comes home importing the authority whose source is in his having been away. He expects to speak and be listened to because of that authority; that authority attaches to his claim to speak to and with the statesman, as well. The difficulty he encounters in speaking *of* the village (to speak *to* it is now impossible) as an emissary of the town and *to* the statesman as an emissary of the village requires that he work out, as if for the first time, the grounds for, the stance enabling, poetic and didactic utterance. The inward events and the political concerns of this poem may be seen, then, as the components of a stylistic search, forced upon a man for whom poetry's connection with culture and politics is more problematical than he had known.[9]

The statesman should not, the poet *cannot* "survey." His encounter with significant inner experience cannot be expressed in the adroit address of a distanced consciousness. This is the stylistic implication of the poet's renunciation of the judge's function even as he demonstrates the judge's power. And insofar as the poet's initial stance had bonded him with the statesman and with the reader, all together in a social and intellectual union distancing them from the villagers, whom they could survey either as statistics or in idealized memory, his rejection of the statesman's judgmental privileges implies also a disruption of his bond with the reader, a disruption of their mutual understanding of the sources and nature of poetry's authority.

But in disrupting his bond with the reader, the poet is now enabled to make a rich discovery of a new source for his speech. This is his discovery of the imagination. For it is the imagination that will now provide the poet with the new perspective that binds him personally and sympathetically to the poor; and, in that bond with the poor, the poet will come to recognize a new authority for speech. With the discovery of this perspective and authority, the powerfully personal experience of desolation embodied in the figure of the solitary widow can be explicitly developed by the poet as his own as well. The poor will now enter the poem more actively than even that ruined figure had, and will be joined to the poet's identity more intimately than had been possible even for her, held at a distance as she had been by the cruelly precise diction—"yon widowed, solitary *thing*" (my emphasis). The stylistic achievement that is to come is, in fact, to free the poet's didactic utterance from the social demands of adroitness, sophistication, and distance—the trappings of judgment narrowly defined—and to found it instead in an intelligence enriched by feeling, openly acknowledged, binding the poet to the poor who are his subjects, and finally the best representatives of his own inner situation.

These substantive and stylistic implications of the poet's rejection of the statesman begin to work themselves out in the curious section that follows that rejection: the account of the urban poor. It is a curious passage because it is not specifically about the plight of Auburn itself. Abruptly enlarged in its scope, the passage connects significantly but indirectly with Auburn's story, for Auburn's people, unlike the subjects of this passage, are not exiled into the British metropolis, but into the American wilderness:

> Where then, ah where, shall poverty reside,
> To scape the pressure of contiguous pride?

If to some common's fenceless limits strayed,
He drives his flock to pick the scanty blade,
Those fenceless fields the sons of wealth divide,
And even the bare-worn common is denied.
   If to the city sped—what waits him there?
To see profusion that he must not share;
To see ten thousand baneful arts combined
To pamper luxury, and thin mankind;
To see those joys the sons of pleasure know,
Extorted from his fellow-creature's woe.
Here, while the courtier glitters in brocade,
There the pale artist plies the sickly trade;
Here, while the proud their long-drawn pomps display,
There the black gibbet glooms beside the way.
The dome where Pleasure holds her midnight reign,
Here, richly deckt, admits the gorgeous train;
Tumultuous grandeur crowds the blazing square,
The rattling chariots clash, the torches glare.
Sure scenes like these no troubles e'er annoy!
Sure these denote one universal joy!
Are these thy serious thoughts?—Ah, turn thine eyes
Where the poor houseless shivering female lies.
She once, perhaps, in village plenty blest,
Has wept at tales of innocence distrest;
Her modest looks the cottage might adorn,
Sweet as the primrose peeps beneath the thorn;
Now lost to all; her friends, her virtue fled,
Near her betrayer's door she lays her head,
And pinch'd with cold, and shrinking from the shower,
With heavy heart deplores that luckless hour
When idly first, ambitious of the town,
She left her wheel and robes of country brown.
   Do thine, sweet AUBURN, thine, the loveliest train,
Do thy fair tribes participate her pain? . . .
Ah, no. To distant climes, a dreary scene,
Where half the convex world intrudes between,
Through torrid tracts with fainting steps they go,
Where wild Altama murmurs to their woe.
               [303–338, 341–344]

In reaching out to include within its scope the suffering of the urban poor, the passage is rendered as a series of scenes, not remembered, not seen, but *imagined*. Neither sight nor memory alone is active here, but rather their fusion in an imaginative power that will soon grow into visionary intensity when the poet once again concentrates his emotional and intellectual attention upon Auburn. This passage on the city poor is crucial to the poem because that final visionary intensity develops from it as the heightened cognitive experience of a man whose imaginative power has grown in association with his sympathetic capaciousness, here demonstrated in part by the generalized scope of his meditations on the city.

The city passage grows as an answer to the poet's question, "Where then, ah where . . . ?" It ponders the narrowing options of the poor by amplifying the second of two answers to that question. Each of these responds to an "if" clause:

> If to some common's fenceless limits strayed,
> He drives his flock to pick the scanty blade,
> Those fenceless fields the sons of wealth divide,
> And even the bare-worn common is denied.
>   If to the city sped—What waits him there? . . .

The response to the first proposition is a simple clause of consequence, rendered as plain statement. But the response to the second—"If to the city sped"—opens out into the fullness of imaginative representation in a series of scenes *envisioned* by the poet as if *seen* by the poor themselves, for the first time now entering the poem with their own power of sight as fully conscious agents. "If to the city sped—What waits him there? / To see . . . To see . . . To see . . ."

The power of sight attributed to the poor is tantamount to the power of judgment. What the poor see are both particularized and generalized scenes of juxtaposed luxury and penury: particularized as in "Here . . . the courtier glitters in brocade," generalized as in "ten thousand baneful arts combined / To pamper luxury, and thin mankind." The play of particularity and generality along with the juxtaposed ("Here" . . . "There") arrangement of the material is important: it registers the activity of mind inherent in the vision of the poor. More than mere gazing, their sight represents their capacity for intelligent insight;

it is seeing that generalizes and compares. Embodying judgment, this kind of seeing, like the statesman's, depends upon perspective. But unlike the "surveying" of the statesman, the perspective of the poor is formed by feeling, by their own suffering involvement in the urban spectacle. They impose a kind of interior perspective upon these scenes in which they see themselves in relation to their economic, sociological, and psychological surroundings. Their sympathetic seeing is most obvious in the lines on the "poor houseless shivering female" whose present plight she herself apprehends in the interior movement of her own consciousness and memory as she "With heavy heart deplores that luckless hour" of her idly ambitious departure from the village.

The achievement of this whole passage is in its simultaneous representation of the speech of the poet and the sight of the poor. Discovering their point of view, yet maintaining his own voice, the poet can in his mind now address the statesman with a newly achieved authority:

> Sure scenes like these no troubles e'er annoy!
> Sure these denote one universal joy!
> Are these thy serious thought?—Ah, turn thine eyes
> Where the poor houseless shivering female lies.

In the manner of these lines we should notice a freedom from the deference that had shaped Goldsmith's earlier address to the statesman as a "friend to truth" whose authority and position were signaled by his function as judge (265–267); this function the poet had renounced, without losing its power. And that power is exercised here, invigorated by the perception that suffering and the capacity for sympathy accompanying it must now be incorporated into any meaningful definition of intelligence, a faculty with which the poor are now seen to be richly endowed. The statesman here is asked to enrich his own judgmental capacity—not merely "to survey" but to see as the poor see, to enter with the poet into the mind and memory of the abandoned girl, to sympathize.

This is an achievement both adroit and generous. The moral and stylistic values of intelligence have been preserved even as they have been enhanced in the sympathetic act that frees the poet's imagination to see as the poor see. The poet can demand a like generosity from the statesman and also from his readers, whose adequacy now is tested in their ability to accept as authoritative a point of view newly discovered by the poet himself. To miss this opportunity, in fact, is to miss the point about poetry itself: its imaginative power and its authority spring from that union of intelligence and sympathy the poet himself has discovered in the process of disengaging himself from the reader and statesman to find the richer perspective they are now free to accept. By freeing his imagination to see as the poor see, the poet is ready for that effort of generous vision adequate to the plight of Auburn's exiles, the subject to which he now can return. In this long interlude, not itself about Auburn, he fully realizes the poetic and personal richness of that motion of the will he had registered in the central passage where he had asserted, without fully understanding, the value of his feelings for the village as he stood before its desolation. In that earlier moment he had opened himself to the play of feelings that only now begin to carry him toward profound discoveries about the source of his poetic power and, along with this, about the personal meaning of his return to his home. Having accepted that play of feelings he has discovered his essential identity with the poor and is empowered therefore to realize more richly his initial intention as a refugee—to tell of all he felt and all he saw—than would have been possible for him in his (fantasized) relation to an idyllic world of story and of play. He had been affectionately bound to that world, but personally aloof from it, distanced by the very consciousness and sophistication he had assumed formed the authority for his position of tale-teller in the fantasized and idyllic economy of story and response.

With rich and significant irony his recognition that the poor themselves are removed from that economy permits him to realize that to tell of all he felt and all he saw is to tell, in fact, of them. It is exquisitely appropriate that Goldsmith should imagine the ruined country girl as one who "once, perhaps, in village plenty blest, / Has wept at tales of innocence distrest." As he imagines her, he concentrates into the portrait the ironies surrounding his own ruined identity as a storyteller, for she is herself an image of his lost audience. More, she is lost to his stories precisely because she forms now their very subject. Indeed, he attributes to her sufficient consciousness to perceive this irony herself. Her consciousness is rooted in her "deploring heart": it is emotional consciousness, at once the source of pain and of self-awareness, and we should hear in these lines significant resonances between her plight, based as it was upon "idle ambition" for the town (335), and the poet's own initially prideful relation to the village as an emissary from the town (89–90).

Perhaps no other moment in the poem so closely courts the dangers of conventional sentimentality and is so intelligently saved from them. It is saved from them first because it risks them, because this risk is an act of intelligence in a poem whose very meaning is in its discovery of the cognitive value of feeling and of the cognitive limitations of mere adroitness and sophistication. And it is saved from them also because it is still adroit and intelligent in its management of the poem's significant ironies, its cognitive material. The adequate reader will accept this moment, just as the poet has risked it, avoiding sophistication's easy invitation to contemn—a ruined maid, her head bowed at her betrayer's door!—because the adequate reader has been feelingly alert to the weight of meaning the moment carries.

Readers will have been alert, that is, to the poet's deepening awareness of the sheer actuality of people he could initially value only as figures in a poet's tale or as listeners to it. They will have seen in the reversal of tale and life, of subject and audience, which forms this moment, a demonstration of the poet's control of his material and not of his abandonment to it. With the girl who now understands herself to be experiencing the suffering for which she once would have wept, a village enters into history. The poet, who had hoped, with a tincture of pride, to find in a village a refuge from history, here registers his discovery that his real story is of a village's ruinous engagement *with history*. He will not, in pride, tell the village of the city; in sorrow he tells the city of the village. He gives us this poem.

The feelings of loss and violation he had carried back with him to the village and which he had thought distinguished him from its innocent and idealized people are now after all indistinguishable from the inner experience of the ruined villagers themselves. To tell of them now is to tell of himself; their story is his. The inner speech that is *The Deserted Village* may be understood then as the enhanced utterance of a man who, in his fantasized retirement, could have functioned only as a narrator. What would have been narration *then* is *now* the enriched, personal, silent speech of a sufferer whose story is really his own; like the story of the ruined maid it is matter only for the inner, overheard speech of the deploring heart. Out of the ruined Auburn, which can no longer assemble itself into an audience for a narration, a new community has been established, a community attuned only in the silent speech generated by suffering and consciousness. In all this loss there is that much gain. For a community of idealized innocence, there is a community of painful experience; for an audience, there are sufferers; for narrative, there is lyric.

In the generalized meditation on the city, the didactic effort of the poem is reshaped by the poet's integration of himself with the poor as now the teller, in lyric utterance, of an inner story that is his as well as theirs. No didactic force has been lost in this transaction; indeed a new manner has been discovered for the richer expression of the lesson. We should recognize, indeed, the sententious force of much of the statement in this section, but the pronouncements have a different structural relation to their context from that of the sententiae toward which previous passages of didactic intent had been directed. Not simple pronouncements, the angry lines are imagined as the record of the judgmental sight of the poor themselves, indistinguishable now from the poet's sympathetic intelligence. Standing in the desolate landscape of Auburn, the poet records in inner speech what he imagines the urban poor to see. His didactic utterance is not now the plain statement that was his presumed right as a figure whose authority was thought to be rooted in the sophisticated consciousness he had imported to the countryside. The poem's earlier manner where it stops, aria-like, to express the well-known declarations of the two paragraphs beginning "Ill fares the land . . ." (50) and "A time there was . . ." (57) is entirely different from the manner of these lines:

> If to the city sped—What waits him there?
> To see profusion that he must not share;
> To see ten thousand baneful arts combined
> To pamper luxury, and thin mankind.

Here the sententiae are embedded within the scene the poet imagines the poor man to see. The poor, that is, are imagined to see with the intelligent dignity that reveals in a scene for the eyes the personified visions that only the mind can make. Their suffering and sympathetic sight raises them to the poet's level, their own sight and silent speech as authoritative as his. In this union of poet and poor is the union of lyric and didactic expression which is the achievement of *The Deserted Village* and which makes possible the charged imaginative vision at the end of the poem, a vision that can be difficult to understand if we do not see what makes it possible. For the final assertion that the exile of the poor is the exile of Poetry itself has been anticipated here already in this passage which attributes to the poor the conscious power and the sympathetic capacity to see poetically.

The claim for the identity of Poetry and Auburn's poor is an enlarged consequence of the identity established between the poet and the urban poor in the meditation on the city. The poem's final movement back to Auburn amplifies this link into explicitness and develops its meaning fully. It recognizes in the union of poetry and poverty a sociological and psychological reality. Indeed, the poet's own poverty is for the first time made explicit as plain fact, a sociological and psychological condition of his identity, as important now as those considerations of status and intelligence which earlier had too much determined his sense of self and audience. The poet sees his own poverty now as a decree of Poetry itself: "Thou source of all my bliss and all my woe, / That found'st me poor at first, and keep'st me so . . ." (413–414). More, this crucial couplet claims Poetry itself as the agency integrating the poet's earlier identity as a villager ("found'st me poor at first") with his present self ("and keep'st me so"). What has often seemed to be an arbitrary assertion is, in fact, nothing else than the fully concentrated articulation of that inner process of growth *toward* the villagers that the poet experiences as he stands alone in the emptied landscape pondering and appreciating their suffering and enhanced selfhood. The lines prove out the integrity of his being, the oneness of his earlier and his present identity, and make good the sentimental risk he took earlier in the poem in conjuring and *adopting* feelings that were compelling though unclear to his understanding. In joining himself with the vanished villagers and with his own village self through the very agency of his poetic power, Goldsmith in fact denies what critics have, in various ways, taken his poem to be: a record of the pathos of one who *cannot* come home again. *The Deserted Village* is nothing if it is not the record of an inner return to the richness and the reality of being once known, lost, and now rediscovered. Indeed, as the lines establish the poet's psychological homecoming, they fully develop the implications of his earlier split with the statesman. It is the statesman's, not the village's world to which he cannot return, now that he has understood such journeying to be interior adventure and has rediscovered the village in the actuality of its exiled people and their capacity for sorrow and consciousness.

If we examine now the passage in which the poet envisions the departure of Auburn's poor, we can see in lines that hardly require explication how justified, as a consequence of the poet's own inner development, are his concluding assertions about the villagers:

> Good Heaven! what sorrows gloom'd that parting day,
> That called them from their native walks away;
> When the poor exiles, every pleasure past,
> Hung round their bowers, and fondly looked their last,
> And took a long farewell, and wished in vain
> For seats like these beyond the western main;
> And shuddering still to face the distant deep,
> Returned and wept, and still returned to weep.
> The good old sire, the first prepared to go
> To new found worlds, and wept for others woe.
> But for himself, in conscious virtue brave,
> He only wished for worlds beyond the grave.
> His lovely daughter, lovelier in her tears,
> The fond companion of his helpless years,
> Silent went next, neglectful of her charms,
> And left a lover's for a father's arms.
> With louder plaints the mother spoke her woes,
> And blest the cot where every pleasure rose;
> And kist her thoughtless babes with many a tear,
> And claspt them close in sorrow doubly dear;
> Whilst her fond husband strove to lend relief
> In all the silent manliness of grief.
>   O luxury! Thou curst by Heaven's decree,
> How ill exchanged are things like these for thee!
>   [363–386]

We need to remember now that these lines record a vision—neither sight nor memory generates it, but the fusion of those faculties by the force of sympathy. The poet still stands alone in a desolated landscape, as he has throughout the poem; but now, in a powerful imaginative effort, following upon his successful effort to see as the poor see, he envisions what their day of departure must have been. The startled exclamation with which the passage begins records not only his sympathy but also, as if in shocked recognition, his full awareness of the reality of these people in their capacity for sorrow. Seeing them as capable of sorrow, the poet sees them also as capable of consciousness, and he develops this crucial insight in a manner that has pointed reference to the poem's idyllic movement, which, for all the affection generating it, had denied significant selfhood to the village folk. But we see them now, pointedly, "every pleasure past," in a situation entirely changed from that in the idyll where their very identity was a function of their sports. Add to this the daughter who "left a lover's for a father's arms" and we see in this envisioned scene the complete devastation of the pastoral idyll earlier presented as a domain of love and of play.

What is the gain? Again, only consciousness. But this is crucial, for in sympathetically envisioning the sorrow of the exile as an increment of consciousness, the poet bridges any significant distance between him and the villagers. It is of the first importance that we recognize how this departure scene is shaped in its essentials as an account of the full consciousness the villagers now possess. The father, for example:

> The good old sire, the first prepared to go
> To new found worlds, and wept for others woe.
> But for himself, in conscious virtue brave,
> He only wished for worlds beyond the grave.
> [371–374]

The mother:

> With louder plaints the mother spoke her woes,
> And blest the cot where every pleasure rose;
> And kist her thoughtless babes with many a tear,
> And claspt them close in sorrow doubly dear;
> Whilst her fond husband strove to lend relief
> In all the silent manliness of grief.
> [379–384]

These lines record the inner growth of the villagers as they submit to their suffering. "In sorrow doubly dear" epitomizes the enhancement of consciousness that necessarily accompanies suffering, and the concluding couplet, picking up the earlier "in conscious virtue brave," yields an image of the father in seriously heroic colors, fully in accord with his enhanced selfhood, intensified suffering, and deepened empathic power: as in the earlier lines he "wept for others woe," he now "strives to lend relief / In all the silent manliness of grief."

The father's silence, perhaps, should catch our attention here. As with the poet the significant locus of his experience is now within, and, as with the poet standing silently in the desolation, the full expression of interiority is sympathy, not declamation or narration. The departure of the villagers, all bearing within them a burden of knowing not earlier accorded them by the poet, in fact raises them to his level. Equal in suffering and therefore equal in consciousness and sympathetic capacity, poet and villagers—devastated, isolated, violated, and abandoned—merge fully. To say, then, that the exile of the people *is* the exile of Poetry itself is simply to record the deepest inner meaning of the poet's return to Auburn, that is, his own growth in sympathy, his own full sight as he sees into an experience as personal as it is public, as lyrical in its stylistic necessities as it is didactic in its intentions. Moreover, the uncompromising force of the poem's didactic expression reaches its fullest strength just in these closing moments when the poem's lyrical direction attains its goal. That goal had been to make the personal suffering of the poet directly expressive of the national theme. It is achieved by his seeing in the plight of the poor an image of his own. The didactic force of these lines is now possible:

> O luxury! Thou curst by Heaven's decree,
> How ill exchanged are things like these for thee!
> How do thy potions, with insidious joy,
> Diffuse their pleasures only to destroy!
> Kingdoms, by thee, to sickly greatness grown,
> Boast of a florid vigour not their own;
> At every draught more large and large they grow,
> A bloated mass of rank unwieldy woe;
> Till sapped their strength, and every part unsound,
> Down, down they sink, and spread a ruin round.
> [385–394]

This force is now possible because the poet is speaking with enhanced and fully legitimated authority, now that authority for speech is no longer limited by unnecessary considerations. With fine and precise modulation these lines merge didactic force with an elegiac, lyrical tonality to produce the most charged imaginative vision of the poem, the vision of the departure of the villagers as the departure of the virtues and of Poetry itself:

> Even now the devastation is begun,
> And half the business of destruction done;
> Even now, methinks, as pondering here I stand,
> I see the rural virtues leave the land:
> Down where yon anchoring vessel spreads the sail,
> That idly waiting flaps with every gale,
> Downward they move, a melancholy band,
> Pass from the shore, and darken all the strand.
> Contented toil, and hospitable care,
> And kind connubial tenderness, are there;
> And piety, with wishes placed above,
> And steady loyalty, and faithful love:
> And thou, sweet Poetry, thou loveliest maid,
> Still first to fly where sensual joys invade . . .
> [395–408]

"As pondering here I stand," that is, facing the desolated landscape, the poet literally sees nothing and says nothing. What he records here rather is the vision that fills his mind, generated from the imagined scene of the domestic leave-taking just preceding. Again, this vision contrasts markedly with memory's earlier identification of the villagers with their sports. Here they are nothing less than the Virtues themselves. In this heightened instant, therefore, the now visionary poet has peopled the depopulated landscape—peopled it with the significant sight of his imagination, which has given us in this scene of the villagers as the Virtues an image of the poor enhanced enough to embody the personal emotional charge of the poem, and, at the same time, the didactic intention linked to that charge of feeling. Lyricism and didacticism are now merged even as the identity of the poet as sufferer has merged with the enlarged selfhood of the villagers.

Raymond Williams, in his incisive evaluation of Goldsmith's poem, perhaps the most important critical notice it has received, comments on the meaning of Goldsmith's concluding identification of Poetry itself with the exiled villagers: ". . . to be a poet is, ironically to be pastoral poet: the social condition of poetry—it is as far as Goldsmith gets—is the idealized pastoral economy. The destruction of one is, or is made to stand for, the destruction of other. And then the village itself becomes a pastoral and a poetic mode."[10] Williams's interest is in the intersection of what he calls the imaginative and the social process, and his sensitive and sympathetic attention to Goldsmith's achievement leads him nevertheless to judge it as untrue to that social process, to the actual history of the English countryside "in which the destruction of the old social relationships [of the village life was] accompanied by an increased use and fertility of land . . ." This actual history

> is overridden [in the poem] by the imaginative process in which, when the pastoral order is destroyed, creation is 'stinted,' the brook is 'choked,' the cry of the bittern is 'hollow,' the lapwing's cries 'unvaried.' This creation of a 'desert' landscape is the imaginative rather than the social process; it is what the new order does to the poet, not to the land. . . . It is not that he cannot . . . see the real social history; he is often especially sensitive to it, as a present fact. But the identification between his own suffering and that of a social group beyond him is inevitably negative, in the end. The present is accurately and powerfully seen, but its real relations, to past and future, are inaccessible, because the governing development is that of the writer himself: a feeling about the past, an idea about the future, into which, by what is truly an intersection, an observed present is arranged. We need not doubt the warmth of Goldsmith's feelings about the men driven from their village: that connection is definite. The structure becomes ambiguous only when this shared feeling is extended to memory and imagination, for what takes over then, in language and idea, is a different pressure: the social history of the writer.[11]

Williams's conclusions are a valuably freshened restatement of perhaps the earliest criticisms the poem attracted. Goldsmith's own prefatory note to Sir Joshua Reynolds acknowledges those contemporary objections to the poem which held that "the depopulation it deplores is nowhere to be seen, and the disorders it laments are only to be found in the poet's own imagination. To this I can scarce make any other answer than that I sincerely believe what I have written."[12] He goes on to assure Reynolds that he has in fact visited the country and that he has taken pains to be certain of his allegations. The value of Williams's criticism is in its recognition of the reality of this issue; in the sympathetic acuity that permits him to stand back from so familiar and favorite a poem and to see that it is, indeed, "baffling," and in his recognition that the poem's vitality is in the complex play of memory, sight, and imagination, all of which work as the agents of the poet's active presence in an actual landscape.

My judgment of Goldsmith's achievement differs from Williams's along lines determined by our differing valuation of those faculties of memory and imagination. The question is how far Goldsmith gets. Williams understands him to stop far earlier than I do—to stop, that is, in his pastoral memories which place him at the center of the idyllic village and which tend to identify poetry itself as pastoral poetry, the utterance of a man who celebrates the innocent communal life of a fantasized social order, or evokes its tears for miseries it knows nothing of. Williams makes no distinction between the action of memory and imagination, defining the first simply as retrospective, the second as projective, as if their yield were the same idealized version of country life. But the action of imagination is a development within the poem itself. It registers the poet's enhanced understanding of the villagers, of himself, and of poetry as he sees their suffering annihilate any significant distance between them and him, so that in the end it is not the pastoral economy *but its destruction* that makes for poetry. The villagers who carry poetry's power away with them are enabled for this responsibility not by their innocence, but by their painful experience, and in the event, the power of poetry itself is shown to reside in its lyric rather than its narrative capacities.[13] The father's silence in manly grief is thus a sign of his inner fullness, an analogue to the silent speech of the poet's which constitutes his poem now as he stands in the landscape, his mind full of vision, so different from the narrator he would have been were he indeed the pastoral poet of his valued fantasy. It is puzzling that Williams, alone among Goldsmith's critics in his alertness to the poetic activity in the poem's play of memory, sight, and imagination, should miss the yield of this activity in the poet's final representation of the enlarged selfhood of the villagers, their maturity, consciousness—in a word, actuality. It is puzzling because Williams's splendid book in its criticism of pastoralism in general makes an important point of the sentimentalizing of the poor inherent in that genre, at least when it has functioned as a self-serving fantasy of the aristocratic order. The sentimentalizing of the poor, which entailed the denial of their actuality as laborers, continued into the eighteenth century with especially baneful effects on pastoral writing, precisely because the tropological and symbolic richness of Renaissance and seventeenth-century pastoral was entirely lost in the later period, for which pastoral consequently became merely an immensely popular means of attitudinizing among the upper classes. Williams correctly notes that "it is basically an eighteenth-century 'discovery' by the educated upper classes—that 'the poor' are not simply a charitable burden, a weight on the economy but the actual producers of wealth" (p. 70). That this discovery did not energize the period's pastoral writing, which was ruined in ignoring it, is a mystery. But this failure in itself should help us to perceive the magnitude of Goldsmith's achievement.

For in abandoning "pastoralism," in growing away from his idyllic memories of the villagers and moving toward them on the strength of his imaginative and sympathetic recognition of their sheer actuality, if not as workers then as sufferers, Goldsmith is in fact true to the deepest meanings inherent in the pastoral kind. Paul Alpers has written about "the sense of the contingency of human utterance [that is the hallmark of Virgil's pastoral poetry]: that it is always dependent on the speaker's (or singer's) situation, powers, and limitations."[14] This is to say that the low, the simple, the natural are, in the best pastoral poetry, not fantasies, nor objects of condescension, but realities capable of representing the acts and choices of real people in real situations. Pastoral song can be tragic or joyous, but it works, when it works, because the poet takes his pastoral material seriously, not needing to allegorize it or disguise it in the dress of a familiar conventionality. In Theocritus's pastoral, as Rosenmeyer shows, the poet does not attitudinize his relation to his material, but invents a style that fully expresses his own ability to merge his consciousness with that of the bower. The values of the bower are real and its life is *the* subject of Theocritean pastoral, not the ironies, perspectives, judgments, and longings that a sophisticated mind can bring to bear on it.

Goldsmith does not merge his consciousness with the bower; he raises the bower into history and joins himself to its devastation, forging an identity with his rural subject that redefines pastoral *and conserves* it. The ruined poet and the ruined audience have learned about the contingency of human utterance, its rootedness in actual life. As they have become the subjects of their own stories, as the contingencies of their lives have made silence their only opportunity, they have, poet and poor, learned to be lyricists. In this respect the claim can be made for *The Deserted Village* that it is a unique achievement in eighteenth-century pastoral writing. In overcoming its initial bond with the reader, it overcomes the fussiness so obvious in its most conventionally pastoral moments. These moments had worked to define the social distance between the poet and the poor. But in bridging that gap, in representing the mature consciousness of the villagers, he demonstrates finally that it is neither the social distance dividing poet and poor, nor the idealized innocence this distance creates, which gives *The Deserted Village* its pastoral character. The distinction of Goldsmith's poem is that in discovering its natural character as a lyric it realizes the profoundest "natural" impulses of pastoral convention. The discovery of pastoral accompanies the discovery of lyric. Like Gibbon's gutted cottage, connected in the historian's mind with the classical art of Greece, the ruined villagers become an emblem of contingency and of art; they deepen our understanding of history, art, and the tragic actualities that link them to one another as the scene and record of suffering individuals. Poetry, in departing from Auburn, leaves only a landscape it never really inhabited, and enters the only domain that matters, the suffering and the silent human heart. This is Goldsmith's lyric discovery.

———◆◆◆———

My reading of Goldsmith's poem asks that the poem be examined as it presents itself: as the interior speech of a man physically present in a landscape, his memory, his sight, his imagination stimulated by that situation. Goldsmith's earlier poem, *The Traveller*, proceeds from a strikingly similar situation, on the strength of strikingly similar feelings. Its very first line—"Remote, unfriended, melancholy, slow"—

virtually defines the lyrical charge of his greater poem. *The Deserted Village*, however, manages a more successful integration of the landscape and the poem, so that the poet's actual situation, "pondering" as he stands, becomes poetically active and is realized as the condition from which the poem proceeds. *The Deserted Village* works itself free from such moments as this one in the earlier work:

> But let us try these truths with closer eyes,
> And trace them through the prospect as it lies:
> Here for a while my proper cares resign'd,
> Here let me sit in sorrow for mankind,
> Like yon neglected shrub at random cast,
> That shades the steep, and sighs at every blast.
> [*The Traveller*, 99–104]

We should be alert here to the distinction the poet draws between his "proper cares" and his "sorrow for mankind." And, indeed, the poem does not successfully integrate the lyric energy of its personal theme with its public and didactic intention; this is because Goldsmith's management of the landscape denies him that opportunity. The landscape functions in *The Traveller* only to provide perspective, to permit the poet to survey, and it is a wildly exaggerated perspective he commands. From atop the Alps, his sight extends to all Europe—here Italy, there France, so that it is literally impossible for the speaker to establish and activate the landscape itself as a focus for the strong lyric charge he brings to the poem. Note how he puts aside his "proper cares" in order to work on his general theme; but note, too, that "neglected shrub." Goldsmith insists upon its physical presence and concentrates into it an intense personal significance; he expects a great deal of poetic work from it. But this disjunction between intense focus and extravagant prospect defines the poem's difficulty in integrating its personal and public themes. The larger landscape becomes entirely a prospect of the mind, the poet's physical presence high in the Alps really no more than a pretext, a mental prospect that can yield sight so extensive as to permit "visions" ranging "Far to the right where Appenine ascends," so that all Italy, as later all Switzerland, and later yet all France and all England come into mental view. The poem's didactic theme—"How small a part of all that human hearts endure, / That part which laws or kings can cause or cure" (429–430)—is a yield of the larger landscape, that extraordinary prospect covering all Europe. But the very insistent lyric impulse underlying the poem is set loosely adrift, fastened only fitfully to such objects as the shrub, such memories as of Goldsmith's brother, and such images as that of a "pensive exile." None of them is physically coordinated with the time and place the poet claims to represent as the occasion of the poem.[15]

The Deserted Village roots its play of memory and vision in the actual situation the poem claims to represent, and more fully realizes itself in the character of an interior monologue with a powerful lyric cast. In integrating its private and public material the poem is a considerable, but not a complete, success. Ralph Rader's account of Goldsmith's formal strategy can help us understand the reasons:

> "Goldsmith's genuinely didactic poem sprang from such deep personal sources that it verged toward lyric, and . . . demanded a special formal solution. All of Goldsmith's formal choices develop his poem steadily in the direction of didactic generality. The opening apostrophe, with its poignant evocation of Auburn's vanished charms, is immediately followed by a prospective statement of the moral ["Ill fares the land," etc.] and then a generalization of the Auburn situation to all of England [57–74]. Only when the overall didactic course of the poem is thus firmly set does Goldsmith develop the sense of lyric presence at the site of the depopulated village . . . and indicate the background of personal suffering which stands behind and implicitly energizes the whole creative act of the poem.[16]

The problem here again has to do with the coordination of didactic and lyric intent. Do we as readers imagine the poem as an imitation of the poet's experience in the landscape, or do we take it as a composition of another kind, freely moving from the moment in the landscape to the moment of composition? This is an important question because much of the poem's didactic delivery is *not* consistent with the moment of the poet's presence in the countryside, not consistent because he stands there alone, literally incapable of speech. Yet the delivery of such lines as "Ill fares the land . . ." and "Ye friends to truth . . ." presupposes another situation: one in which the poet implicitly *represents himself* as a composer at some remove from the initial stimulus of the didactic utterance and with an audience, actually or virtually present, to hear his sententiae.

Rader's assumption is, I think, that this compositional situation governs the whole poem. This is a defensible assumption, not only because it obviously accounts for some features of the structure of the poem we have, but also because that structure is so common to the line of neoclassical landscape meditations in which it can be placed. But to see the poem this way does not adequately account for the poet's specifically insistent effort to locate himself precisely in space ("Near yonder copse," "Beside yon straggling fence," "yon widowed, solitary thing") and in time ("But now the sounds of population fail," "As pondering here I stand"). This effort creates so strongly "the sense of lyric presence at the site of the depopulated village" to which Rader himself is so sensitive. To see the poem's development then as a series of formal choices negotiating between the claims of didactic generality and personal feeling is to assume a compositional manner whose traces are certainly obvious in the poem, but which is not adequate to a mimetic representation of the "sense of lyric presence at the site" the poem so powerfully communicates. Thus Rader explains the concluding identification of Poetry itself with the exiled villagers as that stratagem by which Goldsmith finally links his poem's personal charge with its universalizing, didactic intent. He similarly explains the long meditation on the urban poor as a generalization of Auburn's specific plight, strategically necessary to maintain the poem's continuing series of adjustments between its public and personal, its didactic and lyric, movements.

My reading of the poem does not proceed from a radical disagreement with such a definition of the poem's formal strategies, but rather from my sense of what authenticates them. The meditation on the urban poor, the identification of Poetry with Auburn's exiles—these crucial moments grow from and express the most powerful and distinctive experience the poet undergoes: this is the internalization of his didactic purpose. The poem's composition was not simply a matter of introducing and appropriately positioning passages of alternately personal and general utterance. More than this, the poem records the poet's *developing awareness* of the deeply personal implications for him of the general situation, and the growth of this awareness is a function of the poet's active, imaginative engagement in the landscape he represents himself as inhabiting. The village folk become the enabling agents of the poet's developing awareness, and the poem's lyric charge is fully realized in his representation of the change in his own understanding of them, his own apprehension of their actuality as beings capable of consciousness and suffering. The passage on the urban poor is not then simply a strategic generalization of Auburn's specific plight. It is that, but its special cast alters the poem's perspective on the general subject by attributing to the poor themselves the power of sight and judgment sufficient to apprehend it. Similarly, the assertion that the exile of Auburn's people is the exile of Poetry is not only the strongest statement the poet gives us of the full significance of his lesson on political economy; it is also a sign of the heightened work of his imagination, which, kindled by his sight and his memory as he stands in the ruined landscape, has transformed the villagers from reduced, idyllic figures into enlarged, fully conscious, suffering beings, not in any significant terms different from the poet himself. If the personal feeling energizing the poem is universalized at its conclusion, this is possible because the poet has discovered in the suffering poor an image adequate to that personal feeling; he has seen himself in them, them in himself.

This recognition was not possible for him at the poem's beginning, and for this reason we must read the poem as the record of the poet's inner growth as he fully takes in the import of his experience, pondering the landscape he physically stands in. He internalizes that landscape, and with it the didactic purpose he had brought to it. Significantly, the poem stands as a representation, or an imitation, of a poet's experience in a landscape. Its compositional manner, to be sure, is not entirely consistent with that situation, and his poem's inconsistency reflects the change in the poet's understanding of his task, his authority, his bond with his audience, and his relation to his material, all of which he works out in his poem itself, as he makes it increasingly responsive to his presence in the landscape and the inner moment created by that presence. Once again, there is a question about how far the poet gets. For Williams, Goldsmith stops with "the social history of the poet." Consistent with this view, Rader's analysis of the poem's formal strategy assumes an authoritative speaker, aware of his responsibilities in decorum, skillfully coordinating his personal and public utterance, his poem the moving and finely tooled artifact we might expect from an Augustan craftsman, conscious above all of the social distinctions separating him from the simple people about whom he writes.

But if we are to follow Goldsmith's path in his great poem and adequately judge how far he gets, we shall have to look ahead to the lyric achievement of the next literary generation. As M. H. Abrams did some time ago, we may now trace the genealogy of the "greater romantic lyric" back to Sir John Denham and notice that what distinguishes romantic practice from its neoclassical predecessors also begins to distinguish Goldsmith's poem from that literary line. Abrams describes eighteenth-century local descriptive poetry in the line of *Cooper's Hill* as moralized landscapes, whose central device is to "[couple] sensuous phenomena with moral statements."[17] Abrams understands the romantic lyric to develop from this type by a special intensification of the "coupling" so that the poet, standing in the landscape, does not simply "read" it by associating particular sententiae with particular sensuous details. Instead, he "takes in" the landscape, colors and transforms it in his imagination in an act of "perception which unites the mind to its physical environment." Not reading "Nature's book" but, in fact, writing it, the romantic poet achieves that coalescence of subject and object which is the expression of his poetic power and of his success in overcoming "the separation of mind from nature." In this process Abrams sees the "out-in-out" pattern of the romantic poet's meditation in a landscape:

> The speaker begins with a description of the landscape; an aspect or change of aspect in the landscape evokes a varied but integral process of memory, thought, anticipation, and feeling which remains closely intervolved with the outer scene. In the course of this meditation the lyric speaker achieves an insight, faces up to a tragic loss, comes to a moral decision, or resolves an emotional problem. Often the poem rounds upon itself to end where it began, at the outer scene, but with an altered mood and deepened understanding which is the result of the intervening meditation.[18]

How well *The Deserted Village* accords with this description of romantic procedure is striking, all the more so if we consider Goldsmith's procedure in *The Traveller*. That earlier poem is a series of moralized landscapes: the poet "sees" the topography and then "reads" the character of France, Switzerland, Italy, and England. Two examples should be sufficient. Here is England:

> Where lawns extend that scorn Arcadian pride,
> And brighter streams than fam'd Hydaspis glide.
> There all around the gentlest breezes stray,
> There gentle music melts on every spray;
> Creation's mildest charms are there combin'd.
> Extremes are only in the master's mind!
> [319–324]

Then Switzerland:

> My soul turn from them [Italy], turn we to survey
> Where rougher climes a nobler race display,
> Where the bleak Swiss their stormy mansions tread,
> And force a churlish soil for scanty bread . . .
> Though poor the peasant's hut, his feasts though small,
> He sees his little lot the lot of all . . .
>   Thus every good his native wilds impart,
> Imprints the patriot passion on his heart . . .
> [165–168, 177–178, 199–200]

The movement from the description to the moral here does not depend upon the poet's physical presence in the landscape, and the poet in fact does not insist upon it. As the scene shifts from country to country, it is perfectly clear that a mental stimulus independent of the physical prospect is the agent of new insights: "My soul turn from them, turn we to survey . . ."; ". . . my genius spreads her wing, / And flies where Britain courts the western Spring." But in *The Deserted Village* the poet's mind interacts with the specific locale he stands in, so precisely indicated throughout by the adverbs of place and time which announce the physical immediacy of such objects as the hawthorn bush, the thorn, the fence, and, of course, the solitary widow. In going "out" to these actual phenomena in the landscape, his mind is enabled to draw them "in," to assimilate them to the lyric feelings he has begun to know, and to move "out" again in the imaginative sight that peoples the landscape with the visions that conclude the poem. We must recognize these visions as the mind's yield from its engagement with the physical actuality of the landscape; the poem's mimetic character as the record of a man's physical presence in a landscape is integral with its visionary conclusion.

What then was the innovation that permitted the romantic poet to coordinate better his lyric and didactic intentions, that is, to coordinate his imitation of an actual meditative experience in a landscape with his desire to speak with authority grounded in that experience? I am thinking here of Wordsworth mainly, whose long meditative lyrics resemble Goldsmith's poem at least in their blend of lyricism and didacticism. Briefly, what Wordsworth did was to put his human subjects, such rustic figures as Michael and Margaret, into a central position in that part of the poem devoted to their story. This means that part of the poem, at least, had to be opened up to include dialogue, that is, to record the speech of these figures themselves. Goldsmith does not do this: it is always his voice we hear, even when he alters the poem's perspective so that he is seeing what the poor see. But Wordsworth's practice required yet another formal innovation: Abrams characterizes the language of the greater romantic lyric as "a blank verse which at its best captures remarkably the qualities of the intimate speaking voice, yet remains capable of adapting without strain to the varying levels of the subject matter and feeling."[19] Pope's couplet verse can be similarly described, but Pope pitched his verse in a social scale permitting him a great deal of range in its upper register. The poor do not speak for themselves in his poems. Goldsmith, however, includes social perspectives in his poem which call for a widened expressive range, not yet available to him. When a poet, late in the eighteenth century, did try to reflect a wider social spectrum in his language, as Burns did, he tended to represent the speech of the poor realistically, in dialect contrasting sharply with the literary usage that represented his own voice. But Wordsworth devised a language not distinguishing between his own narration and the dialogue of his rustics, so that between his own speech and his subject's story there were no discordances. Wordsworth's language answers perfectly to his insistence that the sources of his poetic power are in those experiences shared by all "natural hearts."

In Goldsmith's poem we can sense the need for such a language; lacking it, his effort to identify himself and Poetry with the poor who are his subjects does not entirely overcome the limits of a language better suited to represent the poet as one whose special authority for speech tends to distinguish him socially and intellectually from those he seeks to merge with sympathetically. This judgment holds, despite Goldsmith's considerable mimetic success in representing his psychological integration with his actual physical presence in the landscape of the poem, the ruined landscape of the poor.

In evaluating Goldsmith's achievement, then, we must be alert to this decorous awkwardness. It certainly has not been my purpose to award him credits for his approach to romantic procedure and demerits for his neoclassical practice. But we need to see that this profoundly moving poem is very much a poem in process: it records the poet's own discovery of his lyric capacity. As his lyric intention becomes increasingly compelling, the formal character of his task changes, and the awkwardness we can perceive in his procedure reflects the inconsistent impulses behind his expressive effort. *The Deserted Village* ultimately becomes an imitation of a mind's integration with a specific place and time; it begins, however, as the authoritative didactic utterance of an intelligence composing its material at some distance from these. That Goldsmith had to call on Johnson to complete his didactic task is a signal that, by the time he had envisioned the departure of the villagers, his own real work was done.

The label "preromantic" is not new for *The Deserted Village*, and I take some comfort in finding an earlier and familiar judgment useful to my job of explication and evaluation; my effort here may perhaps contribute some precision to it.[20] Goldsmith's poem is preromantic in the sense that it realizes lyric intentions in a way not entirely compatible tonally and structurally with its didactic ones. In doing so, it registers two differing conceptions of a poet's identity, his relation to his material and to his audience. In this mix of intention and discovery we may find the formal discordances that occasionally stand as evidence of an emotional integrity to which a poet's art must make some sacrifice. The continuing acceptance and the evocative power of *The Deserted Village* stand as a proof that such a sacrifice is essential to the power of art, and to its development in time. Goldsmith's poem is not a romantic lyric, but it clarified and freed the impulses that called that new form into existence. It also may be said to stand as evidence for Ralph Rader's definition of the process of art itself, that "primary manifestation of the characteristic freedom of the human spirit, its capacity to invent and develop *in* time forms of imaginative self-discovery and expression which in their aesthetic autonomy are a chief vehicle of its triumph *over* time."[21]

Appendix I

William Shakespeare, *Cymbeline*, IV.ii.215–281

Gui.   Why, he but sleeps!
If he be gone, he'll make his grave a bed.   216
With female fairies will his tomb be haunted,
And worms will not come to thee.
    Arv.   With fairest flowers
Whilst summer lasts and I live here, Fidele,
I'll sweeten thy sad grave. Thou shalt not lack   220
The flower that's like thy face, pale primrose, nor
The azur'd harebell, like thy veins; no, nor
The leaf of eglantine, whom not to slander,
Outsweet'ned not thy breath. The raddock would,
With charitable bill (O bill, sore shaming   225
Those rich-left heirs that let their fathers lie
Without a monument!), bring thee all this,
Yea, and furr'd moss besides. When flow'rs are none,
To winter-ground thy corse—
    Gui.   Prithee have done,
And do not play in wench-like words with that   230
Which is so serious. Let us bury him,
And not protract with admiration what
Is now due debt. To th' grave!
    Arv.   Say, where shall 's lay him?
    Gui. By good Euriphile, our mother.
    Arv.   Be't so;
And let us, Polydore, though now our voices   235
Have got the mannish crack, sing him to th' ground,

As once to our mother; use like note and words,
Save that Euriphile must be Fidele.
    Gui. Cadwal,
I cannot sing. I'll weep, and word it with thee;   240
For notes of sorrow out of tune are worse
Than priests and fanes that lie.
    Arv.   We'll speak it then.
    Bel.   Great griefs, I see, med'cine the less; for Cloten
Is quite forgot. He was a queen's son, boys,
And though he came our enemy, remember   245
He was paid for that. Though mean and mighty, rotting
Together, have one dust, yet reverence
(That angel of the world) doth make distinction
Of place 'tween high and low. Our foe was princely,
And though you took his life, as being our foe,   250
Yet bury him as a prince.
    Gui.   Pray you fetch him hither.
Thersites' body is as good as Ajax',
When neither are alive.
    Arv.   If you'll go fetch him,
We'll say our song the whilst. Brother, begin.
                                    [*Exit Belarius.*]
    Gui. Nay, Cadwal, we must lay his head to th' east, 255
My father hath a reason for't.
    Arv.   'Tis true.
    Gui. Come on then, and remove him.
    Arv.   So. Begin.

                    SONG
    Gui. Fear no more the heat o' th' sun,
         Nor the furious winter's rages,
         Thou thy worldly task hast done,   260
         Home art gone, and ta'en thy wages.
         Golden lads and girls all must,
         As chimney-sweepers, come to dust.

    Arv. Fear no more the frown o' th' great,
         Thou art past the tyrant's stroke;   265

          Care no more to clothe and eat,
          To thee the reed is as the oak.
          The sceptre, learning, physic, must
          All follow this and come to dust.

Gui. Fear no more the lightning-flash.   270
Arv. Nor th' all-dreaded thunder-stone.
Gui. Fear not slander, censure rash.
Arv. Thou hast finish'd joy and moan.
Both. All lovers young, all lovers must
          Consign to thee and come to dust.   275

Gui. No exorciser harm thee.
Arv. Nor no witchcraft charm thee.
Gui. Ghost unlaid forbear thee.
Arv. Nothing ill come near thee.
Both. Quiet consummation have,   280
          And renowned be thy grave.

Reprinted from *The Riverside Shakespeare*, ed. G. B. Evans (Boston: Houghton Mifflin, 1974).

Appendix II

A Song from Shakespear's Cymbelyne
Sung by Guiderus and Arviragus over Fidele, suppos'd to be Dead

I
To fair FIDELE's grassy Tomb
   Soft Maids, and Village Hinds shall bring
Each op'ning Sweet, of earliest Bloom,
   And rifle all the breathing Spring.

II
No wailing Ghost shall dare appear   5
   To vex with Shrieks this quiet Grove:
But Shepherd Lads assemble here,
   And melting Virgins own their Love.

III
No wither'd Witch shall here by seen,
   No Goblins lead their nightly Crew: 10
The Female Fays shall haunt the Green,
   And dress thy Grave with pearly Dew!

IV
The Redbreast oft at Ev'ning Hours
   Shall kindly lend his little Aid:
With hoary Moss, and gather'd Flow'rs,   15
   To deck the Ground where thou art laid.

V
When howling Winds, and beating Rain,
    In Tempests shake the sylvan Cell:
Or midst the Chace on ev'ry Plain,
    The tender Thought on thee shall dwell.   20

VI
Each lonely Scene shall thee restore,
    For thee the Tear be duly shed:
Belov'd, till Life could charm no more;
    And mourn'd, till Pity's self be dead.

Reprinted from *Thomas Gray and William Collins: Poetical Works*, ed. Roger Lonsdale (Oxford, London, New York: Oxford Univ. Press, 1977), pp. 132–133.

Notes

The following abbreviations have been used in the notes:

ECS *Eighteenth-Century Studies*
EIC *Essays in Criticism*
ELH *English Literary History*
HLQ *Huntington Library Quarterly*
YR   *Yale Review*

Introduction: Eloquence and Inwardness in Augustan Writing

1. John Stuart Mill, "Thoughts on Poetry and Its Varieties," *Collected Works of John Stuart Mill*, ed. John M. Robson and Jack Stillinger, 25 vols. to date (Toronto and London: Univ. of Toronto Press and Routledge, Kegan and Paul, 1981), 1:363.
2. As these remarks indicate, M. H. Abrams's account of neoclassical and Romantic critical theories (especially his highlighting of Mill's presentation of the "expressive" position) has been of continuing usefulness to me; see *The Mirror and the Lamp* (New York: Norton, 1958), esp. pp. 21–26, 84–88, 103–114.
3. I ask these questions in the same spirit that S. L. Goldberg, writing about some manifestly romantic features of Pope's mind and art, comments: "To say all this, however, is not to claim that Pope was 'really' a Romantic, nor merely to repeat (what everyone knows) that 'Augustan' and 'Romantic' are very slippery terms. But it does suggest that the English Romantics differed from Pope less in *exhibiting* these characteristics, than in being philosophically conscious of them and of their fundamental importance, and so taking them as a conscious *program* for poetry." See his "Integrity and Life in Pope's Poetry" in *Studies in the Literature of the Eighteenth Century*, 2, ed. R. F. Brissenden (Canberra: Australia National Univ. Presses, 1973). My reference is to the reprint of this piece in *Pope: Recent*

Essays by Several Hands, ed. Maynard Mack and James A. Winn (Hamden, Conn.: Archon, 1980, p. 41.)
4. Anne Williams in her important book, *Prophetic Strain* (Chicago: Univ. of Chicago Press, 1984), has sought to open up discussion of lyric impulse and lyric form in eighteenth-century poetry. Williams too is especially interested in poems not ostensibly lyric, but with strong lyric presence nonetheless, and she is willing to say that the most interesting of these in the eighteenth century, whether epistles or satires or elegies, are really all versions of what she calls the "greater lyric"—in period discussion usually called the "greater ode." In the poems she chooses for discussion, Williams emphasizes as a sign of their lyric character their presentation of a central consciousness, generally emerging as a prophetic voice, as it shapes and is shaped by its engagement with the "abiding issues about man, nature, and human life which have always occupied serious poets in their most ambitious work" (p. 2). A limitation of this valuable book, perhaps, is that in its emphasis on the prophetic voice of Augustan lyricism it misses the essentially social origins and commitments of that expression, and consequently the powerfully autobiographical cast, whether feigned or "actual," of its representations of inwardness. Lyricism for Williams is essentially a sign of consciousness coming to itself by transcending the social. In the poems I explore, the process usually involves a continuing negotiation between the inward and the social.

Donald Davie's succinct discussion of Augustan lyricism in his introduction to his collection of poems of that title has been very useful to me. Davie's interest, however, is not in the lyric of inwardness, but in the quite different "public" lyric, which in its various forms—the patriotic song, the hymn, the ballad—stood in essential contrast to the period's satire, and had its sources in attitudes toward public and religious experience more positive than those which gave rise to satire. Moreover, Davie focuses on the lyric that is "composed either to match an existing piece of music, or in the expectation and hope of a musical setting being contrived for it." See *The Augustan Lyric* (London: Heinemann, 1974), esp. pp. 2–6.
5. See Davie, pp. 7–8: "It is Horace above all who matters; the Horace of the *carmina*. For the pre-Augustan Catullus, the eighteenth century as a whole had less liking than the seventeenth century before it or the nineteenth century after. . . . It is the Horace of the *carmina* who stands for most of the eighteenth century as the type of the lyric poet." Davie emphasizes that aspect of Horace which Prior takes over and gives expression to in "A Better Answer to Cloe Jealous," for instance, that is, the "urbanity . . . which is neither more nor less than tact and sympathy and

sureness in the handling of human relations within the decorous proprieties insisted on by a civilized society. . . . The more trivial the overt occasions [of these poems], the more the lesson goes home, for what is involved is precisely *nuance,* a nicety of human attention for which no occasion . . . is too trivial to be worth taking care about."

6. A point regularly made in Horace studies is that the autobiographical actuality of Horace's representations of his own personal experience is a difficult matter for his reader to be confident about. Horace is a poet of extraordinary elusiveness, yet one who nevertheless *seems* so often *to sound* as though *he might be* telling about *himself* (whatever *himself* might be taken to mean). Gordon Williams has explored this matter and has commented on the "immediacy that approximates to autobiography" to be found in some places in the *Satires,* and also on the markedly enhanced opportunities for self-presentation which Horace's originality in the verse epistle provided him. Entirely original to Horace's epistle was its accommodation to "any and every mood, any tone, and, being completely dependent upon the personality of the poet in relation to the particular addressee, it offered a form which was infinitely sensitive and responsive to autobiographical expression." But commenting in another place on Horace's self-representation in the love poetry, Williams writes: "There is much that is left unsaid in Horace's love-poetry. It is never sheer self-expression; always the poet's personality is away out of reach. . . . There is point and balance and objectivity of statement, delight in contrasts and contradictions, mockery, often self-mockery, never self-revelation or confession without an ulterior motive." See *Tradition and Originality in Roman Poetry* (Oxford: Clarendon, 1968), pp. 438, 565.

7. *Q. Horatii Flacci: Carminum Libri IV, Epodon Liber,* ed. T. E. Page (London: St. Martin's, 1977), pp. 23–24. The translation, with some changes of my own, is by C. E. Bennett, *Horace: Odes and Epodes* (Cambridge, Mass., and London: Harvard Univ. Press and Heinemann [Loeb Classical Library], 1978), p. 69.

8. On the separation between Virgil and Horace in this ode, see Steele Commager, *The Odes of Horace: A Critical Study* (New Haven and London: Yale Univ. Press, 1962), pp. 287–290. Commager goes too far, I think, in saying that Horace's "cry of grief yields, by the poem's end, to an assertion of the order that grief defies." But Commager is certainly right to state that "Neither is absolute. Only the powerful balance is final: *frustra . . . heu.*"

9. John Traugott's comment is pertinent here: "As sentimentalism is a cultural attitude, neither a philosophy nor a disease, it is futile to seek a definition that is more precise than such text-book cliches as 'delicacy of feeling and perception,' 'benevolism,' 'tender, romantic, or nostalgic feel-

ing'; together with their pejorative analogues, 'preciousness,' 'bathos,' 'self-indulgent emotivity.' When we have repeated the cliches we have little more to say" ("Heart and Mask and Genre in Sentimental Comedy," *Eighteenth-Century Life*, 10, n.s. 3 [1986]: 140).

10. Gray's solemn and agile masking of his inner life all the while he presents it as his central subject still seems a phenomenon cognate with the heartier playfulness of sentimental comedy. Here the triumphant fantasy is that the pure-hearted and transparent sincerity preferred by the sentimentalist, and the masking preferred by the worldly, can find an accord. Traugott writes: "In sentimental comedy, worldliness and sentiment, though opposites, seem to feed on one another. If the world is composed of nothing but masks the pretended desire of sentiment to penetrate the mask and spy out the naked heart is just another mask. The age did not choose between worldliness and sentiment; it chose both as paradoxical necessities. They could live together in the fantasy of triumph of the best comedy" (p. 143). On Gray's articulation of all that he needs to say about himself at the same time that he hides almost everything, see Bertrand Bronson, "On a Special Decorum in Gray's 'Elegy'" in *Facets of the Enlightenment* (Berkeley and Los Angeles: Univ. of California Press, 1968), pp. 157–158.

11. Please see Appendix I for the scene from *Cymbeline*, Appendix II for A *Song from Cymbelyne* by William Collins.

12. Note how the word "renowned" in the following citation suggests the possibility of something *public*, something known and noted emerging from all the silence and peace ordained by the prayer-like wishes, each of which describes not an event but the absence of one.

13. "Even the striking depiction of the Furies as 'that rav'ning Brood of Fate / Who lap the Blood of Sorrow' is interrupted by an asterisk . . . which refers the reader to a scholarly note on the *Electra*. The passage in short announces its politeness in ways that seem designed to prevent the reader from confusing Collins' artificial vision with the naive enthusiasm of its Cibberian equivalent" (satirized by Pope in *Dunciad* III.235–252). See Steven Knapp, *Personification and the Sublime: Milton to Coleridge*, (Cambridge, Mass., and London: Harvard Univ. Press, 1985), p. 94.

14. "Gray thought his language more poetical as it was more re\ ote from common use: finding in Dryden *honey redolent of Spring*, an expression that reaches the utmost limits of our language, Gray drove it a little more beyond common apprehension, by making *gales* to be *redolent of joy and youth*" (*Lives of the Poets*, ed. G. B. Hill, 3 vols. [Oxford: Clarendon, 1905], 3:435.)

15. See M. H. Abrams, "Structure and Style in the Greater Romantic Lyric," in *From Sensibility to Romanticism*, ed. F. W. Hilles and H. Bloom

(London, Oxford, New York: Oxford Univ. Press [Galaxy Books], 1965), p. 539: In the Eton College ode "Gray deliberately rendered both his observation and reflections in the hieratic style of a formal odic *oratio*. The poet's recollection of times past . . . is managed through an invocation to Father Thames . . . and the language throughout is heightened and stylized by the apostrophe, exclamation, rhetorical question and studied periphrasis. . . . Both reminiscence and reflection are depersonalized, and occur mainly as general propositions which are sometimes expressed as *sententiae* . . . and at other times as propositions . . . converted into the tableau and allegory form . . ."

1: Pope and Augustan Lyricism

1. At least since Maynard Mack's seminal "The Muse of Satire," (YR, 42 [1951]: 80–92) Pope's readers have been aware of that element in the poems that is most obvious as "performance." Mack's emphasis was on the rhetorical presentation of a fictive speaker taking on a set of roles, all in the name of winning the approval of the reader. Whether the reader chose to call that fictive speaker "Pope" or not was to Mack a matter of indifference. But not all of Pope's readers have been comfortable setting aside their sense of the presence of a "real" Pope. S. L. Goldberg some time ago assented to Mack's assertion that Pope "always reveals himself as a character in a drama, not as a man confiding in us" (Mack, p. 88), but for Goldberg Pope's dramatic performance was the very vehicle of self-discovery and self-scrutiny. "It is Pope the 'dramatist' that matters, and the relevant kind of impersonality to seek in his work is that manifested in the greatest dramatic 'masterpieces'—an integrity and plenitude of dramatic *and* personal realisation" ("Integrity and Life in Pope's Poetry" in *Pope: Recent Essays by Several Hands*, ed. Maynard Mack and James A. Winn (Hamden, Conn.: Archon, 1980), p. 19, reprinted from *Studies in the Literature of the Eighteenth Century*, 2, ed. R. F. Brissenden (Canberra: Australian National Univ. Presses, 1973). My chapter can be taken as an endorsement of Goldberg's understanding of Pope's rhetorical and dramatic performance.

Much work on Pope in the past few years has emphasized the autobiographical intention in the poetry, and its concurrent representation of deeply inward states of mind. See especially Howard Erskine-Hill's chapters on Pope's Horatian poems in *The Augustan Idea in English Literature* (London: Arnold, 1983) and Frank Stack's *Pope and Horace: Studies in Imitation* (Cambridge: Cambridge Univ. Press, 1985). Stack calls attention to Shaftsbury's view of Horace as a poet of inwardness and demonstrates the complexity Pope's imitations took on as they responded fully to the opportunity Horace's models provided for self-scrutiny and self-exploration. See esp. pp. 16–17, and chap 7, passim, where Stack's fine reading of Pope's imitation of *Epistle II. ii.* presents Pope's poem "as a profound discovery of the inner self" (p. 18). See also F. V. Bogel, *Acts of Knowledge: Pope's Later Poems* (Lewisburg, Pa.: Bucknell Univ. Press, 1981), chap. 3 passim.

2. All references to Pope's poems are to *The Twickenham Edition of the Poems of Alexander Pope*, ed. John Butt et al., 11 vols. (London: Methuen, 1939–1969).

3. Compare lines 35–36: "To laugh were want of Goodness and of Grace, / And to be grave, exceeds all Pow'r of Face." Here too Pope understands reading and judging as essentially social acts continuous with private impulses. Once again, the inwardness of the impulse to laugh is registered as a social judgment. In the name of politeness the good critic restrains the impulse, with the result that he "sits in *sad* [my emphasis] civility"—in some sense untrue to himself—but free of the "weeping" that marks his stronger response to Atticus. The distinction between sad civility and weeping is a sign of the distinction between the comic failure of the bad writer, and the moral failure of the good one.

4. Geoffrey Tillotson some time ago commented on the absence of "organic unity" in Pope's poetry and emphasized rather the special richness of its "horizontal continuity of . . . argument"; its segments joined by the artistry of Pope's transitions, the argument works to create an affective as well as logical line, "as if the preceding emotions have ended by pressing a switch and so have brought new forces into play" (*On the Poetry of Pope*, 2d ed. (Oxford: Clarendon, 1950), pp. 55, 52). See pp. 43–55 passim. And of Pope's transitions in *An Epistle to Dr. Arbuthnot*, Frederick Keener has remarked that "useful as it is to distinguish the voices Pope employs, the meat of his art is in the transitions between them" (*An Essay on Pope* [New York: Columbia Univ. Press, 1974], p. 84). Tillotson's sense of the construction of Pope's poems accords nicely with Stack's description of the special achievement of the Horatian imitations. Referring specifically to *Epistle II. ii.*, Stack writes that its distinction is "the openness of [its] response to the Horatian text. [Pope's] involvement with each of Horace's themes is intense, and yet his own movement from one 'subject' to another is fluid. . . . His poetry rises to rhetoric and falls to conversation, sharpens in irritation, and becomes still in the resonances of meditation. As such it represents an impressive internalization of both the themes and the form of one of Horace's most challenging epistles. . . . Together [the Horatian original and Pope's imitation] suggest that the art

of poetry is never to rest in one position, never to close on its subject" (p. 149). See also Erskine-Hill, p. 313, on Pope's emotional shaping of his epistles.
5. Erskine-Hill discusses the emotional range of the *Epistle to Arbuthnot* in *The Augustan Idea in English Literature*, p. 314.
6. Of the surprising swings of mood and tone in this poem, Bogel has written: "In the early part of the poem especially, as in one or two of Pope's other epistles, there is a more than Horatian abruptness about the transitions. This abruptness, a kind of reflective hiatus between paragraphs, is often found in poetry of an intense inwardness, which subordinates temporal structure to the reflective 'now' of the speaker's consciousness" (p. 119). On this particular moment in Pope's *Epistle II. ii*, Erskine-Hill has written that "Pope's expansion of Horace's famous passage is more than poignant . . . [in lines 78–79] above all we feel the steady, prolonged enjambed rhythm: eight uninterrupted iambic beats, brought up short, almost at the end of the couplet, by the emphatic deferred pause, and the lonely contrast of the final three words. What is there which can fill that sudden silence? [But then with] 'But after all what wou'd you have me do?' (1.80) Pope relaxes his manner, and leads us from that unnerving silence almost thankfully back into the world of folly" (p. 320). See also Stack, p. 126: in this passage "in place of Horace's *brevitas* we have a short but powerful elegy on time, loss, and the self . . . These famous lines are not in themselves 'Horatian'—the pathos is held a little too long for that—but they suggest a profoundly Horatian awareness of the inner self."
7. G. K. Hunter, "The Romanticism of Pope's Horace," in *Essential Articles: Alexander Pope*, ed. Maynard Mack (Hamden, Conn.: Archon, 1968), p. 592, reprinted from *EIC*, 10 (1960): 390–414. See also n. 1 above. This view has been most aggressively put forth by Howard Weinbrot in his reading of Pope's imitation of *Epistle II. i* (To Augustus). In asserting his sense of the sharp distinctions between Pope and Horace as political satirists, Weinbrot, however, fails to account for those qualities of sensibility they obviously share. See *Augustus Caesar in "Augustan" England: The Decline of a Classical Norm* (Princeton: Princeton Univ. Press, 1978), pp. 182–217 passim.
8. "Pope and Horace: *The Second Epistle of the Second Book*," in *Restoration and Eighteenth-Century Literature*, ed. Carroll Camden (Chicago: Univ. of Chicago Press, 1963), pp. 319–320.
9. In Horace's poem is a strong sense that these questions are directed with some sharpness to Florus, the epistle's addressee. Pope's imitation drops such a possibility altogether: this is clearly a moment of self-absorption. See Stack, p. 145–146.

10. Erskine-Hill is right to say that "despite the human range of the poem, its gravity, sadness and acknowledgment of suffering, Pope at last brings it firmly back into the world of fools" with this satirically colored ending. But he goes on to say that in the concluding representation of that world of fools "the deprivations dealt with by the poem . . . assume their least daunting form. This challenge can be met on the level of social deportment, and no more need be said" (p. 324). This assertion misses the intensity of Pope's self-assertion here, the sense he establishes of his lonely authority to dismiss that world of fools. It is not social deportment Pope emphasizes here, but something closer to heroism.

11. Stack has very well said about Pope's "renunciation" of poetry in *Epistle II. ii.* that "if the art of poetry must give way to the art of life, it must not do so before it has illumined as nothing else can what that greater art might be" (p. 135). Bogel, also writing on the portrayal in *Epistle II. ii.* of Pope's self-discovery and its connection with his commitment to poetry, comments that it "is a mark of Pope's increased awareness that poetry, which was earlier described as an 'unweary'd Mill,' is no longer an isolable talent but at one with the liberated self. More important, it is at one with the moral self. The quest for self-knowledge is nothing more or less than a quest for that 'God of Nature' which, once discovered and accepted, is indifferent to the particular forms through which the moral self is articulated" (p. 122). But this view underplays Pope's struggle to accommodate the aggressive energy of his imagination, realized in his career in satire, to the "moral self." It was the essence of the matter that his was the life of wit, and that he saw that life as a "warfare upon earth." The lyric and elegiac power of *Epistle II. ii.* is entirely a function of Pope's need to articulate the moral self in that particular form.

12. On self-possession as a subject of Pope's poetry in general, see Goldberg, pp. 188–189.

2: Swift as Lyricist

1. Not so Thackeray to the audience for his lecture on Swift; to those in it fortunate enough not to have read the fourth voyage "I would recall the advice of the venerable Mr. Punch to persons about to marry, and say 'Don't.'" Excerpted in *Discussions of Jonathan Swift*, ed. J. L. Traugott (Boston: Heath, 1962), p. 19, from Thackeray's lecture in *The English Humorists of the Eighteenth Century*.

2. Samuel Johnson, "Swift," *Lives of the Poets*, ed. G. B. Hill, 3 vols. (Oxford: Clarendon, 1905), 3:52.

3. Ibid., p. 62.

4. A good example of our poise and its useful results is A. E. Dyson's excellent definition of the value to us of an art as playful and as subversive in its play as Swift's: "On a final balance, I fancy that we have to compromise: agreeing that *Gulliver* ends by destroying all its supposed positives, but deducing, from the exuberance of the style and the fact that it was written at all, that Swift did not really end in Gulliver's position . . . he always . . . enjoyed the technique of irony itself, both as an intellectual game, and as a guarantee of at least some civilized reality. Very often, even at the most intense moments, we may feel that pleasure in the intellectual destructiveness of the wit is of more importance to him than the moral purpose, or the misanthropy that is its supposed *raison d'être*. Irony, by its very nature, instructs by pleasing: and to ignore the pleasure, and its civilized implications, is inevitably to oversimplify, and falsify the total effect" ("Swift: The Metamorphosis of Irony," *Essays and Studies*, n. s. 11 [1958]: 67). The escape route here, of course, is quite properly Swift's artistry, and Dyson's judgment is in accord with Irvin Ehrenpreis's characterization of Robert C. Elliott's argument in *The Power of Satire* (Princeton: Princeton Univ. Press, 1960): "the element of satire which belongs to imaginative literature is the element that invites not action but contemplation" (*Swift: The Man, His Works and the Age*, 3 vols. [London: Methuen, 1962–1983], 2 [1967]: 295). John Traugott's studies of Swift have all emphasized the increment of consciousness which Swift's irony yields, but Traugott is especially alert to the danger of Swift's games. "Irony asks to be saved from itself by an arbitrarily imposed 'stop' . . . [but] the peculiar quality of Swift's irony is that he does not impose a stop." Instead he gives us laughter. "The terminal thing for Swift is a joke to remind us that though our case is hopeless we are alive. The jokes about Gulliver's stable-pleasures put to rout all philosophical instabilities that have to do with hatred of the Yahoo and love of the Houyhnhnm. It is a characteristic end-game, a trick, a feat of aesthetic legerdemain, not a faith. We need not forget to be" ("Gulliver in the Doll's House: *Gulliver's Travels* the Children's Classic," *Yearbook of English Studies*, 14 [1984]: 148).
5. John Traugott, "Swift's Allegory: The Yahoo as Man of Mode," *Univ. of Toronto Quarterly*, 33 1 (Oct. 1963): 5.
6. "For every Whig or Tory exterminator and every modest proposer that Swift invents and exposes, there is counterbalancing evidence of a primary Swiftian feeling which is unsettlingly similar, a Kurtz-like underside . . . wishing extermination, now of 'all the brutes,' now of selected types" (C. J. Rawson, "Nature's Dance of Death: Part I: Urbanity and Strain in Fielding, Swift and Pope," *ECS*, 3 [Spring 1970]: 317).
7. The dark side of this positive fantasy was, of course, clear to Swift; he

reveals it in the questions he raises but does not bother to answer. Gulliver may be obtuse and evil when he attributes the giant king's horror at gunpowder to narrow principles and short views but, as Traugott asks, "Eschewing force, how did the King establish his rule of the Good, [and] maintain it? How is a lawyer to be kept to one interpretation of the law? Following Platonic utopias, the citizens presumably simply love the Good once they see it. But also following Platonic utopia, those who have not eyes to see are eliminated" as is demonstrated by the "chill and master-race eugenics of the Houyhnhnms or the genocide in store for the Yahoos" (pp. 147, 149).

8. *The Drapier's Letters and Other Works*, ed. Herbert Davis, The Shakespeare-head edition of Swift's *Prose Works*, 14 vols. (Oxford: Blackwell, 1939–1968), 10: 3, 4, 5, 7, 11. Subsequent references to this volume and others in this edition are cited as *Prose Works*.

9. *Prose Works*, 9:159.

10. *Prose Works*, 12:114.

11. Edward Said argued that Swift's intentionally "literary" writing was less significant to him than the work he did in service to the Tory ministry. Said speaks of Swift's purely literary writing as "indicting itself in his mind for being an appendage to reality. . . . Correct writing for Swift did not merely conform to reality. . . . It was reality . . . an event necessitated by other events. . . . The Tory policy Swift supported and wrote about was policy in the world of actuality: the Whig opposition was projection, mere scribbling. . . . After 1714, Swift occupied no place except as outsider. . . . He had become the scribbler and projector he had once impersonated and attacked" ("Swift's Tory Anarchy," *ECS*, 3/1 (Fall 1969): 48, 54, 56–57. Following Said, it seems to me that Swift's overtly didactic writing, as in the sermons and *The Drapier's Letters* would conform to his sense of what correct, ethical, and authentic expression could be.

12. Rawson comments that even the "Church of England man, an unusually sustained portrait of virtuous moderation . . . becomes at moments which are kindled by a real Swiftian intensity, a faintly unreal figure. And Swift's most powerfully realized moderates are not virtuous, but calm upholders of the world's wickedness, modestly proposing a nominal Christianity, or mass murder. Behind them stands a Swift whose more absolute moral denunciations . . . turn indistinct under strange pressures of self-implication and self-conccalment" (p. 320).

13. *Prose Works*, 2:4.

14. Ibid., pp. 27–28.

15. Northrop Frye, *Anatomy of Criticism* (Princeton: Princeton Univ. Press, 1957), pp. 226, 234.

16. Ehrenpreis's is the most comprehensive account we have of the *Argument*, discussing at length the difficult ironies of its endorsement of hypocrisy: "Swift cannot mean simply that it is absurd for men to keep the name when the thing it designates is gone; for in his scheme, nominal Christianity is parallel to the nominal communion demanded of officeholders by the Test Act; and we can be certain that the author wishes to defend the act. On the other hand, not only do we not like to suppose that he is counselling hypocrisy, but also we can hardly interpret the bitterly ironical style of the pseudo-defense, throughout the essay, as expressing anything but a ferocious derogation of *nominal* Christianity as contrasted with *real*." Ehrenpreis seeks to solve this dilemma by "looking into history," and recording that at the time of the writing of An *Argument against Abolishing Christianity* there were those "who felt indignant at the perversion of the sacrament" entailed in "occasional conformity," who "agitated for passage of the bill against occasional conformity," but who, "while they awaited this consummation, . . . felt no impulse to relax the law already in operation." In the terms of the *Argument* these were the "real Christians" to whom Swift appealed: they had no respect for nominal Christianity but they did not "see how its mere abolition 'unmitigated' by some form of coercive invigilation [could] do other than weaken the real institution" (2:282–284).

But it is not clear to me that this appeal to history for a solution to the "problem" of the *Argument* does anything but restate that problem. For there is no "solution" to be sought, no argument to be unraveled. In the satire Swift allows himself the freedom of his own deepest disdain for the institution he is committed to defending. The piece is remarkable because it can express also his contempt for (what he represents as) the debased and cowardly sophistication—the "radical chic"—of the Church's opponents. *An Argument against Abolishing Christianity* is, after all, not a problem to be solved. It is a great fiction about the shattering of a traditional culture, and its power is not in the convolutions of its argument in favor of hypocrisy, or even in the exuberance of its comic satire, but rather in its wide-ranging and freely distributed contempt both for what is destroyed as well as for the destroyers.

17. "The Yahoo's Overthrow" (1733–1734) in *The Poems of Jonathan Swift*, ed. Harold Williams, 2d ed., 3 vols. (Oxford: Clarendon, 1958), 3:814–817. Subsequent references to Swift's poems are to this edition and are cited by volume and page, where needed, and by line numbers.

18. *Prose Works*, 5:227.

19. John Irwin Fischer writes of Swift's account of Stella's care for him: "Pained by his pain she accepts her pain and turns it to good. . . . [In her minis-

tering to Swift] she catches entire that 'True Honour' which comprehends all virtues and which, amidst man's allotted pain and frailties, both gives and receives blessings" (*On Swift's Poetry* [Gainesville: Univ. of Florida Press, 1978], pp. 143–44.) But Fischer dismisses the severe didacticism of the poem's first half as both "silly" and "unfortunate" (p. 142), missing, I think, its importance within the poem's dramatic and lyric *development* of its didactic material.

20. Robert Uphaus has correctly pointed to this poem as an example of Swift's capacity for a "poetry of approval": Uphaus sees the poem as a "reaffirmation of the stability of friendship and proof of the invulnerable wholeness of a virtuous life" ("Swift's Poetry: The Making of Meaning," ECS, 5/4 (Summer 1972): 576–578.) I would not argue against this as a general judgment, but such terms as "proof" and "invulnerable" are not quite adequate to the strain with which Swift experiences and expresses his affirmations—his *need* for affirmation is more accurate—in this beautiful and trying poem.

21. Samuel Johnson, *Diaries, Prayers, and Annals*, ed. E. L. McAdam, Jr., with Donald and Mary Hyde, in the Yale edition of *The Works of Samuel Johnson* (New Haven and London: Yale Univ. Press and Oxford Univ. Press, 1958), 1:383–384 (12 Aug. 1784).

3: Teaching and Pleasing: Johnson's Lyric of Reason

1. Jean Hagstrum, for example, acknowledged that Johnson "has impressed many as the most crudely and directly didactic of all great critics," and then insisted that this didacticism is a lapse from Johnson's "basic position": *Samuel Johnson's Literary Criticism* (Chicago and London: Univ. of Chicago Press, Phoenix Books, 1967), p. 72. And David Tarbet, though he vindicated Johnson's capacity as a coherent thinker on aesthetics, then went on to ask why Johnson often suspended his interest in aesthetic matters when his interest in a work involved him in questions of morality and religion. Tarbet answered his own question by saying that Johnson's separation of poetry and religion, for example, "must not be given undue importance. It allowed Johnson to concentrate on aesthetic questions without confusing them with *sub voce* objections to the manners or beliefs of the poet he was judging" ("Lockean Intuition and Johnson's Characterization of Aesthetic Response," ECS, 5/1 [Fall 1971]: 76, 78). This is sometimes true, of course, but it often is not, and in emphasizing the point we are forgiving Johnson for an attitude he would not have thought required forgiveness: his sense that aesthetic matters could not be very importantly discussed if they were dissociated from moral ones. Leopold

Damrosch has remarked that we are getting a smaller yield from our efforts to sidestep Johnson's didacticism, though Damrosch himself believes that the *Preface to Shakespeare* is a lesser achievement because of it than the best of the *Lives of the Poets*. See *The Uses of Johnson's Criticism* (Charlottesville: Univ. of Virginia Press, 1976), p. 2, and chap. 5 passim.
2. *Johnson on Shakespeare*, ed. Arthur Sherbo, in the Yale edition of *The Works of Samuel Johnson* (New Haven and London: Yale Univ. Press, 1968), 8: 704. Further references to Johnson's works unless otherwise noted are to the Yale edition and are cited as *Works*.
3. R. D. Stock comments on Johnson's discussions of poetic justice in *King Lear*: "it is true that ours is a fallen world, and we cannot fairly deny the artist his right to copy it. But . . . we are reasonable and moral beings; our sense of justice is superior to the real justice which prevails in the world, but is not this sense, too, a part of our experience, and fittingly to be imitated by the poet?" (*Samuel Johnson and Neoclassical Dramatic Theory* [Lincoln: Univ. of Nebraska Press, 1973], p. 122).
4. S. H. Butcher, trans., *Aristotle's Theory of Poetry and Fine Art* (New York: Dover, 1951), p. 39. The quote is from section 9 of *the Poetics*.
5. *Works*, 7:71.
6. Shakespeare's real power, for example, according to Johnson, is to be found not in particular passages, but in the progress of his fable and the tenor of his dialogue; Johnson advises against recommending him by select quotation. In Shakespeare's mingled drama, Johnson points to the "successive evolution of the design." In observing that Shakespeare's plays preserve the unity of action, Johnson notes that "his plan has commonly what Aristotle requires, a beginning, a middle and an end; one event is concatenated with another, and the conclusion follows with easy consequence." Johnson can even defend Shakespeare's introduction of an underplot in *King Lear* by arguing that "the injury done by Edmund to the simplicity of the action is abundantly recompensed by the addition of variety, and by the art with which he is made to co-operate with the chief design" (*Works*, 7: 62, 67, 75). And in the life of Milton Johnson's first comment on *Paradise Lost* declares that "with respect to design it may claim the first place . . . among the productions of the human mind." There is no need to demonstrate Johnson's alertness to matters of form and design. Rather, in what matters most to Johnson, art's obligation to instruct by pleasing, these considerations do not figure prominently and never vindicate a work Johnson sees as morally inadequate.
7. *Works*, 7:67.
8. Murray Krieger, "Reason, Nature and Literary Kinds in Johnson's Criticism of Shakespeare," *ECS*, 4 (1971): 194, 198.

9. In *Rambler* 37, *Works*, ed. W. J. Bate and Albrecht B. Strauss, 3: 204–205.
10. Irving Howe, "Reading Lionel Trilling," *Commentary*, 56 (Aug. 1973): 69.
11. Lionel Trilling, *Sincerity and Authenticity* (Cambridge, Mass.: Harvard Univ. Press, 1972), pp. 99–100.
12. On Johnson as an exemplar of authenticity of this kind, see F. V. Bogel, *Literature and Insubstantiality in Later Eighteenth-Century England*, (Princeton: Princeton Univ. Press, 1984), pp. 177–178. See also S. L. Goldberg, "Integrity and Life in Pope's Poetry," in *Studies in the Literature of the Eighteenth Century*, 2, ed. R. F. Brissenden (Canberra: Australian National Univ. Presses, 1973), reprinted in *Pope: Recent Essays by Several Hands*, ed. Maynard Mack and James Winn (Hamden, Conn.: Archon, 1980), pp. 43–45. Goldberg holds that the term "integrity" is more appropriate than Trilling's "authenticity" for denoting the strenuous self-fashioning that, as portrayed in English literary tradition, need not undo one's social being.
13. Ralph W. Rader, "Literary Form in Factual Narrative," *Essays in Eighteenth-Century Biography*, ed. Philip B. Daghlian (Bloomington and London: Univ. of Indiana Press, 1968), p. 35.
14. James Boswell, *Life of Samuel Johnson*, ed. R. W. Chapman, Oxford Standard Authors (London, New York, and Toronto: Oxford Univ. Press, 1953), p. 1296 (12 June 1784). All references to the *Life of Samuel Johnson* are to this edition, hereafter cited as *Life*. Wherever possible, I have cited Boswell's dating of incidents and anecdotes in order to facilitate reference to other editions.
15. *Life*, pp. 54, 97 (aet. 20, 29).
16. *Life*, pp. 955–959 (17 Apr. 1778).
17. Patrick O'Flaherty, "Johnson as Satirist: A New Look at *The Vanity of Human Wishes*," *ELH*, 34 (1967): 78–91; Howard Weinbrot, *The Formal Strain* (Chicago: Univ. of Chicago Press, 1969), chap. 8 passim.
18. As most of Johnson's readers have done, Patrick O'Flaherty, in the article cited above, recognized that *The Vanity of Human Wishes* is far more complex tonally than its designation as a satire would allow. Whereas most readers have sensed a source of the poem's richness in this, O'Flaherty claimed to take a new look at the poem and concluded that its tonal complexity demonstrates Johnson's unfitness for satire, hence his poem's inauthenticity (e.g., "once we as readers realize that the indignation expressed at the beginning is fake, a 'suspicion of falsity' hangs over the entire poem", p. 88). But readers who have commented most interestingly on this issue have seen in Johnson's willingness to "mix" his genres a source of his poem's power. See n. 36, below.
19. F. R. Leavis, *Revaluation* (London: Chatto and Windus, 1936), p. 117.

20. *Life*, p. 139 (aet. 40).
21. *Life*, p. 812 (the date of Boswell's letter is 22 Apr. 1775).
22. *Life*, pp. 153–154 (aet. 41).
23. *Life*, p. 242 (aet. 50).
24. *The History of Rasselas*, ed. Geoffrey Tillotson and Brian Jenkins (London, New York, and Toronto: Oxford Univ. Press, 1971), chap. 16. Hereafter cited as *Rasselas*.
25. James L. Clifford, *Young Sam Johnson* (New York: Oxford Univ. Press, A Hesperides Book, 1961), chap. 10 passim.
26. *The Satires of Juvenal*, trans. Rolfe Humphries (Bloomington: Indiana Univ. Press, 1958), p. 121.
27. *Poems*, ed. E. L. McAdam, Jr., with George Milne (*Works*, 6 (1964): 91–92, lines 1–6. Subsequent references to *The Vanity of Human Wishes* are cited by line number.
28. *The Latin Poets*, ed. R. B. Godolphin, The Modern Library (New York: Random House, 1949), p. 572 (lines 1–10).
29. Patricia M. Spacks has commented on Johnson's purpose and manner here: "Having *seen* the world in some systematic fashion, the observer is able to *say* what its nature is. Juvenal makes no distinction between seeing and saying; that Johnson does is characteristic of an age highly aware of the difficulties and importance of moral activity. The effort at articulation is a moral activity" ("From Satire to Description," YR, 58/2 [Winter 1969]: 238).
30. On the question-and-answer pattern in *The Vanity of Human Wishes* Lawrence Lipking has commented that "Johnson's questions are by no means purely rhetorical. They aim at a refinement of the questioning process itself, at a mode of inquiry where 'suspense' will be replaced by 'Petitions' [to a God] whose powers of observation are not indifferent or uninvolved" and who "sees within as well as without, into the hearts of men as well as their scene" ("*The Vision of Theodore* and *The Vanity of Human Wishes*," ELH, 43 [1976]: 532). See also Howard Weinbrot, "No 'Mock Debate': Questions and Answers in *The Vanity of Human Wishes*," *Modern Language Quarterly*, 41 (1980): 250–251, 261, 266. Weinbrot sees the reader escorted by the poem's questions through a series of mistaken ideas or improper feelings to the more edifying position Johnson prepares for him at the poem's end. This particular "reader-response" pattern, reminiscent of Stanley Fish's sense of Milton's manipulation of the reader in *Paradise Lost*, seems to me not present in Johnson's poem or characteristic of Johnson's way in general, by which he seeks to engage as intimately as possible with the reader's undeluded, inquiring, and unmanipulated consciousness.
31. Anne Williams, in her very interesting discussion of the lyricism of *The*

Vanity of Human Wishes (whose imaginative character she characterizes in her chapter title, "Satire into Lyric"), has sought to define this lyricism as an effect of what seems to her the prophetic attitude of the poem's conclusion, itself emerging from the poem's preceding representations of mankind as questing, as sick, as assailed. Williams therefore emphasizes the poem's apparent impersonality, perhaps missing its most interesting feature, and the most difficult to explain: the strange sense we have of the local immediacy and intimacy of that very authoritative and public voice of the poem's speaker. Acknowledging that the prophetic mode is displaced "into the realm of purely human experience" and expressed by "commonplace 'Augustan' language," Williams, I think, is then mistaken to characterize the poem "as prophecy . . . poised somewhere between the biblical and the Romantic versions of the poet/Prophet." See *Prophetic Strain* (Chicago: Univ. of Chicago Press, 1984), pp. 90–92. The poem is pitched at the level of heightened social speech, and though its speaker is anonymous, it is neither possible nor pleasurable to take it in without knowing that its author is Samuel Johnson. Although difficult to account for, this is a rhetorical as well as a biographical fact.

32. Ralph W. Rader, "The Concept of Genre and Eighteenth-Century Studies," *New Approaches to Eighteenth-Century Literature*, ed. Phillip Harth (New York and London: Columbia Univ. Press, 1974), pp. 101–102.

33. Leavis, p. 119.

34. This moment in the poem seems to exemplify Rachel Trickett's claim that the poem expresses "a feeling of community, of a man writing for men . . . from a recognition of their common humanity and its deeper concerns" (*The Honest Muse* [Oxford: Oxford Univ. Press, 1967], p. 246). Trickett emphasizes Johnson's ability to enlist conventional attitudes and habits of language in order to create this "feeling of community." It is hard, however, to share her sense that the poem seems not to be presented to an audience. See also J. D. Needham, "'The Vanity of Human Wishes' as Tragic Poetry," *Journal of the Australasian Universities Language and Literature Association*, 46 (1976): 217.

35. "Since power resides in the eyes of others, [Wolsey] invests his entire being in appearances, and essentially . . . he simply ceases to exist. For all his trappings of power, he is essentially a transparent man." D. V. Boyd, "Vanity and Vacuity: A Reading of Johnson's Verse Satires," *ELH*, 39 (1972): 399.

36. Patrick O'Flaherty (n. 18 above) cites Frye's judgment that satire "breaks down when its content is too oppressively real to permit the maintaining of the fantastic or hypothetical tone" (*Anatomy of Criticism* [Princeton: Princeton Univ. Press, 1957], p. 224), and recognizes, as most of John-

son's critics have, that in *The Vanity* compassion replaces anger. This leads O'Flaherty to his odd judgment that the poem is a failure because of Johnson's disinclination to proceed as a satiric poseur, disguising his compassion in order to arouse the reforming spirit in his readers. W. J. Bate has commented more interestingly on Johnson's resistance to satire: noting first Johnson's *predisposition to satire*, Bate points out that "Johnson was unable merely to observe, but had to participate and share; and . . . his own participation sets a bar to satire. The result, time and again in all of his moral writing, is that we have anger, protest, even ridicule, always in the process of turning into something else." Bate describes the movement from satire in *The Vanity of Human Wishes:* the satiric objects "all begin to stumble and weaken. Disease, misfortune, old age begin to club or push them imperceptibly into weariness, defeat, staleness, illness and finally death. In short Johnson starts to sympathize and to share. And this strange, powerful poem, this apparent satire . . . softens its mockery by dissolving it within a wider understanding" ("Johnson and Satire Manqué," *Eighteenth-Century Studies in Honor of Donald F. Hyde*, ed. W. H. Bond [New York: The Grolier Club, 1970], pp. 150, 155). See also W. J. Bate, *Samuel Johnson* (New York: Harcourt, Brace, Jovanovich, 1975), pp. 493–497. J. D. Needham attributes to an essentially tragic vision this inclination of Johnson's to deflect his attack from its ostensible targets to the world around them: "In all the stories one's attitude to the protagonist is complicated by the fact that he is the victim of the world's cruelty as well as his own folly" (p. 211). Johnson, however, seems not sufficiently distant from his own material to be able to see it as tragedy; that would be to make it over too much merely to "literature."

37. But David Boyd (n. 35 above), in response to O'Flaherty's contention that the poem lacks an object of satire, argued instead that it "lacks any objects *except* those of satire. The piercing eye finds vanity everywhere it turns, finds vanity, in fact, apparently a precondition of human existence" (p. 401). Boyd's important article overemphasized the bleakness of Johnson's vision, seeing in it only the uncompromising insistence that for humanity the choice of life is between "vanity and vacuity." I think Boyd misses the rich composition of feeling and insight that Johnson creates by insisting on something more from his reader than "the piercing eye"; the composition of rational and sympathetic sight, the author's *and* the reader's, is richer than satiric vision alone, and yields more to the eye of reason than a vision of vanity and vacuity.

38. "Johnson insists on some solution for man that makes possible the useful focusing of strong emotion; he wishes a proper object for hope and fear, for dislikes and desires. . . . Johnson's hero is not passive even in his devo-

tion . . . the state which makes prayer possible is one of vigor" (Spacks, p. 244).
39. Boyd (n. 37 above) concludes that the poem's final "appeal to faith . . . signals the bankruptcy of its initial appeal to observation" (p. 403). But in Johnson's account, prayer as an intense expression of will, fervor, and *reason* seems to unite the power of observation to the fervors of devotion, not to repudiate it. The strong emphasis on mind *and* devotion confirms the adequacy of our rational energy even in the face of the "vanity and vacuity" that are the mind's first but not final discoveries. Robert Voitle, who emphasized Johnson's orthodox insistence upon the rational basis of morality, on the other hand, had difficulty in connecting this aspect of Johnson's moral thought to what Voitle claimed was the dominating pessimism of Johnson's great poem, missing, I think, the full experience the poem provides in mitigation of its pessimistic doctrine. See Robert Voitle, *Samuel Johnson, The Moralist* (Cambridge, Mass.: Harvard Univ. Press, 1961), chap. 2 passim. John Hardy's discomfort with the poem's closing has a similar basis: it seems inadequate to the intensity of Johnson's portrayal, throughout the poem, of the sheer painfulness of experience. "Does not the assertiveness of the rhetoric [of the apparently affirmative] lines suggest something desperate about the claim being made," Hardy asks, and then goes on to answer his own question by noting the honesty of the closing lines, expressed in the play of "make" against "find": "Whatever happiness may be manufactured to soothe the sense of unhappiness, the mind realises that, apart from this, there is no happiness to be found. This is an insight true to the experience of the poem and the observations on life it contains" ("Johnson's 'Vanity of Human Wishes'" in *Studies in the Literature of Eighteenth Century*, 4, ed. R. F. Brissenden (Canberra: Australian National Univ. Presses, 1979), pp. 97–98. See also Hardy's earlier essay, "Hope and Fear in Johnson," *EIC*, 26/4 (1976): esp. 296–297. For an attempt to understand in existentialist terms the tensions between Johnson's doubts and his efforts at affirmation, see Max Byrd, "Johnson's Spiritual Anxiety," *Modern Philology* (1981), 368–378.
40. *Works*, 7:77.
41. Ian Watt, "Dr. Johnson and the Literature of Experience," *Johnsonian Studies*, ed. Magdi Wahba (Cairo, 1962), pp. 15, 19–20; reprinted from *The Listener*, Sept. 24, 1959.
42. From Book 3 of *The Republic*, excerpted in *Critical Theory since Plato*, ed. Hazard Adams (New York, Chicago, Atlanta, and San Francisco: Harcourt, Brace, Jovanovich, 1971), pp. 29–30. The translation is Benjamin Jowett's, *The Dialogues of Plato*, 4th ed. (Oxford: Clarendon, 1953).
43. *Works*, 4:9.

44. I am aware that in Freudian terms, Johnson, as I read him, confuses suppression with repression, the latter being Freud's designation of a process whose pathological force is so intense precisely because it deals with matters inaccessible to consciousness, indeed makes them so. But what I say of Johnson seems justified by what he himself says, and Johnson's special power to move us may have much to do with the freedom he attributes to us in our rational will as well as with his awareness of the pain this freedom entails.
45. *Rasselas*, chap. 46.
46. J. W. Krutch, *Samuel Johnson* (New York: Holt, 1944), pp. 314–315.
47. Jean-Paul Sartre, "Existentialist Psychoanalysis," *Existentialism and Human Emotions* (New York: The Wisdom Library, 1957), p. 82. This is a section from *Being and Nothingness*, trans. Hazel E. Barnes.
48. Compare Sartre, ibid., p. 73: reflection "is penetrated by a great light without being able to express what this light is illuminating. . . . All is there, luminous . . . [but without] the means which would ordinarily permit *analysis* and *conceptualization*." Perhaps Johnson's powerful personifications are instruments of analysis and conceptualization.
49. *Rasselas*, chap. 12.
50. "Shakespeare's plays are not in the rigorous and critical sense either tragedies or comedies, but compositions of a distinct kind; exhibiting the real state of sublunary nature, which partakes of good and evil, joy and sorrow, mingled with endless variety of proportion and innumerable modes of combination; and expressing the course of the world, in which the loss of one is the gain of another; in which, at the same time, the reveller is hasting to his wine, and the mourner burying his friend; in which the malignity of one is sometimes defeated by the frolick of another; and many mischiefs and many benefits are done and hindered without design. . . . That the mingled drama may convey all the instruction of tragedy or comedy cannot be denied, because it includes both in its alterations of exhibitions, and approaches nearer than either to the appearance of life, by shewing how great machinations and slender designs may promote or obviate one another, and the high and the low cooperate in the general system by unavoidable concatenation" (*Works*, 7:66).
51. Two studies emphasizing the action of inquiry in *Rasselas* are Harold Pagliaro, "Structural Patterns of Control in *Rasselas*," *English Writers of the Eighteenth Century*, ed. J. H. Middendorf (New York: Columbia Univ. Press, 1971), esp. p. 211; and Eric Rothstein, *Systems of Order and Inquiry in Later Eighteenth-Century Fiction* (Berkeley and Los Angeles: Univ. of California Press, 1975), pp. 23–62 passim.
52. "The poetry of Pope . . . frequently articulates a pattern of *concordia dis-*

cors but it also demonstrates the poet's struggle to maintain or recover it, and this effort is as much a part of the meaning of his poetry as the more static pattern of 'reconcil'd extremes.' . . . In contrast, the greatest writers of the latter half of the century have abandoned, or lost, or freed themselves from an understanding of paradoxical substantiality. More central than substantial paradox to the literary expression of this period are figures whose ontological import, in practice, tends in quite the opposite direction, figures like dilemma and contradiction" (F. V. Bogel, *Literature and Insubstantiality*, p. 38). See Bogel's earlier article on this subject, "Structure and Substantiality in Later Eighteenth-Century Literature," *Studies in Burke and His Time*, 15 (Winter 1973–1974): 151, 152. In this earlier version of his argument, Bogel says that Pope's rhetoric works to maintain and reconcile paradox and is thus evidence of a mind not disabled by (in R. D. Laing's parlance) "ontological insecurity." Not commanding such psychological and philosophical confidence in the structure of experience, Johnson, as Bogel put it, "fashioned a prose style that invested reductive abstractions with such weight and power as to make them reasonable substitutes" for the large and integrated philosophical or metaphysical vision he lacked.

53. *Lives of the Poets*, ed. G. B. Hill, 3 vols. (Oxford: Clarendon, 1905), 3:229.
54. *Rasselas*, chap. 28.
55. Paul McGlynn interprets Johnson's doublets as rhetorical devices that help to create an hypothetical treatise structure in his poem; they do this by acting as compressed catalogs, rather than logical discriminations, thereby giving to us the sense that the author of the feigned treatise commands an exhaustive range of moral experience and knowledge. But why see feigned catalogs in what are plain doublets? Why see a *hypothetical* treatise in what is a *real* didactic poem, a poem in which the effort to reason is not hypothetical but actually managed in the author's parallel and antithetic doublets? Why should Johnson feign an inclusive or exhaustive vision when he tells us plainly that such is not to be had? Johnson's distinction—and difficulty—as an artist is his aversion to feigning, and his real doublets are not fictional catalogs. To be sure, *The Vanity*'s initial perspective is one of great range (China to Peru), but in its progress the results of distanced inquiry into so much moral geography are assimilated to the spectacle of particular cases. The knowledge we finally get is an amalgam of wide sight and particularized response; as we come closer to each case our sympathies complicate our vision, not obscuring it, but enriching it, requiring us to revise our initial apprehension of distanced typicalities. First we *see* Wolsey from afar; at the end of his section, we are close enough to

overhear him. He becomes a man, not an instance, and we are properly prevented from responding to him as merely another case in point, as merely another example of Johnson's merely (hypothetical) command of his sententious wisdom. See Paul McGlynn, "Rhetoric as Metaphor in *The Vanity of Human Wishes*," *Studies in English Literature*, 15 (1975): 473–482.
56. *Rasselas*, chap. 29.
57. On this incident, and on dilemma generally in later eighteenth-century writing, see Bogel, *Literature and Insubstantiality*, p. 38.
58. Rothstein, p. 56: "Each privation and demonstration of worldly vanity should have been as painful or more painful than it has been; but it also should have been, not a counsel of despair or a chance for self-delusion, but a small signpost pointing toward providential eternity. This is what happens in Chapter 48, which leaves the assembly silent and collected, and then sententious."
59. Sheldon Sacks, *Fiction and the Shape of Belief* (Berkeley and Los Angeles: Univ. of California Press, 1964), pp. 49–60 passim.
60. *Rasselas*, chap. 6.
61. *Rasselas*, chap. 18. See W. J. Bate's brief discussion of this incident in "Johnson and Satire Manqué" (n. 36 above), pp. 151–152. Sheldon Sacks also has written on how Johnson's management of the incident plays against the satirical possibilities inherent in it (pp. 14–15).

4: Goldsmith's Discovery of Lyric

1. Edward Gibbon, *The History of the Decline and Fall of the Roman Empire*, ed. William Smith, 8 vols. (London: John Murray 1854), 3: 198–199.
2. All references to *The Deserted Village*, Goldsmith's preface to that poem, and to *The Traveller* are to the texts in *Collected Works of Oliver Goldsmith*, ed. Arthur Friedman (Oxford: Clarendon, 1966), vol. 4. The passage here is p. 297, lines 251–258.
3. Morris Golden in his account of Goldsmith's use of the "family wanderer" theme said of *The Deserted Village* that "here Goldsmith seems finally to give up as comfortless the yearning for the past, for security, for the placid family of childhood. He had discovered, at least sub-consciously, that you can't go home again, because home no longer exists" ("The Family-Wanderer Theme in Goldsmith," *ELH*, 25 [1958]: 188–189). Goldsmith's recognition that Auburn is gone seems quite explicit to me, very much on the level of consciousness. Golden developed these thoughts more richly in a later essay in which he touched briefly but valuably on

the literary shape (and strain) Goldsmith's inner motives imparted to his work (see below, n. 7). For a more recent and emphatically (and excessively) psychoanalytic account of the poem's preoccupation with loss, see Anne Williams, *Prophetic Strain* (Chicago: Univ. of Chicago Press, 1984), pp. 118–119, and passim. More compelling than her Freudian reading is Williams's sense of the poem's lyric structure of feeling and expression: "The speaker of *The Deserted Village* is a *penseroso* who believes himself a prophet" (p. 111). "Prophet" is not right, but Williams catches the strangeness of Goldsmith's rhetorical stiuation, declaiming within a solitude. He is no prophet, but at the poem's close, he is certainly capable of vision, as I demonstrate below.

4. Among the more important studies of the pastoral character of *The Deserted Village* are Ricardo Quintana, *Oliver Goldsmith: A Georgian Study* (New York: Macmillan, 1967), pp. 131–136; Earl Miner, "The Making of 'The Deserted Village'" *HLQ*, 22 (1959): esp. 138–141; Leo Storm, "Literary Convention in Goldsmith's 'Deserted Village'" *HLQ*, 33 (1970): 243–255, where it is argued that "What is often called pastoral in *The Deserted Village* is, in fact, georgic" (p. 246). Common to these discussions is the association they seek to establish between Goldsmith's attraction to pastoral and his conservative, Tory, Augustan cast of mind. This usually involves deemphasizing the poem's powerfully self-expressive quality and intention, as if the availability of a recognized convention or genre necessarily provided an opportunity to all poets to depersonalize all poetry, and as if, moreover, a conservative, Tory, or Augustan cast of mind would necessarily mute a writer's strong self-expressive impulses. This critical prejudice may explain the reasons for which efforts to understand Goldsmith's poem in the light of its pastoral elements have not yielded rich returns. A significant exception is Raymond Williams's very important discussion in *The Country and the City* (London: Chatto and Windus, 1973); see at n. 10. Anne Williams also has correctly insisted upon the bond joining the poem's pastoral and lyric impulses, but she has identified its pastoral impulses too simply with its overidealization of the remembered village. For her, the departure of the villagers stands for the death of the pastoral genre itself, whose idealizing habits can no longer accord with a harsh historical reality (*Prophetic Strain*, esp. pp. 121–122). But the pastoral genre and Goldsmith's use of it are more complex and rich than that, by no means incapable of engaging the human experience of loss within history.

5. Thomas G. Rosenmeyer, *The Green Cabinet: Theocritus and the European Pastoral Lyric* (Berkeley and Los Angeles: Univ. of California Press, 1969), pp. 52–53, 136–139, and chaps. 3 and 6 passim.

6. Morris Golden notes that the parson's "positive actions . . . involve children; his serious thoughts are with heaven, which one assumes is a permanent and even more idyllic Auburn; he has no work or force as an adult." The parson's presentation is thus consistent with that of Auburn: "an extinct childhood paradise, a static and innocent word [that contrasts] with every environment in which adults must act" ("The Broken Dream of *The Deserted Village*," *Literature and Psychology*, 9 [1959]: 42).
7. Golden (ibid., p. 43) points out Goldsmith's tendency to seek identification with "other objects shown in the same circumstances . . . Symbolically, [the old woman] is doing all along what Goldsmith is: supporting herself by gleaning alone in the wilderness. She is even metaphorically, as he is in fact, 'The sad historian of the pensive plain.'"
8. Though my judgment of Goldsmith's achievement differs from Williams's, I am indebted to his discussion of *The Deserted Village* for its emphasis on the play of memory, sight, and imagination within the poem. See *The Country and the City*, pp. 74–79.
9. Readers may wish to compare with mine Richard Jaarsma's exploration of the shape Goldsmith's poem takes from the impress of its author's "Augustanism." Jaarsma tends to ignore the difficulties Goldsmith's Augustanism could cause him, and to see the poem as an armory of doctrinal self-assurance, just as the studies of pastoralism cited above (n. 4) tend to see in Goldsmith's employment of pastoral a sign of literary and political toughness. See Richard Jaarsma, "Ethics in the Wasteland: Image and Structure in Goldsmith's *The Deserted Village*." *Tennessee Studies in Language and Literature*, 13 (1971): 447–459. Such notions of what it means to be an "Augustan writer" receive their definitive rebuttal in Roger Lonsdale's "A Garden and a Grave: The Poetry of Oliver Goldsmith," in *The Author in His Work: Essays on a Problem in Criticism*, ed. Louis L Martz and Aubrey Williams (New Haven: Yale Univ. Press, 1978), pp. 3–30. Lonsdale is especially responsive to the personal and lyric expressiveness of *The Deserted Village*.
10. R. Williams, p. 78.
11. Ibid., pp. 79, 78. My quote reverses the order of these sections in Williams.
12. In so defining the sources of lyric self-awareness, what Goldsmith has begun to do in poetry may be compared with the achievement of John Clare as Raymond Williams defines it: in reacting "to a country from which any acceptable social order has been removed[,] Clare goes beyond the external observation of the [eighteenth-century] poems of protest and of melancholy retrospect. What happens in him is that the loss in internal" (p. 141).
13. Cf. R. Williams, p. 70.

14. Paul J. Alpers, "The Eclogue Tradition and the Nature of Pastoral," *College English*, 34 (Dec. 1972): 335.
15. On Goldsmith's difficulty in integrating the personal and the political elements in *The Traveller*, see Lonsdale, pp. 14–19.
16. Ralph W. Rader, "The Concept of Genre and Eighteenth-Century Studies," *New Approaches to Eighteenth-Century Literature*, ed. Phillip Harth (New York and London: Columbia Univ. Press, 1974), p. 99. Rader's sensitive, brief account of the poem's formal organization is to be recommended particularly for its alertness to the personal impulses the poem's form answers to.
17. M. H. Abrams, "Structure and Style in the Greater Romantic Lyric," *From Sensibility to Romanticism*, ed. F. W. Hilles and Harold Bloom (London, Oxford, and New York: Oxford Univ. Press, 1965), p. 537.
18. Ibid., pp. 527–528.
19. Ibid., p. 531.
20. The preromanticism of *The Deserted Village* has been characterized in many ways: for Ralph Wardle the poem's "ideas were related to the Romantic primitivism which was already gaining ground. The poet's praise of rural life, his appreciation of nature, his humanitarianism, and his subjectivity all found sympathetic readers in his own time and, even more, in the generation which followed. Whether he wished to or not, Goldsmith virtually anticipated the Romantic Revival in all but his adherence to neoclassical diction" (*Oliver Goldsmith* [Lawrence: Univ. of Kansas Press, 1957], p. 204). This way of putting the case has, perhaps quite properly, aroused the responses of those who fiercely emphasize Goldsmith's "Augustanism." The issue has occasionally been addressed in stylistic terms. Morris Golden recognized the stress between Goldsmith's desire for self-revelation and his adherence to the ideal of a public literary decorum ("The Broken Dream," p. 44) and in a report of a talk by Ian Jack are these observations: "Idealised, sentimentalised, Arcadian though its picture of the past might be, the main part of *The Deserted Village* could be regarded as the only great Augustan pastoral, with a characteristic passage of satirical and didactic poetry somewhat incongruously added. It was a transitional poem, if ever there was one" (*New Rambler*, ser. C, 3 (June 1967): 4.) See also Anne Williams, p. 121: "*The Deserted Village* is as paradoxical in poetic technique as it is in theme . . . entirely Augustan in diction and versification, and also quintessentially lyrical in organization."
21. Rader, p. 115.

Index

Abrams, M. H., 182, 184, 193 n2, 196 n15
acknowledgments, in Johnson, 111, 113–115, 117
aesthetic vs. moral, in Johnson, 96, 204 n1
Alpers, Paul J., 176
anger, in Swift, 79, 81
Aristotle, 96
audience, 1–2, 21–22; in Goldsmith, 143, 180; in Gray, 20; in Johnson, 49; in Pope, 30; in Swift, 56, 69, 76–77, 83
Augustan lyricism, 1–2, 4, 23, 93, 194 n4
authenticity, 99–100; in Johnson, 101–104, 107, 129, 137, 206 n12; in Swift, 65
authority, of poet: in Goldsmith, 143, 160–162, 165, 173; in Johnson, 48–49, 119; in Pope, 27–28, 30, 33, 43, 45, 200 n10; in Swift, 62
authority, of subject, in Goldsmith, 156–157

Bate, W. J., 209 n36, 213 n61
Bogel, F. V., 199 n6, 200 n11, 206 n12, 212 n52, 213 n57
Boswell, James, *Life of Samuel Johnson*, 102–107, 109, 129

Boyd, David V., 208 n35, 209 n37, 210 n39
Bronson, Bertrand, 196 n10
Burns, Robert, *The Cotter's Saturday Night*, 21
Byrd, Max, 210 n39

celebrative style, in Swift, 74–75
character: in Johnson, 129; in Swift, 62–66; vs. personality, in Johnson, 122, 125; in Plato, 54, 127; in Swift, 56, 64, 89
Clare, John, 215 n12
Clifford, James, 111
Coleridge, Samuel Taylor, 97–98
Collins, William: *Ode to Fear*, 19, 196 n13; *A Song from Shakespear's Cymbelyne*, 11–19, 190–191
comedy: in Pope, 33; in Swift, 74
Commager, Steele, 195 n8
consciousness, function of: in Goldsmith, 147–148, 153, 156, 166, 168, 171–172; in Johnson, 126–128; in Pope, 27; in Theocritus, 176; vs. feeling, 17–20, 166, 168
"covert" lyricism, 22
criticism: function of, for Johnson, 97; modern, and Johnson, 94, 107; and Swift, 52–53
critical intelligence, in Johnson, 128

217

culture, role of: in Goldsmith, 49, 144–145, 148; in Johnson, 48–49, 114; in Pope, 34, 37, 39, 42, 47; in Swift, 51

Damrosch, Leopold, 204 n1
Davie, Donald, 194 nn4&5
declamation, 20–21
"democracy of the bower," 151–152
design: in Johnson, 97, 99–101, 205 n6; in Pope, 132
desire, in Johnson, 135–136
didactic address, 21–22; in Goldsmith, 159, 168, 172; in Johnson, 48–49; in Pope, 30, 43–47; in Swift, 50–51, 56, 62, 69, 75, 77
didactic purpose: in Goldsmith, 148, 180–181; in Johnson, 132; in romantic poets, 184; in Swift, 76
didactic stance: in Pope, 27–28; in Swift, 92
didacticism, 2; in Goldsmith, 142; in Horace, 12; in Johnson, 94, 97–99, 101, 107, 117, 120, 128, 204 n1; in Pope, 40–42; in Shakespeare, 12; in Swift, 69, 85, 92, 204 n19
didacticism and lyricism, 48; in Goldsmith, 142, 168–169, 173, 179–180, 184; in Johnson, 123; in Swift, 86, 90; in Wordsworth, 184
dignity: in Johnson, 137; in Swift, 72, 93
dilemma, in Johnson, 136, 213 n57
doctrine, in Swift, 79–80, 89
doublets, in Johnson, 129–132, 135–136, 212 n55
dramatic action: in Collins, 11, 16; in Pope, 25; in Shakespeare, 14
Dyson, A. E., 201 n4

Edwards, Oliver, 104–106
Ehrenpreis, Irvin, 201 n4, 203 n16
Elliott, Robert C., 201 n4
eloquence, 9–10, 15; in Collins, 18; in Gray, 20; and inwardness, 1–22
eloquent and reticent speech, in Horace, 7–9
empiricism, in Johnson, 48, 98–99, 101, 104, 134
Empson, William, 39
epigrams, in Johnson, 113
Erskine-Hill, Howard, 197 n1, 199 nn4&5, 200 n10
experience, role of: in Goldsmith, 154–155, 175; in Johnson, 48; in Pope, 37, 46

fame, for Johnson, 105
feeling: in Collins, 16, 18; in Goldsmith, 143–156, 165–167; in Johnson, 117; in Pope, 25; in Swift, 87; vs. consciousness, 17–20, 166, 168
fiction, 54; in Johnson, 134, 137; in Swift, 57, 203 n16
fictions: for Johnson, 121, 126; for Plato, 121
Fielding, Henry, 141
figurative language, in Johnson, 132
Fischer, John Irwin, 203 n19
form, in Johnson, 108, 137
freedom: in Johnson, 211 n44; in Swift, 61–62
Freud, Sigmund, 211 n44
Frye, Northrop, 61, 208 n36

Gibbon, Edward, *The History of the Decline and Fall of the Roman Empire*, 139–142
Gifford, William, 111–112

Goldberg, S. L., 193 n3, 197 n1, 200 n12, 206 n12
Golden, Morris, 213 n3, 215 nn6&7, 216 n20
GOLDSMITH, Oliver, 48; *The Deserted Village*, 22, 49–50, 142–186, 213 n3, 214 n4, 215 nn6,7,8&9, 216 nn16&20; *The Traveller*, 177–179, 183, 216 n15
Gray, Thomas: *Elegy in a Country Churchyard*, 10–11, 196 n10; Eton College ode, 20, 196 nn14&15
"greater ode," 194 n4

Hagstrum, Jean, 204 n1
Hardy, John, 210 n39
hatred, function of, in Swift, 52–53
heroic tone: in Johnson, 128; in Swift, 74–75, 81–82
history, role of, in Goldsmith, 149–150, 174
hope and desire, in Johnson, 135
Horace, 40, 194 n5, 195 n7, 198 n1; *Epistle II, i* (To Augustus), 199 n7; *Epistle II, ii* (To Florus), 28, 32–34, 43–45, 198 n4, 199 nn6&9; *Ode I.24*, 4–10, 194 n5, 195 nn6&8; *Satires*, 195 n6
Howe, Irving, 99
Hunter, G. K., 31, 199 n7

ideal: in Johnson, 122; vs. actual, in Goldsmith, 167; in Swift, 80–81
identity, of poet: in Goldsmith, 142–143, 152, 155–157, 166, 169, 177, 185; in Johnson, 122; in Pope, 24–25, 31, 36–47; in Swift, 55, 62–65, 77, 89
imagination, in Goldsmith, 158–159, 162, 164–166, 169–170, 173, 175–176, 181

inarticulateness, 9–11
inner drama, in Pope, 27–28, 40, 43, 47
inner speech, in Goldsmith, 150, 167–168, 177, 179
inquiry, in Johnson, 131–134, 211 n51, 212 n55
intelligence: in Goldsmith, 165–168; in Johnson, 128, 137. *See also* consciousness; judgment
intimacy: in Johnson, 208 n31; in Swift, 74
intricacy: in Horace, 9; in Collins, 11
inward experience, representation of: in Collins, 16; in Goldsmith, 146, 157, 161, 181; in Horace, 10
inwardness, 1–23, 31, 40, 44, 48, 50, 100, 117, 197 n1, 199 n6; and eloquence, 1–22; and experience, in Johnson, 48
irony, 18; in Gibbon, 140–141; in Goldsmith, 149, 166; in Pope, 30; in Swift, 57, 62, 64, 79, 201 n4

Jaarsma, Richard, 215 n9
Jack, Ian, 216 n20
Johnson, Esther, 67–69
JOHNSON, Samuel, 47–49, 93, 94–138, 185, 196 n14, 203 n3, 206 n12, 207 n30, 209 nn37&38, 211 nn44&48, 212 n52, 213 nn57, 58&61; criticism, 94–99, 204 n1; essays, 137; *The History of Rasselas*, 107, 109–110, 124, 129–138, 211 n51; life of Milton, 205 n6; *Life of Pope*, 132; life of Swift, 53, 55, 65; *London*, 111; *Preface to Shakespeare*, 49, 130, 211 n50; *The Rambler*, 107, 109;

JOHNSON, Samuel (*continued*)
  Rambler 4, 134; *Rambler* 32 (on endurance), 128–129, 135; *Rambler* 71 (on procrastination), 123, 129; *The Vanity of Human Wishes*, 22, 107–109, 110–124, 127, 135, 137, 206n18, 207nn29, 30&31, 208nn34&36, 210n39, 212n55
judgment, 19–21, 24, 98, 139; vs. sympathy, in Goldsmith, 149, 152–155, 160–165
Juvenal: tenth satire, 111–112, 207n29; third satire, 111

Keats, John, 96
Keener, Frederick, 198n4
Knapp, Steven, 196n13
Krieger, Murray, 98
Krutch, J. W., 125

language: in Goldsmith and Wordsworth, 184–185; in Johnson, 132; in Swift, 57
Leavis, F. R., 50, 108, 113
Lipking, Lawrence, 209n30
Lonsdale, Roger, 215n9
lyric poetry proper, 10, 182
lyricism, 1–4, 22–23, 93, 141, 194n4; in Collins, 16; in Goldsmith, 177, 185; in Horace, 9; in Johnson, 101, 118, 207n31; in Pope, 23, 25; in Shakespeare, 13; in Swift, 51

McGlynn, Paul, 212n55
Mack, Maynard, 197n1
masking, in Gray, 196n10
maturity, in Goldsmith, 147, 159
meaning: for Johnson, 99–100; for Swift, 55, 57, 61

meditation, 110, 113
memory, function of: in Goldsmith, 151–152, 156; with sight and imagination, 158, 170, 175–176, 215n8
Mill, John Stuart, 2–3, 193n1
mind and will, in Johnson, 126–128. *See also* consciousness
Miner, Earl, 214n4
mixed drama, 131
modernism, 99
moral economy, in Goldsmith, 153–154
moral lyricism, 6, 29
moral vs. aesthetic, in Johnson, 96, 204n1
morality: in Johnson, 65, 95, 99, 102, 108, 113–114, 207n29, 210n39; in Pope, 200n11; in Swift, 82, 89

Needham, J. D., 208nn34&36

O'Flaherty, Patrick, 108, 206n18, 208n36
orthodoxy, in Johnson, 102–104
"overheard" utterance, 2–3; in Collins, 16; in Goldsmith, 167; in Horace, 9; in Johnson, 118, 212n55; in Pope, 25, 27; in Swift, 93

Pagliaro, Harold, 211n51
panegyric, in Swift, 70
paradox, 212n52
pastoral, in Goldsmith, 151–152, 154, 176–177, 214n4
pathos: in Collins, 18; in Johnson, 117
personal/public expression. *See* public/private expression

personality: in Johnson, 118–119, 123; in Swift, 126; vs. character, 54–56, 64, 89, 122, 125, 127
personifications, in Johnson, 127, 211n48
perspective, in Goldsmith, 145, 158–162, 165–166, 178
pity, 152; in Goldsmith, 153, 156; in Johnson, 116, 118, 127
Plato, *The Republic*, 54, 65, 121–122, 126–127
play, in Swift, 52, 57, 61–62, 65, 71, 126
pleasure: in Goldsmith, 143; in Johnson, 95–96, 98, 101, 109, 113, 137
poet, function of, 2; in Goldsmith, 49, 175; in Pope, 31–37, 40, 43, 46; in Swift, 62, 75
poetic justice, for Johnson, 95, 120, 205n3
poise, 53–54, 87, 201n4
politics, in Goldsmith, 160
POPE, Alexander, 21, 23–47, 184, 193n3, 200n12, 211n52
—"Atticus," 23–24, 198n3
—*The Dunciad*, 47
—*Epilogue to the Satires*, 37, 47
—*An Essay on Criticism*, 34–40
—*An Essay on Man*, 43, 132
—Horatian imitations, 22, 31, 197n1, 198n4; *Epistle to Burlington*, 25–28, 43, 150; *An Epistle to Dr. Arbuthnot*, 25, 33, 198n4, 199n5; *The Second Epistle of the Second Book of Horace*, 28–47, 198n4, 199nn6&7, 200nn10&11
—*Moral Essays*, 21
prayer, in Johnson, 118–119, 123, 135, 210n39

preromanticism, in Goldsmith, 185, 216n20
principle of measure, in Johnson, 129, 134
Prior, Matthew, 194n5
public/private expression, 4–5, 9, 22, 48; in Goldsmith, 50, 142, 178–180; in Gray, 20; in Johnson, 108–109, 123, 125, 208n31; in Pope, 23–24, 30, 37, 44–47; in Swift, 86–87, 92–93
public/private identity: in Johnson, 122; in Swift, 62–63, 77

questions, in Johnson, 115, 118, 207n30
Quintana, Ricardo, 214n4

Rader, Ralph W., 102, 113, 179–181, 185–186, 216n16
rational will: in Johnson, 119–120, 123–125, 128, 211n44; in Swift, 90
Rawson, C. J., 201n6, 202n12
realism: in Shakespeare, 13–14; in Swift, 74
reason, in Johnson, 104. *See also* rational will
repression, for Johnson, 123–127, 211n44
reticent eloquence, 7–10; in Collins, 15–16
rhetoric: in Johnson, 110, 129, 132, 134, 212n52; in Pope, 132, 212n52
risk: in Goldsmith, 167; in Johnson, 107, 117
romantic criticism, 97; lyric, 184; "primitivism," and Goldsmith, 216n20
Rosenmeyer, Thomas G., 151, 176

Rothstein, Eric, 211n51, 213n58

Sacks, Sheldon, 137, 213n61
Said, Edward, 202n11
Sartre, Jean-Paul, 126, 211n48; *La Nausée*, 100
satire, 208n36; in Johnson, 108, 111, 208n37; in Pope, 40, 44, 46; in Swift, 50–51, 56–57, 61, 63, 70, 201n4
seeing and saying, in Johnson, 112–113, 115–117, 127, 137, 207n29
self, experience of: in Johnson, 65, 128, 135; in Pope, 38, 40, 45, 46, 200n11; in Swift, 50–51, 56
self-assertion: in Goldsmith, 149; in Johnson, 135; in Pope, 200n10
self-awareness: in Collins, 16; in Goldsmith, 215n12; in Johnson, 95, 120, 125–126, 138; in Pope, 25, 27, 199n6
self-discovery, 48; in Goldsmith, 142, 156, 166, 181, 186, 215n7; in Johnson, 118, 128; in Pope, 31, 36, 40, 42, 44, 197n1, 200n11; in Swift, 51, 92
self-exploration, in Pope, 30–31, 47, 197n1
self-possession, in Pope, 43, 46, 200n12
self-renunciation, in Swift, 80
self-revelation, 11; in Goldsmith, 216n20; in Horace, 195n6; in Johnson, 101, 104, 107; in Pope, 23–24, 28, 31, 37; in Swift, 65, 86, 92
self-scrutiny: in Goldsmith, 154; in Pope, 24, 28, 40, 197n1
sentimentalism, 10, 13–14, 195n9, 196n10

sentimentality, in Goldsmith, 146, 167
Shakespeare, William, 49, 98, 211n50; *Cymbeline*, 11–12, 14, 187–189; *King Lear*, 95–96, 205nn3&6
Sidney, Sir Philip, 96
sight, in Goldsmith, 164, 168, 183. *See also* perspective; seeing and saying
"socialized viciousness," in Swift, 79
sophistication: in Burns, 21; in Collins, 19, 196n13; in Goldsmith, 167
Spacks, Patricia M., 207n29, 209n38
speech: in Collins, 11, 18; in Goldsmith, 150; in Horace, 7–9; proper, in Johnson, 116, 118, 137; in Shakespeare, 13–14
speech/inarticulateness, 9–11
Stack, Frank, 197n1, 198n4, 199n6, 200n11
stance, in Goldsmith, 142, 148, 158, 162
Sterne, Laurence, *A Sentimental Journey*, 141
Stock, R. D., 205n3
Storm, Leo, 214n4
style: in Gibbon, 141; in Johnson, 132, 212n52
SWIFT, Jonathan, 48, 50–93, 126, 200n1, 201nn4,5&6, 202n12
—*An Argument against Abolishing Christianity*, 55, 58–61, 64, 203n16
—*Cadenus and Vanessa*, 74
—*The Drapier's Letters*, 55–57, 76, 202n11

—*An Epistle to a Lady* . . . , 66
—*Gulliver's Travels*, 201 n4
—*The Legion Club*, 62
—*A Modest Proposal*, 54–58, 64
—pamphlets, 21
—poems to Stella, 22, 51, 67–93; *Stella's Birthday, March 13, 1726/7*, 86–92, 204 n20; *To Stella, Visiting Me in My Sickness*, 77–86, 203 n19; *To Stella, Who Collected and Transcribed His Poems*, 69–70, 75
—satire, 50–51, 56–57, 92
—*The Sentiments of a Church of England Man*, 55, 58–60
—sermons, 55, 202 n11
—*Verses on the Death of Dr. Swift, D.S.P.D.*, 62
sympathy: in Gibbon, 139; in Goldsmith, 144, 154–155, 157–159, 166, 172; in Johnson, 126, 138; vs. judgment, in Goldsmith, 152–155, 160–165

Tarbet, David, 204 n1
Tate, Nahum, *King Lear*, 95–96
Thackeray, William, 200 n1
theatricality, in Pope, 23–24, 27–29, 197 n1
Theocritus, 176
Tillotson, Geoffrey, 198 n4
tonal shift: in Goldsmith, 144, 146; in Pope, 29, 199 n6; in Swift, 87

tone: in Johnson, 206 n18; in Pope, 46; in Swift, 72, 75
tragedy, 95–96
transitions, in Pope, 28, 198 n4, 199 n6
Traugott, John, 54, 126, 195 n9, 196 n10, 201 n4, 202 n7
Trickett, Rachel, 208 n34
Trilling, Lionel, *Sincerity and Authority*, 99–101

Uphaus, Robert, 204 n20
urbanity: in Gibbon, 140–141; in Swift, 88, 92

Voitle, Robert, 210 n39

Wardle, Ralph, 216 n20
Watt, Ian, 121
Weinbrot, Howard, 108, 199 n7, 207 n30
will: in Goldsmith, 147, 166; in Johnson, 122, 129, 135. *See also* rational will
Williams, Anne, 194 n4, 207 n31, 214 nn3&4, 216 n20
Williams, Aubrey, 43
Williams, Gordon, 195 n6
Williams, Raymond, 174–176, 214 n4, 215 nn8,11&12
wit: in Johnson, 113–114, 119, 132; in Swift, 78
Wordsworth, William, 184